CAREER DISCOVERY ENCYCLOPEDIA

2
BOR
DENTA

FERGUSON PUBLISHING COMPANY
CHICAGO, ILLINOIS

Library of Congress Cataloging-in-Publication Data
Career discovery encyclopedia.—4th ed.
p. cm.
Includes index.
Summary: Eight volumes with over 500 articles on all categories of occupations present such information as job descriptions, salaries, educational and training requirements, sources of further information, and other pertinent facts.
ISBN 0-89434-275-4
1. Vocational guidance—Dictionaries--Juvenile literature. [1. Vocational guidance—Dictionaries. 2. Occupations.] I. Ferguson Publishing Company.

HF5381.2.C37 2000
331.7'02—dc21

99-055994

Web: http://www.fergpubco.com

Printed in the United States of America
X-2

CONTENTS

VOLUME 2

Border Patrol Officers 2
Botanists 4
Bounty Hunters 6
Bricklayers and Stonemasons 8
Broadcast Engineers 10
Business Managers 12
Buyers 14
Cable Television Technicians 16
Cardiologists 18
Cardiovascular Technologists 20
Career Counselors 22
Carpenters 24
Cartographers 26
Cartoonists 28
Cashiers 30
Caterers 32
Cement Masons 34
Ceramic Artists 36
Ceramics Engineers 38
Certified Nurse-Midwives 40
Chemical Engineers 42
Chemical Technicians 44
Chemists 46
Child Care Workers 48
Child Life Specialists 50
Chiropractors 52
Choreographers 54

Cinematographers 56
Circus Performers 58
City Managers 60
City Planners 62
Civil Engineering Technicians 64
Civil Engineers 66
Clerks 68
Clinical Chemists 70
Clowns 72
Coal Mining Technicians 74
Collection Workers 76
College Administrators 78
College Professors 80
Columnists 82
Comedians 84
Communications Equipment Mechanics .86
Composers 88
Computer Aided Design Technicians 90
Computer and Electronics Sales Representatives 92
Computer and Office Machine Technicians 94
Computer and Video Game Designers 96
Computer Network Specialists 98
Computer Operators 100
Computer Programmers 102
Computer Security Specialists 104
Computer Systems Analysts 106
Computer Trainers 108
Congressional Aides 110
Conservators and Conservation Technicians 112
Construction Inspectors 114
Construction Laborers 116
Cooks, Chefs, and Bakers 118
Coremakers 120
Corrections Officers 122

Cosmetologists 124
Cost Estimators 126
Costume Designers 128
Counter and Retail Clerks 130
Court Reporters 132
Creative Arts Therapists 134
Crime Analysts 136
Cruise Ship Workers 138
Customer Service Representatives 140
Customs Officials 142
Dancers 144
Database Specialists 146
Demographers 148
Dental Assistants 150
Dental Hygienists 152
Dental Laboratory Technicians 154
Glossary . . . . *.156*
Index . . . . *.158*

BORDER PATROL OFFICERS

SCHOOL SUBJECTS:
GEOGRAPHY, FOREIGN LANGUAGE

PERSONAL SKILLS:
LEADERSHIP/MANAGEMENT

MINIMUM EDUCATION LEVEL:
HIGH SCHOOL DIPLOMA

OUTLOOK:
FASTER THAN THE AVERAGE

OTHER ARTICLES TO LOOK AT:

Customs Officials
Deputy U.S. Marshals
Detectives
FBI Agents
Police Officers
Security Guards

WHAT BORDER PATROL OFFICERS DO

To preserve the well being of the citizens of the United States, the federal government has established laws that describe which persons and which products can enter the country. However, many attempts are made to break these laws and cross the border illegally. *Border patrol officers* have a mission to prevent illegal entry into the United States at the borders, and to deport or arrest people who attempt illegal entry.

Border patrol officers are federal law enforcement officers, a group that also includes U.S. marshals, FBI agents, and others. They all have a duty to enforce the laws of the U.S. government. Under U.S. law, people from other countries who wish to enter the country must apply to the government for this privilege. Those who are visiting or wish to work or study here must obtain visas. Those who wish to live here permanently must apply for residency status. Border patrol officers are on guard to make sure that people follow these rules.

Along the U.S. border with Mexico and the border with Canada, border patrol officers work 24 hours a day. To catch people sneaking over the border, they use many different tactics. They patrol the border in jeeps and, in more rugged terrain, on horseback. They routinely fly helicopters over areas where many people try to come into the country. At night they scan the horizon with special night vision goggles. They also work at regular border crossings to be sure that people are not coming in illegally inside cars and trucks.

When people are caught trying to cross the border illegally, border patrol officers will deport them back across the border. Because of their duties, border patrol officers need to know about the laws of apprehension, arrest, detention, search and seizure, and other specialized regulations.

In recent years the prevention of drug smuggling has become a major part of the border patrol officer's job. Officers sometimes use drug-sniffing dogs to help find where drugs have been hidden.

Border patrol officers take their orders from their sector chiefs. With experience and training, border patrol officers can advance to higher positions. They may become *inspectors* who work at border crossings, airports, and other entry points into the United States, checking passports and visas. They may become *plain-clothes investigators* who work on large-scale projects, such as attempting to stop smuggling rings. They may also choose to shift from the law enforcement to the service functions of their agency, and administer examinations and interviews to people who wish to become citizens.

EDUCATION AND TRAINING

Applicants for the job of border patrol officer must take an entrance exam. They are then accepted into training based on their test scores. A high school diploma or its equivalent is required to take the exam. Students can prepare for this career by taking courses in English, history, communications, and Spanish.

Like other federal law enforcement officers, border patrol officers are trained at the Federal Law Enforcement Training Center at the Glynco Naval Air Station in Georgia. They take a 16-week course, in which they learn the laws they will need in the course of their duties. They will also undergo physical training and learn the safe use of firearms. They must also study Spanish, a requirement unique to this branch of law enforcement. After graduation, all border patrol officers are initially stationed along the Mexican border.

EARNINGS AND OUTLOOK

A beginning border patrol officer earns between $27,500 and $39,700 per year. With more experience, the salary increases to around $45,000 per year. There are many opportunities for working overtime, which results in extra pay. Officers in certain cities, such as New York, Los Angeles, Boston, San Francisco, Chicago, Washington, DC, and others are entitled to receive additional locality pay, which adds roughly 16 percent to the base salary.

There will be an increased demand for border patrol officers through 2006, due to the continuing war on drugs and the economic problems of Latin American countries, which force many people to try to cross the U.S. border illegally.

A border patrol officer leads an illegal alien to a waiting bus that will take him and others back across the border.

FOR MORE INFORMATION

For more information about a career as a border patrol officer, contact:

Immigration and Naturalization Service
425 I Street, NW
Washington, DC 20536
Tel: 202-514-2000
Web: http://www.ins.usdoj.gov

The following Web site has all the information you need on the history, mission, and organization of the border patrol, complete with links to other sites, an online museum, email addresses of more than 100 agents and trainees nationwide, a library of articles on the border patrol, short stories, journal entries written by officers, and more.

The Unofficial U.S. Border Patrol Web Site
Web: http://www.usbp.com

BOTANISTS

SCHOOL SUBJECTS
AGRICULTURE, BIOLOGY

PERSONAL SKILLS:
HELPING/TEACHING
TECHNICAL/SCIENTIFIC

MINIMUM EDUCATION LEVEL:
BACHELOR'S DEGREE

OUTLOOK:
FASTER THAN THE AVERAGE

OTHER ARTICLES TO LOOK AT:

Biologists
Ecologists
Foresters
Naturalists
Soil Conservation Technicians
Soil Scientists

WHAT BOTANISTS DO

Botanists study plant life from cell structure to reproduction, from how plants are distributed to how rainfall, climate, and other conditions affect them, and more.

Botany is a major branch of biology. Studies in botany reach into many areas of biology, including biophysics, genetics, and other specialized studies. Botanists play an important role in modern science and industry. Their work affects agriculture, agronomy (soil and crop science), conservation, forestry, horticulture, and more. In recent years, the role of the botanist has taken on more importance as society demands new drugs to treat disease, more food resources in developing countries, and solutions to environmental problems.

The primary work of botanists is in research and applied science. They study every aspect of plant life: cell structure, heredity, anatomy, growth reproduction, how plants are distributed on the earth, and how rainfall, soil, elevation, and climate affect them. These studies are used to help humans and the environment.

In most cases, botanists focus on a specific problem or set of problems in their research. They may try to develop new varieties of crops that better resist disease or improve the growth of other crops such as high-yield corn. Other botanists focus on a specific type of plant species, such as ferns (pteridology), or plants that are native to a specific area, such as wetland or desert. Botanists who work in private industry, such as a food or drug company, may focus on developing new products, testing and inspection, or other areas.

Research takes place in a wide variety of settings such as research stations at colleges and universities and botanical gardens. Botanists who work in conservation or ecology often do their work out in the field. They help recreate lost or damaged ecosystems, direct pollution cleanups, and inventory species.

There are many specialties in botany. *Ethnobotanists* study the use of plant life by a particular culture or ethnic group in order to find medical uses of certain plants. An example would be the study of Native Americans' use of herbs and other plant products to treat illnesses. *Ecologists* study the connection between plants and animals and the physical environment. They restore native species to areas, repair damaged ecosystems, and work on problems of pollution. Forest ecologists focus on forest species and their habitats, such as forest wetlands. *Mycologists* study fungi and apply their findings to medicine, agriculture, and industry for development of drugs, such as antibiotics, molds and yeasts. *Plant cytologists* use powerful microscopes to study plant tissues in order to determine such things as why some cells become malignant and cause the plant to get sick or die. *Plant geneticists* study the origin, transmission, and development of inherited traits, such as size and color.

EDUCATION AND TRAINING

Education requirements for botanists are rigorous. Nonresearch jobs require a bachelor's degree, while research and teaching positions usually require at least a master's or even a doctoral degree. At the undergraduate level, there are numerous degrees in botany or biology (which includes studies in both botany and zoology). A master's degree requires more specialized study—for example, a master's in conservation biology focuses on the conservation of specific plant and animal communities.

High school students interested in botany should take courses in biology, mathematics, and other science subjects.

EARNINGS AND OUTLOOK

According to the Botanical Society of America, graduates with bachelor's degrees earn average starting salaries of $24,000 per year. Graduates with master's degrees start at nearly $31,000 a year. Botanists who work in private industry earn average annual salaries of $35,085, while those in government earn $41,754 a year.

Employment for botanists is expected to increase faster than the average for all other occupations through 2006. Botanists will be needed to help with environmental, conservation, and pharmaceutical issues. Botanists work in such a wide variety of fields that some type of employment is almost guaranteed.

A Forest Service botanist takes a close look at one of the plants in the Sand Dunes area of the Hiawatha National Forest in Michigan.

FOR MORE INFORMATION

Contact the following organization for a free booklet on careers in botany:

Botanical Society of America
Business Office
1735 Neil Avenue
Columbus, OH 43210-1293
Tel: 614-292-3519
Web: http://www.botany.org/

Contact this group about volunteer positions in natural resource management:

Student Conservation Association
PO Box 550
Charlestown, NH 03603
Email: ask-us@sca-inc.org
Tel : 603-543-1828
Web: http://www.sca-inc.org/

BOUNTY HUNTERS

SCHOOL SUBJECTS:
ENGLISH, GOVERNMENT

PERSONAL SKILLS:
FOLLOWING INSTRUCTIONS

MINIMUM EDUCATION LEVEL:
HIGH SCHOOL DIPLOMA

OUTLOOK:
ABOUT AS FAST AS THE AVERAGE

OTHER ARTICLES TO LOOK AT:

Corrections Officers
Deputy U.S. Marshals
Detectives
FBI Agents
Parole Officers
Police Officers

WHAT BOUNTY HUNTERS DO

Bounty hunters, or *bail enforcement agents*, track down and return individuals who are fugitives from justice. They work in conjunction with bail bondsmen and the court system. The scenario plays out as follows: An individual is arrested for breaking a law. The individual is given the chance to be freed from jail if he guarantees his presence in court on a certain date by posting a large amount of money. Most people who are arrested don't have these large sums of money on hand, so they enlist the services of a bail bondsman who provides the money to the court. The individual must pay the bondsman a fee—usually 10 percent of the actual posted bond. If the individual does not show up on the court date, the bondsman can either try to bring the person in or hire a bounty hunter to track the person down. The bounty hunter is paid only if the fugitive is returned to court.

After the bounty hunter is on the case, his or her main goal is to locate the fugitive as quickly and as safely as possible. Although the timeframe varies from state to state and court to court, bounty hunters usually have 90 days at the most to bring back the fugitive. Locating a fugitive requires research, detection, and law enforcement skills. It can involve many days of interviewing people, tracing paper trails, and sitting in vehicles for countless hours of surveillance. Bounty hunters can use almost any means possible to re-arrest a fugitive. In most states they can enter the homes of fugitives if they believe, beyond a reasonable doubt, that the fugitive is inside. Most bounty hunters use weapons to persuade a fugitive to return peacefully and to protect themselves. After the fugitive is found, the bounty hunter makes a private arrest of the individual and takes the fugitive back to jail to await trial. Although most bounty hunters re-arrest the fugitive themselves, some locate the fugitive and then alert the local law officials to make the actual arrest.

EDUCATION AND TRAINING

Although you won't find a class at school called Bounty Hunting 101, there are some courses that can help you prepare for a job in this field. Classes in government, political science, communication, and business will help you prepare for the legal and business side of bounty hunting. Self-defense or martial arts courses can give you skills you might need when capturing a fugitive. Foreign languages may come in handy as well, depending on the area of the country where you may be working.

Although a college education is not required to become a bounty hunter, you should have at least some sort of training in law

At times, bounty hunters must show a great deal of patience in their tracking of fugitives. These two bounty hunters wait in their car after being given a tip about where to find a fugitive.

enforcement and criminal justice. If a college degree or vocational school is in your future, aim for criminal justice studies or police academy training. If you want to focus immediately on bail enforcement, some training opportunities are available. The National Institute of Bail Enforcement in Arizona provides a series of training seminars. The Bail Enforcement Agency in California also trains bail enforcement agents all over the country with classes taught by private investigators, SWAT team members, and fugitive recovery agents.

EARNINGS AND OUTLOOK

Bounty hunters who start their own businesses should expect to lose money at the beginning, according to the Fugitive Apprehension Select Team in Missouri. The bounty hunting business, like any other, takes time to develop. The National Center for Policy Analysis states that beginning bounty hunters earn $20,000+ per year, while more established bounty hunters and business owners can earn over $30,000 per year.

Employment for bounty hunters is increasing about as fast as the average for all other occupations, although this field has a narrow niche in the bail bonding business. Competition among bail enforcement agents continues to propel the field as a profession and as an asset to our legal system. Because private bail bonding and bail enforcement agents are working instead of public officials, there is no cost to the taxpayer for the apprehension of these fugitives.

FOR MORE INFORMATION

American Bail Enforcement Association, Inc.
PO Box 33244
Austin, TX 78764
Tel: 512-719-3595
Web: http://www.pimall.com/nais/n.dm.html

BRICKLAYERS AND STONEMASONS

SCHOOL SUBJECTS:
MATHEMATICS, TECHNICAL/SHOP

PERSONAL SKILLS:
FOLLOWING INSTRUCTIONS
MECHANICAL/MANIPULATIVE

MINIMUM EDUCATION LEVEL:
HIGH SCHOOL DIPLOMA
APPRENTICESHIP

OUTLOOK:
ABOUT AS FAST AS THE AVERAGE

OTHER ARTICLES TO LOOK AT:

Carpenters

Cement Masons

Construction Laborers

Marble Setters, Tile Setters, and Terrazzo Workers

Plasterers

WHAT BRICKLAYERS AND STONEMASONS DO

Bricklayers construct walls, floors, fireplaces, and other structures with brick, cinder, or concrete block. *Stonemasons* build stone walls and stone exteriors and floors. They usually work on large building projects, such as public buildings, hotels, and office buildings.

Before starting a job, bricklayers and stonemasons work with blueprints (plans drawn out on paper) to determine where to construct a wall or other object and how big it should be. To shape bricks and chisel stone, bricklayers and stonemasons use a variety of hand tools, such as hammers, chisels, and brushes. They may also use electric drills and saws.

Bricklayers must know how to mix mortar, which is made of cement, sand, and water, and how to spread it so that the joints throughout the structure will be evenly spaced with a neat appearance. They may have helpers who mix the mortar as well as move materials and scaffolding around the work site.

When laying bricks, bricklayers spread a layer of mortar, place the brick on the mortar bed, and then tap it into place. Care must be taken when starting the building process. Bricklayers continually measure the bricklaying to make sure that it is straight. They cut bricks with a hammer and chisel to fit around windows, doors, and other openings.

When constructing a stone wall or floor, stonemasons set the first level of stones in a layer of mortar. They build a wall by alternating layers of mortar and stone, and they set a stone floor by placing stones over the mortar surface. They use measuring devices so that the work remains straight. To make various shapes and sizes, masons use a special hammer to cut each stone.

EDUCATION AND TRAINING

Bricklayers and stonemasons must be able to read blueprints and other building specifications and closely follow instructions. They need to be skillful in using hand tools, power tools, and measuring devices.

The best way to become a bricklayer or stonemason is to complete a three-year apprenticeship. To become an apprentice, you need the approval of the local apprenticeship committee and you must be 17 years old, in good physical condition, and have a high school diploma. High school coursework should include classes in mathematics, mechanical drawing, and blueprint reading. Take precollege engineering classes if your school offers them.

With a string as a guide for leveling, a bricklayer sets a brick in mortar.

EARNINGS AND OUTLOOK

The average salary for bricklayers and stonemasons is about $25,000 per year, with a range between $13,000 and $48,000. Most make between $18,000 and $32,500. Earnings for those who work outside can be affected by bad weather, and earnings are lower for workers in areas where the local economy is in a slump.

Over the next eight years, employment opportunities for bricklayers and stonemasons are expected to rise at rates about the same as the average for all other occupations. There will probably be increased construction of many kinds of buildings because of population increases, business growth, and the growing popularity of brick and stone, especially ornamental brickwork and stonework on building fronts and in lobbies. During economic downturns, bricklayers and stonemasons, like other workers in construction-related jobs, can expect to have fewer job opportunities and perhaps be laid off.

FOR MORE INFORMATION

For information on training and apprenticeship programs, contact:

Associated General Contractors of America
1957 E Street, NW
Washington, DC 20006
Tel: 202-393-2040
Web: http://www.agc.org

The National Association of Home Builders offers education and training programs for workers in the home building industry.

Home Builders Institute
1090 Vermont Avenue, NW, Suite 600
Washington, DC 20005
Tel: 202-371-0600; 800-795-7955
Web: http://www.hbi.org

BROADCAST ENGINEERS

SCHOOL SUBJECTS:
COMPUTER SCIENCE, MATHEMATICS

PERSONAL INTERESTS:
MECHANICAL/MANIPULATIVE
TECHNICAL/SCIENTIFIC

MINIMUM EDUCATION LEVEL:
SOME POSTSECONDARY TRAINING

OUTLOOK:
ABOUT AS FAST AS THE AVERAGE

OTHER ARTICLES TO LOOK AT:

Audio Recording Engineers
Cable Television Technicians
Electronics Engineering Technicians
Film Editors
Telecommunications Technicians

WHAT BROADCAST ENGINEERS DO

Broadcast engineers, also called broadcast technicians, operate the electronic equipment that sends radio and television signals to the public. They are responsible for the operation, installation, and repair of the equipment.

While many broadcast engineers work in the studio, others, called *field technicians,* set up and operate portable radio and television transmitting equipment at locations away from the main station. For example, a radio station may broadcast several hours of programming from a record store that is having a grand opening or a television station may broadcast a news report live from city hall.

Field technicians link up microphones, mini-cameras, and amplifiers with the main station by using telephone lines. If the location of the broadcast is too far away for a telephone connection, the broadcast engineers will set up, test, and operate portable microwave transmitters. Sometimes these transmitters beam their signals directly to the main station's receivers; at other times, the engineers aim the transmitter's signals up toward an orbiting satellite. The satellite then relays the signal back down to the main stations.

Engineers doing maintenance work may have to climb poles and antenna towers, while those on the ground might set up heavy equipment.

Field technicians usually travel to the site of a remote broadcast in a specially equipped van. The van carries the transmitting equipment, microphones, cameras, lighting equipment, and power sources needed for the broadcast. The van also carries any tools or parts the technicians may need to make minor repairs. These technicians must also be able to use electrical test meters to make sure their equipment is operating properly.

The broadcast engineer monitors the transmitting equipment as the broadcast is being sent back to the main station. Often, a broadcast is taped for later use.

EDUCATION AND TRAINING

In high school, students interested in a career as a broadcast technician should take courses in mathematics, physics, the physical sciences, and computers.

After high school, students should enter at least a two-year program of training in a community college or technical school. Courses offered will include electronics and radio and television theory.

Broadcast engineers must be good with electrical and mechanical systems. This requires good manual dexterity with precise, coordinated hand movements. Beginners usually learn from experienced technicians while on the job. They may start out at a smaller station while learning important skills, and then move on to a larger station where this experience can help them land a job.

EARNINGS AND OUTLOOK

Broadcast engineers earn average salaries of about $30,000 per year. Those working for smaller stations may earn considerably less, while those working for larger stations could earn more. For chief engineers, salaries average $46,000 per year.

Broadcasting technology is rapidly advancing in both radio and television broadcasting. According to the U.S. Bureau of Labor Statistics, the overall employment of broadcast engineers is expected to grow about as fast as the average through the year 2006. Growth in the number of stations and number of programming hours should increase demand.

However, due to increased technology, some positions may be eliminated due to laborsaving technical advances like computer programming and remote control transmitters. Many new jobs will result from the need to replace existing engineers who often leave the industry for other jobs in electronics.

FOR MORE INFORMATION

Students interested in a career as a broadcast engineer should participate in school clubs or activities that deal with electronics or involve working with camera or video equipment.

Two broadcast engineers run a news program from the central control room at a television station.

Contact BEA for scholarship information and a list of schools offering degrees in broadcasting. Visit their Web site to sign up for a free monthly email newsletter that contains useful information about broadcast education and the broadcasting industry.

Broadcast Education Association (BEA)
1771 N Street, NW
Washington, DC 20036-2891
Tel: 202-429-5354
Email: fweaber@nab.org
Web: http://www.beaweb.org

For more information about a career as a broadcast engineer, contact the following organizations:

National Association of Broadcast Employees and Technicians
501 3rd Street, NW, 8th Floor
Washington, DC 20001
Web: http://nabetcwa.org

Society of Broadcast Engineers
8445 Keystone Crossing, Suite 140
Indianapolis, IN 46240-2454
Tel: 317-253-1640
Web: http://www.sbe.org

BUSINESS MANAGERS

SCHOOL SUBJECTS:
BUSINESS, COMPUTER SCIENCE

PERSONAL SKILLS:
HELPING/TEACHING
LEADERSHIP/MANAGEMENT

MINIMUM EDUCATION LEVEL:
BACHELOR'S DEGREE

OUTLOOK:
ABOUT AS FAST AS THE AVERAGE

OTHER ARTICLES TO LOOK AT:

Buyers
Cost Estimators
Office Administrators
Property and Real Estate Managers
Retail Store Managers

WHAT BUSINESS MANAGERS DO

Nearly all organizations have what is called a management hierarchy. This means that in addition to the person who heads the entire organization, there are also people who manage different parts of the organization. For example, a large corporation will usually have a *president* or *chief executive officer* (CEO). Helping and supporting the president are different *vice-presidents* or officers who oversee various aspects of the company. The *chief financial officer* manages the financial, or money, part of the company. The *chief operating officer* usually manages all the day-to-day operations of the company. The *chief information officer* oversees the information technology systems of the company, such as computer networks and Internet access.

These vice-presidents or officers supervise the work of various *business managers*. Managers, in turn, have people working under them. The larger the corporation, the more specific each person's area of responsibility is. In a very large company, one business manager may be in charge of planning conferences, while another business manager may work with personnel.

In smaller firms, the business manager may oversee all the administrative needs of the company. These may include personnel, financial records, mail, information processing, data processing, ordering supplies, and supervising the clerical staff.

Business managers may have to prepare financial reports, oversee the flow of cash, and develop information to measure the stability of the company. Some business managers develop overall plans, set goals and deadlines, and develop procedures.

EDUCATION AND TRAINING

Because business managers are part of the management team, they should be able to cooperate with a group of people and have good communication skills. Young people considering a job as a business manager should enjoy working with numbers, because much of the job is keeping track of finances. Computer knowledge is also very helpful. Useful courses of study in high school include English, mathematics, and business. A college degree in business administration or accounting is usually a requirement to be hired as a business manager, and many colleges offer specific management courses. Work experience is usually considered necessary before a manager can supervise the work of others.

Managers and vice-presidents may specialize in certain areas of business. Sales managers usually have worked in the sales department, for example; public relations managers have a background in public rela-

Business managers often call meetings of their staff, like the one shown here, to explain new policies and procedures that are to be implemented in the workplace.

tions. Specialists have a combination of education and training in the area that they are promoted into.

EARNINGS AND OUTLOOK

The salaries of business managers vary greatly depending on the responsibilities, length of service, and the size, location, and type of company. According to a 1998 survey by the American Management Association, the average annual salary is about $92,000. The average salary for company presidents or CEOs is $144,000. For managers at lower levels, an average salary is $55,000 to $60,000. Managers may also receive bonuses, company stock, and other extra benefits.

The job outlook for business managers is expected to be average through the next decade. There will be heavy competition for the best jobs.

FOR MORE INFORMATION

While still in school, students can join clubs such as Junior Achievement, which introduces them to community business leaders. Any activity that gives students an opportunity to exercise their organizational and planning skills is excellent preparation for a future business manager.

To learn more about a career as a business manager, contact:

Junior Achievement
One Education Way
Colorado Springs, CO 80906
Web: http://www.ja.org

American Management Association
1601 Broadway
New York, NY 10019-7420
Web: http://www.amanet.org

National Management Association
2210 Arbor Boulevard
Dayton, OH 45439-1580
Web: http://nmal.org

BUYERS

SCHOOL SUBJECTS:
BUSINESS, ECONOMICS, MATHEMATICS

PERSONAL SKILLS:
COMMUNICATION/IDEAS
LEADERSHIP/MANAGEMENT

MINIMUM EDUCATION LEVEL:
HIGH SCHOOL DIPLOMA

OUTLOOK:
LITTLE CHANGE OR MORE SLOWLY THAN THE AVERAGE

OTHER ARTICLES TO LOOK AT:

Auctioneers
Cashiers
Counter and Retail Clerks
Retail Managers
Retail Sales Workers
Services Sales Representatives

WHAT BUYERS DO

Buyers purchase the merchandise that is sold in local stores or by chains of stores. Sometimes buyers specialize in one kind of merchandise, such as clothing or toys. The goal of all buyers is the same: to find and buy the best products at the best price for the store or chain that employs them.

In some stores buyers are responsible for both buying goods and supervising the selling of goods. In other stores they are involved only with buying.

All buyers must be experts in the products they buy. They order goods months before the store will sell them, and they must be able to predict how many will be sold. To do this, they must know all about the product—what it is used for, how well it is made, what it looks like, and who will buy it. In addition, they need to know the best sources for purchasing the product.

In making their purchases, buyers must understand what type of merchandising the store owners prefer. Do they want to sell a large number of lower priced goods or a smaller number of higher priced goods? Buyers must clearly understand how much profit the owners are trying to make. This will help them determine how much risk they are allowed to take in the type and quantity of products bought. Large quantities of unsold goods do not make for profits.

If buyers are to be successful, they also must understand their customers—the kind of goods they like, how much they can afford, and the times they prefer to buy. Buyers need to know the sizes, colors, and other features that will most satisfy their customers' needs.

Buyers may deal directly with traveling salespeople, or they may order by mail or telephone from a manufacturer or wholesaler. Some travel to other cities to visit showrooms. Buyers of such specialized goods as glassware or china may make yearly trips to other countries. Some buyers attend trade shows where manufacturers of similar items display their products.

EDUCATION AND TRAINING

Most buying positions require a high school diploma. Although a college degree is not always required to become a buyer, those candidates who have bachelor's degrees have a better chance of getting a job as a buyer.

While in high school, students should take courses, such as mathematics and English. In college, students should take courses in business administration, marketing, retailing, purchasing, and economics.

EARNINGS AND OUTLOOK

How much a buyer earns depends on various factors, including the employer's sales volume. Mass merchandisers, such as discount or chain department stores, pay among the highest salaries.

Most buyers earn between $23,300 and $49,9000 a year, depending on the size of their store and its geographic location. Some buyers, primarily at large department stores, earn as much as $63,000 a year. Most buyers receive the usual company benefits, such as vacation, sick leave, life and health insurance, and pension plans. They generally also receive an employee's discount of 10 to 20 percent on merchandise purchased for personal use.

The increased use of computers by buyers for maintaining records and ordering merchandise has meant that each buyer can do more and stores need fewer buyers overall. Because of this, the number of people employed as buyers is expected to grow only slightly through 2006.

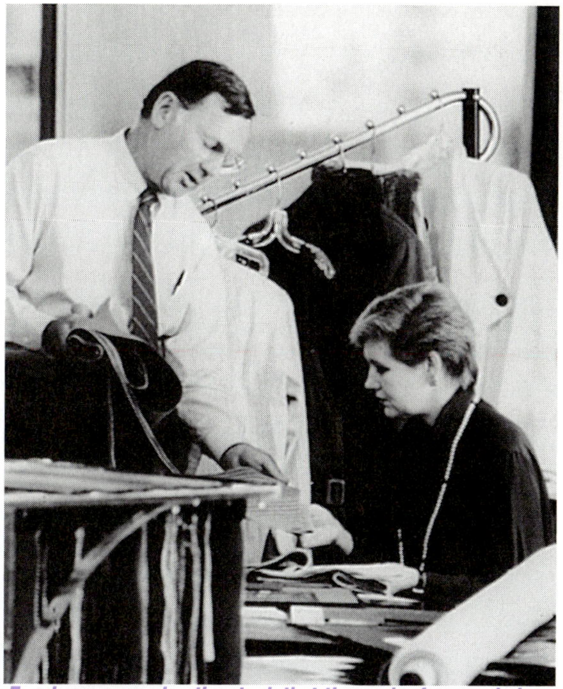

Two buyers examine the stock that they order from a wholesaler for their store.

FOR MORE INFORMATION

For materials on educational programs in the retail industry, contact:

National Retail Federation
325 7th Street, NW, Suite 1000
Washington, DC 20004
Tel: 202-783-7971

For career information, send a request marked "Careers" to:

American Purchasing Society
30 West Downer Place
Aurora, IL 60506
Tel: 630-859-0250
Web: http://www.amercian-purchasing.com

For information on the magazine, Your Future Purchasing Career, *lists of colleges with purchasing programs, and bios of people in the field, contact:*

National Association of Purchasing Management
Customer Service
2055 East Centennial Circle
PO Box 22160
Tempe, AZ 85285
Tel: 800-888-6276, ext. 401
Web: http://www.napm.org

CABLE TELEVISION TECHNICIANS

SCHOOL SUBJECTS:
MATHEMATICS, TECHNICAL/SHOP

PERSONAL SKILLS:
FOLLOWING INSTRUCTIONS
MECHANICAL/MANIPULATIVE

MINIMUM EDUCATION LEVEL:
HIGH SCHOOL DIPLOMA

OUTLOOK:
LITTLE CHANGE OR MORE SLOWLY THAN THE AVERAGE

OTHER ARTICLES TO LOOK AT:

Communications Equipment Mechanics

Electrical and Electronics Engineers

Electricians

Telecommunications Technicians

WHAT CABLE TELEVISION TECHNICIANS DO

For many years after its invention, television was beamed, or broadcast, into homes from tall transmitter towers. Technical advances later made possible the addition of satellite television transmission. Today, many of the programs available to television viewers are transmitted directly over wires, or cables, by a process called cable television. *Cable television technicians* inspect, maintain, and repair the antennas, cables, and amplifying equipment used in cable television transmission systems.

Television cables usually are strung along telephone poles in rural and suburban areas and through tunnels in cities. Some cable technicians regularly inspect these cables to look for signs of damage or wear. This means climbing telephone poles or working in small spaces underground. These technicians also use blueprints and other technical drawings to locate problems along the cable route. When breakdowns occur, the technicians repair or replace the affected cable. Cable television technicians also work at pole-mounted amplifiers. These amplifiers make the signal running along the cable stronger. The cable television technicians use electronic meters and miniature television sets to make sure that the signal provides the best reception possible.

In addition to working directly with television cables, cable television technicians also listen to customers' questions and complaints about reception. The technicians must be able to discover the reasons for the problems and then make the necessary repairs.

Cable television technicians use a variety of instruments and tools in their work. For example, they use electrical measuring instruments, such as voltmeters, ohmmeters, and capacity meters. They also use electricians' hand tools.

EDUCATION AND TRAINING

To work as a cable television technician, you should be physically fit. Some heavy lifting is involved, as well as climbing and working in small spaces. In addition, you must have excellent eyesight and color perception.

In high school, take classes in English, mathematics (particularly technical math), and shop. After high school, you can take a one- or two-year technical training program at a community college or a technical institute. Classes in these programs provide hands-on training and cover the basics of electrical wiring and electronics, broadcasting theory and practice, reading blueprints and schematic drawing, and physics.

EARNINGS AND OUTLOOK

The Women in Cable and Telecommunications Foundation and *Cablevision Magazine* conducted a survey in 1998 to examine salary parities between men and women in the telecommunications industry. In entry-level professional/technical positions, men had average annual salaries of $26,779 and women had salaries of $26,034. At the associate level, men made $29,902 a year, while women made $31,133. At the senior level, men averaged $36,857 and women averaged $36,803.

Companies offer a variety of benefit packages, which can include any of the following: paid holidays, vacations, and sick days; personal days; medical, dental, and life insurance; profit-sharing plans; 401(k) plans; retirement and pension plans; and educational assistance programs.

The 1996 Telecommunications Act, a government deregulation of the telecommunications industry, has allowed cable companies to expand into other areas. Some cable operators are now offering telephone service, high-speed Internet access, and digital television. To make way for these changes, cable companies have been investing billions of dollars in facility improvements. As a result, experienced cable technicians with an understanding of new technology have had the best job opportunities.

FOR MORE INFORMATION

For information on careers, educational programs and seminars, and certification, contact:

Society of Cable Telecommunications Engineers
140 Philips Road
Exton, PA 19341
Web: http://www.scte.org

A cable television technician tightens connectors at a junction box.

For technician training course information and to receive a NCTI Info Kit, contact:

National Cable Television Institute
801 West Mineral Avenue
Littleton, CO 80120
Tel: 303-797-9393

For information on careers and the cable industry, contact:

National Cable Television Association
1724 Massachusetts Avenue, NW
Washington, DC 20036
Tel: 202-775-3550
Web: http://www.ncta.com

For information about conferences, special programs, and membership, contact:

Women in Cable and Telecommunications
230 West Monroe, Suite 730
Chicago, IL 60606
Tel: 312-634-2330
Web: http://www.wict.org

CARDIOLOGISTS

SCHOOL SUBJECTS:
BIOLOGY, CHEMISTRY, PSYCHOLOGY

PERSONAL SKILLS:
HELPING/TEACHING
TECHNICAL/SCIENTIFIC

MINIMUM EDUCATION LEVEL:
MEDICAL DEGREE

OUTLOOK:
FASTER THAN THE AVERAGE

OTHER ARTICLES TO LOOK AT:

Allergists
Dermatologists
General Practitioners
Geriatricians
Physicians
Surgeons

WHAT CARDIOLOGISTS DO

Cardiologists are physicians who specialize in the diagnosis and treatment of heart disease. In most instances, cardiologists consult with a patient to determine if the symptoms the patient has are signs of heart disease.

During their initial interview with a patient, cardiologists review the patient's medical history and then perform a physical examination. This is their first opportunity to listen to the patient's heart. Often, a cardiologist can tell if there is a cardiac problem by just listening to the rhythm of the heartbeat. For example, when examining a patient for a heart murmur (an abnormal heartbeat), cardiologists are able to tell if it is an innocent murmur, or if it could cause problems.

If necessary, cardiologists send their patients for specific tests that aid in evaluating and diagnosing their symptoms. The most common test is the electrocardiogram (ECG or EKG). An ECG measures the electrical activity produced by heart contractions and prints out a graph for the cardiologist to review. Many problems can be detected through ECGs.

Cardiac catheterization is another test. A small tube is inserted through a blood vessel into or near the heart. This procedure is used to take pictures of the heart that cardiologists can use for diagnosis as well as to evaluate the body's electrical system. This procedure may also be used in some cases to remove obstructions.

Another form of test is the echocardiogram. During this procedure, high-pitched sounds, inaudible to the human ear, are sent into the body. Their echoes are plotted and create a picture of the heart. A stress echocardiogram evaluates the heart by measuring the supply of blood going to the muscles before and after exercise.

Cardiologists do not perform heart surgery; thoracic surgeons do this. Many surgeons, however, often consult with a cardiologist in the preoperative phase of treatment.

Also, cardiologists often provide information and advice to their patients regarding the prevention of cardiac disease through diet and exercise.

EDUCATION AND TRAINING

Students interested in becoming cardiologists should take courses in biology, chemistry, and health in high school. Classes in communication and foreign language are also recommended.

You must first earn a bachelor's degree from a college, and then you must earn your M.D. degree and become licensed to practice medicine (See *Physicians*). To become a cardiologist, you must take seven to eight more years of additional training. This includes an internship that may last from one to two years and a six-year residency program.

Cardiologists spend three years in a residency program in internal medicine and another three years in a residency program in the subspecialty of cardiology.

Cardiologists should be board certified by the American Board of Internal Medicine (ABIM) in both internal medicine and in the cardiology subspecialty. To be certified in internal medicine, you need to complete medical school and at least three years of additional training and also pass a comprehensive exam. Certification in cardiology requires at least three more years of accredited training (in cardiology), proven clinical competence, and passing another comprehensive exam. In 1990, the ABIM began issuing certificates that carried time limitations. This was done to ensure that all certified doctors maintain a high level of competency. For continuing medical education, cardiologists can attend conferences, lectures, or specialized readings.

EARNINGS AND OUTLOOK

According to a 1998 survey conducted by the American Medical Association, the mean net income for internal medicine physicians is roughly $185,700, but salaries may begin around $116,306. Cardiologists can expect a higher income considering it is a subspecialty of internal medicine and demands a higher level of training.

The influence of managed care is being felt in the field of cardiology. The usual inpatient time for someone who has suffered a heart attack has been greatly reduced. Years ago it was common for heart attack patients to remain in the hospital for a month. However, inpatient hospital time has been steadily decreasing. Today patients may stay in the hospital for only two to five days.

Another influence on cardiology is the constant research that is being performed in the field. With the influx of new information, the field is continually evolving. According to the *Occupational Outlook Handbook*, physicians' jobs are expected to grow faster than the average through the year 2006.

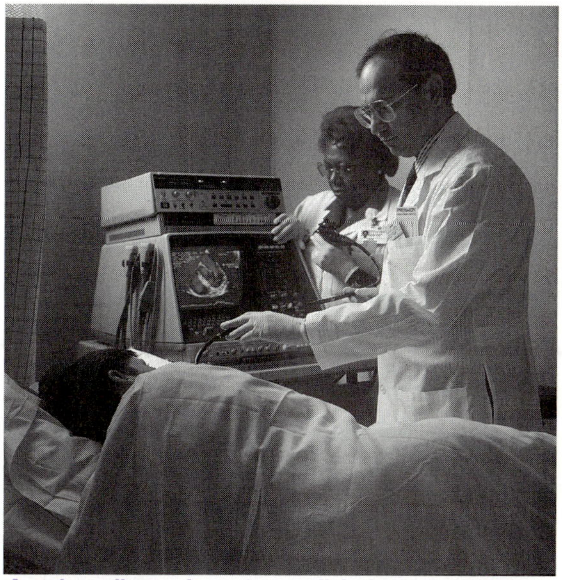

An echocardiogram is one test cardiologists use to diagnose heart problems.

FOR MORE INFORMATION

Following are organizations that provide information on the field of cardiology and sources of certification information.

American Board of Internal Medicine
510 Walnut Street, Suite 1700
Philadelphia, PA 19106-3699
Tel: 800-441-ABIM
Web: http://www.abim.org

American College of Cardiology
9111 Old Georgetown Road
Bethesda, MD 20814
Tel: 800-253-4636, ext. 630
Web: http://www.acc.org

CARDIOVASCULAR TECHNOLOGISTS

SCHOOL SUBJECTS:
BIOLOGY, HEALTH

PERSONAL SKILLS:
HELPING/TEACHING
TECHNICAL/SCIENTIFIC

MINIMUM EDUCATION LEVEL:
SOME POSTSECONDARY TRAINING

OUTLOOK:
FASTER THAN THE AVERAGE

OTHER ARTICLES TO LOOK AT:

Biomedical Equipment Technicians

Electroneurodiagnostic Technologists

Perfusionists

Surgical Technologists

X-Ray Technologists

WHAT CARDIOVASCULAR TECHNOLOGISTS DO

Cardiovascular technologists assist physicians in diagnosing and treating ailments of the heart and blood vessels. Cardiovascular technologists work in hospitals in intensive-care units, cardiac-care units, emergency rooms, and cancer wards. They also may work in nonhospital settings such as clinics, mobile medical services, or private doctor's offices.

There are many possible specialties for cardiovascular technologists. *Electrocardiograph technicians*, often known as *EKG technicians*, operate electrocardiograph (EKG) machines that show how a person's heart is beating. These machines reveal important information about the condition of the heart, including irregular heartbeats or the presence of blocked arteries. EKGs can be used to diagnose heart disease, check the progress of treatment, or check the patient's condition after recovery.

Holter monitor technologists fasten electrodes to a patient's chest and a small monitor to their waist, in order to record the heart during activity. The monitor records the heart as the patient stands, sit, sleeps, or performs any other activity. When the patient returns to the hospital the holter monitor technician removes the monitor and puts it in a scanner that produces audio and visual representations of heart activity. The technician then analyzes the data and passes it on to a physician.

Stress test technologists record the heart's activity during physical activity. In one type of stress test, the technician hooks up the patient to an EKG machine and attaches electrodes to the patient's arms, legs, and chest. They take a reading of the patient's blood pressure and heart at rest, then as the patient walks on a treadmill. The rate of exercise is increased and the technician monitors the heart's responses.

Cardiology technologists assist surgeons and physicians in cardiac catherization (tubing) procedures. An example of this would be an angiogram, where a tube is inserted into the heart to diagnose the condition of the heart's blood vessels, and to see problems such as blockage. Cardiology technologists also assist with angioplasties. In this procedure, a tube with a balloon at the end is inserted into an artery to clear blockage and expand the artery.

Vascular technologists and *echocardiographers* use ultrasound equipment to obtain and record information about the condition of the heart. Ultrasound equipment is used to direct sound waves to a part of the body that needs to be studied. The waves bounce back to create an image of the body organ in question.

Cardiac monitor technicians perform many of the same duties as EKG technicians.

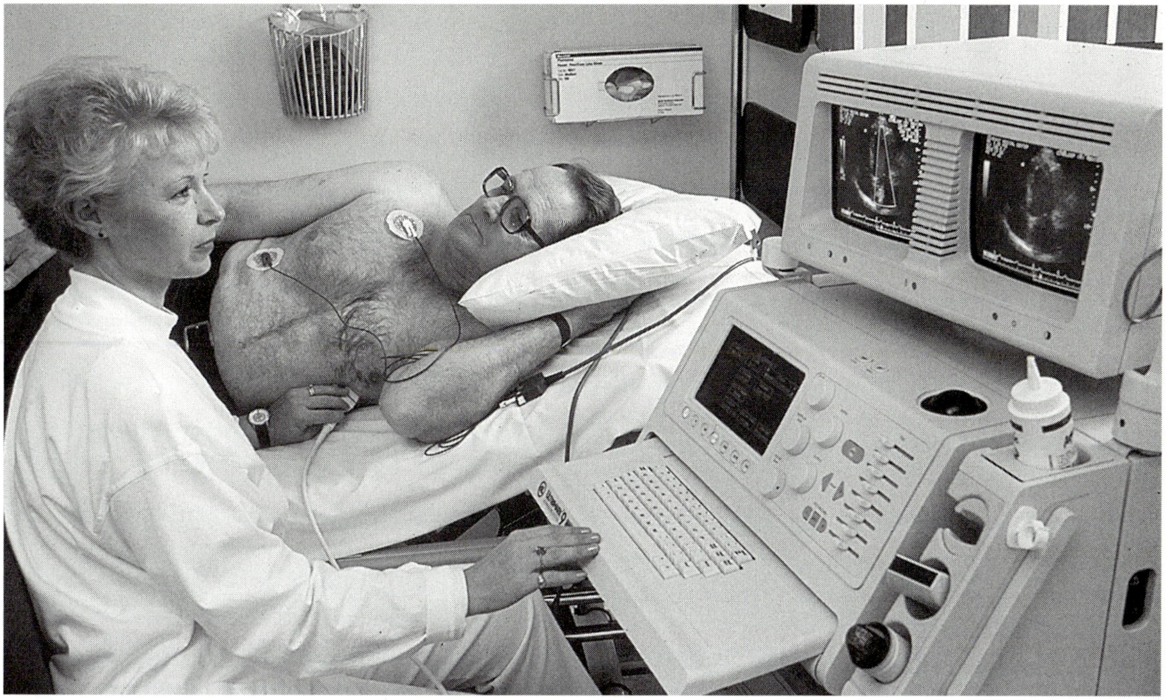

A cardiovascular technologist sits before a row of screens reviewing the status of a heart patient.

They watch cardiac monitors to ensure that the patient's heart is beating as it should.

EDUCATION AND TRAINING

Cardiovascular technologists need to be high school graduates. In addition, they must receive on-the-job training that lasts from six months to two years.

Cardiovascular technologists need to have training in mathematics, including algebra and geometry, and must be able to solve problems having to do with ratios, proportions, and percentages. They should have good reading skills to be able to understand training manuals and other written instructions.

EARNINGS AND OUTLOOK

A typical starting salary for a cardiovascular technologist is around $15,200 a year. For experienced cardiovascular technologists, who can do more complicated kinds of work, a salary of $32,000 is typical.

Job opportunities for cardiovascular technologists vary by specialty. Openings for EKG technicians will decline as equipment and procedures continue to become more efficient. However, employment of cardiology technologists is expected to grow faster than the average in the next decade.

FOR MORE INFORMATION

For more information about a career as a cardiovascular technologist, contact:

American Society of Cardiovascular Professionals/Society of Cardiovascular Management
120 Falcon Drive, Unit 3
Fredericksburg, VA 22408
Tel: 540-891-0079

CAREER COUNSELORS

SCHOOL SUBJECTS:
BUSINESS, PSYCHOLOGY, SOCIOLOGY

PERSONAL SKILLS:
COMMUNICATION/IDEAS
HELPING/TEACHING

MINIMUM EDUCATION LEVEL:
BACHELOR'S DEGREE

OUTLOOK:
ABOUT AS FAST AS THE AVERAGE

OTHER ARTICLES TO LOOK AT:

Adult and Vocational Education Teachers

Executive Recruiters

Guidance Counselors

Office Administrators

Personnel Specialists

WHAT CAREER COUNSELORS DO

Career counselors help people discover their occupational interests and skills so that they may make informed career decisions. First, counselors must establish a friendly working relationship and find out what kind of information and guidance is needed. The counselors determine what abilities people already have and what areas may need strengthening. To determine this, counselors sometimes administer tests, including standardized achievement and aptitude tests. The results of the tests help the counselors provide better guidance.

Employment counselors also help people make decisions about what kinds of work they want to do. Employment counselors work with employers to help them hire people for specific job openings. They gather descriptions of the particular positions that employers need to fill, and, using these descriptions, the counselors tell qualified job seekers about suitable jobs available.

Guidance counselors help students, mostly in junior and senior high school, to choose courses that will prepare them for jobs and careers. They also help students with educational, social, and personal problems. Sometimes suggestions and encouragement are all that students need. But if a student has a serious problem, the guidance counselor may refer the student to a social welfare agency, child guidance clinic, health department, or other community service agency.

Career counselors have enormous responsibilities as they assist people in making major life decisions. They must enjoy working with people of all ages, backgrounds, and sexes. In addition, they should have a thorough knowledge of education, training, employment trends, the job market, and career resources to best assist their clients.

EDUCATION AND TRAINING

Nationally certified career counselors must have at least a master's degree in counseling (or a related field, such as psychology), experience as a supervised counselor, and a minimum of three years of full-time independent career counseling. A doctorate is generally recommended for the best jobs, and ongoing education in the field is a requirement for certificate renewal by the National Board of Certified Counselors.

New career counselors are often considered trainees for the first six months to a year of their employment. They may work for schools, colleges, or public health agencies, in business and industry, or maintain their own private practices. Opportunities for advancement are excellent, and many counselors go on to become supervisors, administrators, or directors of career development projects.

A director of financial aid consults with a student about her financial aid package.

EARNINGS AND OUTLOOK

Annual earnings of career and placement counselors vary greatly among educational institutions, with larger institutions offering the highest salaries. The average salary is approximately $35,000 per year at educational institutions. In private practice, the range is wider yet. Some counselors earn as little as $20,000 per year, others as much as $100,000. This range includes the many agency counselors who also work part-time in private practice.

There should be good growth in the field of employment counseling through the year 2006, according to the U.S. Department of Labor. Although only moderate opportunities are anticipated for employment and rehabilitation counselors in state and local governments, rapid growth is expected in the development of human resource and employment assistance programs in private business and industry, which should produce more jobs.

FOR MORE INFORMATION

School or public librarians can direct interested students to reading material about work as a career counselor. Talking to a school guidance counselor about the nature of counseling work is a good start.

For more information about a career as a career counselor, contact:

Career Planning and Adult Development Network
PO Box 1484
Pacifica, CA 94044
Tel: 650-359-3089

National Board for Certified Counselors
3 Terrace Way, Suite D
Greensboro, NC 27403-3660
Web: http://www.nbcc.org

CARPENTERS

SCHOOL SUBJECTS:
MATHEMATICS, TECHNICAL/SHOP

PERSONAL SKILLS:
FOLLOWING INSTRUCTIONS
MECHANICAL/MANIPULATIVE

MINIMUM EDUCATION LEVEL:
HIGH SCHOOL DIPLOMA
APPRENTICESHIP

OUTLOOK:
MUCH FASTER THAN THE AVERAGE

OTHER ARTICLES TO LOOK AT:

Bricklayers and Stonemasons
Cement Masons
Construction Laborers
Drywall Installers and Repairers
Plasterers
Roofers

WHAT CARPENTERS DO

Carpenters cut, shape, and fasten together pieces of wood, wallboard, plywood, and insulation. Most carpenters work on constructing, remodeling, or repairing houses or other kinds of buildings. Some carpenters work indoors, some outdoors, and some work both indoors and outdoors. Carpenters work with hand tools, such as hammers, saws, measuring devices, and screwdrivers, and with power tools, such as electric saws and drills.

There are two basic kinds of carpentry work. Rough carpentry involves constructing and installing the parts of a building that are usually covered up by the time the rooms are finished, such as the wooden framework of the building and the frames inside walls. Because the sturdiness of the building depends on how well this is done, care must be taken. Rough carpentry also includes building various temporary structures needed on construction sites. Among these are scaffolds, the wooden platforms that workers stand on; wooden chutes used as channels for wet concrete; and wooden molds or forms that the concrete is poured into to make foundations for buildings.

Finish carpentry involves building and installing wooden floors, shelves, cabinets, and other visible pieces of woodwork that make rooms look complete. Finish carpenters can specialize in one particular structure. Stair fabricators and cabinetmakers are two types of carpenter with advanced artistic skills in carpentry. *Finish carpenters* must be especially precise in their work, since it not only must be strong and well-built; it must also have a good appearance.

EDUCATION AND TRAINING

If you're considering a career as a carpenter, begin your planning with high school. A high school education is not required for a good job as a carpenter, but most contractors and developers prefer applicants with a diploma, or the equivalent, a GED. Classes you should consider taking include carpentry and woodworking, as well as other shop classes; algebra, geometry and other applied mathematics courses; science; and mechanical drawing, among others.

After high school, the best way to become a carpenter is to complete an apprenticeship program, which lasts four years. Applicants to these programs typically are required to be high school graduates and at least 17 years old. During training, apprentices work at a variety of jobs, learning both rough and finish carpentry. In addition, they receive classroom instruction about different kinds of construction materials; about how buildings are built; about how to use and care for tools; and about how to read blueprints, make sketches, and do the mathematical calculations that often are required on the job.

Rather than complete an apprenticeship, many carpenters learn their skills informally on the job. How thorough their training is depends on their employer and the kinds of experience that the job provides. People who become carpenters in this way sometimes do not learn as much, and it may take them longer to become considered skilled carpenters.

EARNINGS AND OUTLOOK

According to the federal Bureau of Labor Statistics, the majority of carpenters who did not own their own businesses made between $20,780 and $40,039 in 1997, the most recent year for which statistics are available. The mean annual wage that year was $30,800. (Apprentices make at least 40 percent of this wage at the start of this training, and receive increases each year of the program). These carpenters often are hired just for particular projects, rather than being full-time employees.

In the late 1990s, the construction trades experienced a severe shortage of qualified workers, making the outlook for a job in this field excellent in the next 10 to 15 years. It's important to remember, however, that the availability of steady employment generally depends on economic conditions in the area where carpenters want to work. In areas where the economy is strong and there is a lot of building going on, well-qualified carpenters can find good job opportunities. Today, jobs are plentiful all over the country. However, when local economic conditions are less favorable, jobs are harder to find, and earnings are lower.

A carpenter cuts a board with a hand saw while working on construction of a home.

FOR MORE INFORMATION

For more information about a career as a carpenter, contact the following organizations.

Home Builders Institute
1090 Vermont Avenue, NW, Suite 600
Washington, DC 20005
Tel: 202-371-0600 or 800-795-7955
Web: http://www.hbi.org

National Association of Homebuilders
1201 15th Street, NW
Washington, DC 20005-2800
Tel: 202-822-0200
Web: http://www.nahb.com

Associated General Contractors of America
1957 E Street, NW
Washington, DC 20006
Web: http://www.agc.org

CARTOGRAPHERS

SCHOOL SUBJECTS:
GEOGRAPHY, SOCIAL STUDIES

PERSONAL SKILLS:
ARTISTIC
TECHNICAL/SCIENTIFIC

MINIMUM EDUCATION LEVEL:
BACHELOR'S DEGREE

OUTLOOK:
LITTLE CHANGE OR MORE SLOWLY THAN THE AVERAGE

OTHER ARTICLES TO LOOK AT:

Geographers
Geophysicists
Oceanographers
Photographers
Surveying and Mapping Technicians

WHAT CARTOGRAPHERS DO

Cartographers are mapmakers. They use information about the world's surface to create maps that graphically represent what the world looks like. Cartographers use photographs taken from space and survey information collected on the ground to make these visual representations.

Cartographers use the skills of photogrammetrists to interpret and obtain geographic measurements from photographs taken from airplanes or satellites. They also use the information gathered by surveyors to determine the distances between areas, the height of mountains and other landforms, and the precise locations of valleys, lakes, and other geographic features. Cartographers then draw a map that shows all this information in detail. Cartographers prepare maps through a hand technique called scribing. Scribing is a process in which a sharp tool is used to cut away the surface coating of a plastic sheet. By using this process the cartographer creates lines and indentations that represent the features of the earth. These sheets are then made into maps.

Cartographers not only make maps from new information, they also make maps from other maps. For example, a cartographer might take a large map of the world and use it to make a map of France or another country. To do this, the cartographer must interpret the symbols on the original map (like numbers used to represent how high mountains are) and redraw those features in greater detail.

Cartographers are increasingly using computers to draw maps and collect and interpret geographic information. In addition to making maps, cartographers also study them. A cartographer may be asked to look at a map and help determine where it would be best to drill for oil. Cartographers are also constantly reviewing maps to ensure that they are correct. For instance, new photographs from space might show that a large forest has been cut down. This information must be transferred onto the new map.

EDUCATION AND TRAINING

Cartographers should know how to read and understand detailed photographs or drawings and be able to use drafting tools to draw accurate maps. They also should be skilled in the use of computer technology. Computer-mapping software and data-merging software permit huge amounts of data to be collected and displayed using overlays on one map. Cartographers have to work with other mapping scientists, so they should have good communications skills and be able to get along with others.

The best way to become a cartographer is to get a college degree in engineering or a physical science such as geography. Some people, however, may become cartographers after graduating high school and getting a job as a cartographer's assistant. High school courses should include geography, mechanical drawing, and as many computer courses as possible. Many times cartographers will receive on-the-job training before taking on the full responsibilities of mapmaking.

EARNINGS AND OUTLOOK

Most of the approximately 5,000 cartographers in the federal government earn between $16,900 and $61,600 annually, with the average about $33,800 per year. An entry-level cartographer in the private sector may earn $18,000 per year, while a highly trained cartographer could easily earn $42,000 or more annually. Cartographers with specialized skills earn the highest salaries.

Through the year 2006, some growth in employment of cartographers and other mapping scientists may occur in the private sector. The increasing demand for sophisticated land and sea maps will require specialized mapping skills. Little or no growth is expected in employment by departments and agencies of the federal government. The greatest growth in employment will be in geographic information systems (GIS), which involve sophisticated mapping systems.

FOR MORE INFORMATION

For more information, contact:

North American Cartographic Information Society
6010 Executive Boulevard, Suite 100
Rockville, MD 20852

A cartographer works on a historical map of Washington, DC.

American Congress on Surveying and Mapping
5410 Grosvenor Lane, Suite 100
Bethesda, MD 20814
Tel: 301-493-0200

General information on careers in photogrammetry and a pamphlet entitled "Careers in Photogrammetry" are available from:

American Society for Photogrammetry and Remote Sensing
5410 Grosvenor Lane, Suite 210
Bethesda, MD 20814
Tel: 301-493-0290

CARTOONISTS

SCHOOL SUBJECTS:
ART, COMPUTER SCIENCE, HISTORY

PERSONAL SKILLS:
ARTISTIC, COMMUNICATION/IDEAS

MINIMUM EDUCATION LEVEL:
HIGH SCHOOL DIPLOMA

OUTLOOK:
FASTER THAN THE AVERAGE

OTHER ARTICLES TO LOOK AT:

Art Directors
Artists
Cinematographers
Graphics Designers
Special Effects Technicians

WHAT CARTOONISTS DO

Cartoonists draw the illustrations for a variety of publications and sources, including comic strips, political cartoons, comic books, magazines, greeting cards, and advertisements. As a cartoonist, you'll translate ideas into pictures to communicate to an audience. Sometimes these ideas are meant to be funny, as in the comic strips. Other times they are meant to carry a political or social message, as in editorial cartoons in a newspaper. Sometimes cartoonists tell a longer story, as in a comic book. Still other times, cartoonists are hired to sell a product, as in a television commercial.

If creating a comic strip, panel, or book, you'll first need an idea. Like most writers, you'll draw from your own life, and enhance the details with your imagination. Or you may choose to comment on current or historical events. For inspiration, you may read other comic strips, read the newspaper, or listen to music. Most artists have very individual approaches to their work. You'll make sketches in a drawing pad, "roughing out" ideas. Once you have something you're happy with, you'll then set out to prepare the drawing for publication. You are likely to have a favorite kind of paper and pencil to use. Some cartoonists work in offices, but many freelance, working from drawing desks at home.

After you've drawn up the rough strips, you'll then add the lettering, giving words to your characters. When you're satisfied with your work, you can then ink in the lines. This can be a painstaking process and requires patience and a steady hand. The ink will easily run or smear if you don't work with a clean nib (the end of the ink pen), letting the ink dry in stages as you draw. Once the ink is completely dry, you'll erase the pencil lines.

You may choose to use a computer to add shading to your drawing, or you may do so manually with special shading materials from an art store. When using the computer, you'll scan the drawing, then bring it up in a special computer program. Shading can be added using special software, as can color.

Because most artists work freelance, they can set their own hours. However, when meeting deadlines, they may have to put in extra time.

EDUCATION AND TRAINING

In high school, you should take all the art and drawing classes you can. Photography classes also will help you to develop visual composition skills. English composition and literature classes will help you develop creative writing skills.

Cartoonists don't necessarily need a college education, but they should have some formal art training. In addition to being creative, cartoonists must have a good grasp of contemporary life, so it would be useful to study political science, history, and social studies.

Many cartoonists begin by selling cartoons to small publications such as community newspapers. Another way to start your career is to put together a collection, called a portfolio, of your best work and send it to publishers, syndicates, or advertising agencies. Cartoonists' success depends on how much the public likes their work.

EARNINGS AND OUTLOOK

Freelance cartoonists and animators may earn anywhere from $50 to $1,200 per assignment, but higher figures are usually reserved for very well known artists. Comic strip cartoonists are usually paid according to the number of newspapers that carry their strip and can earn $100,000 or more in a year. Those who create very popular strips and characters may share in the profits of merchandise such as toys, dolls, calendars, and games inspired by the strip.

Employment for cartoonists is expected to grow faster than the average, but it will still be hard to break into the market. Because of the freelance nature of the work, it can be very difficult to earn a steady wage and work full-time. The most opportunities will be with advertising departments or graphic arts agencies. Having your work published in magazines and newspapers will require great persistence and great luck. The syndicates (those companies that sell strips to newspapers) reject thousands of artist portfolios every year.

FOR MORE INFORMATION

If your school has a newspaper or some other publication, submit some of your best drawings and ask the editors to use you as a cartoonist. You might also draw posters for school or sporting events.

A cartoonist finishes the coloring on a panel for a comic strip.

The NCS has an Education Committee, and publishes an "Occupation and Education Guide." The Web site is also very informative, with quotes from cartoonists and information about syndicates.

National Cartoonists Society (NCS)
Columbus Circle Station
PO Box 2067
New York, NY 10023
Tel: 212-627-1550
Web: http://www.reuben.org

For general information on illustrators, contact:

Society of Illustrators
128 East 63rd Street
New York, NY 10021-7303
Web: http://www.societyillustrators.org

CASHIERS

SCHOOL SUBJECTS:
BUSINESS, MATHEMATICS

PERSONAL SKILLS:
COMMUNICATION/IDEAS
HELPING/TEACHING

MINIMUM EDUCATION LEVEL:
HIGH SCHOOL DIPLOMA

OUTLOOK:
ABOUT AS FAST AS THE AVERAGE

OTHER ARTICLES TO LOOK AT:

Bank Services Occupations
Bookkeepers
Counter and Retail Clerks
Retail Sales Workers
Retail Store Managers
Services Sales Representatives

WHAT CASHIERS DO

Cashiers receive money paid by customers for a product or service. They also make change, fill out credit-card slips, and provide receipts to customers. Cashiers are known by many different names in different businesses. In a supermarket, for instance, cashiers are called *check-out clerks*, *grocery clerks*, or *checkers*. In theaters, cashiers may be called *ticket sellers* or *box-office cashiers*. And in railroad or bus stations, cashiers may be called *ticket agents*. Wherever cashiers work, they must keep records of the amounts of money collected during their shifts so that end-of-day totals can be figured.

In drug stores, grocery stores, and department stores, cashiers may bag or wrap merchandise and, when time is available, put prices on merchandise, restock shelves, or do other jobs. In some businesses, cashiers prepare bank deposits, sales-tax reports, and paychecks for employees. Cashiers working in restaurants, theaters, and hotels may answer phone calls, take reservations, and sometimes are in charge of candy counters.

Cashiers usually operate some type of cash register in their work. These may be very simple machines that add up amounts, print them on a paper tape, and open the cash drawer. More frequently, cashiers work with some form of computer terminal that feeds information about the transaction into a central computer, shows a digital read-out of prices, and provides an itemized bill for the customer. In some cases, cashiers use electronic devices called optical scanners. The cashier passes the product label over the scanner, which reads a code on the package and transmits the code to the cashier's terminal. The price of the item is then automatically displayed at the terminal and added to the customer's bill.

EDUCATION AND TRAINING

Some employers require that cashiers be high school graduates; others do not. High school courses that are most likely to help prepare a student for this work include bookkeeping, typing, business-machine operations, and business arithmetic. For some kinds of more complicated cashier jobs, employers may prefer applicants who are graduates of two-year community colleges or business schools, especially those programs that include some on-the-job experience as part of their training program.

Cashiers spend most of their time working with customers, and so they need to have a pleasant personality. They should also be good at mathematics and be accurate. Although the work is not strenuous, cashiers usually have to be able to stand for long periods of time.

A customer pays a cashier for her purchases.

EARNINGS AND OUTLOOK

Experienced, full-time cashiers who belong to the United Food and Commercial Workers International Union average about $27,900 per year, but beginners average about $5.90 per hour. Cashiers who work in restaurants generally make less than those in other businesses do. Some cashiers receive insurance benefits and paid vacation days, although these are usually only available to full-time cashiers. More than half of all cashiers work part-time.

Job opportunities for cashiers are expected to grow at an average pace through 2006. Opportunities will be especially good for applicants with good mathematical and language skills. Competition will be strongest for the higher-paying cashier jobs, such as those in department stores.

Factors that could limit job growth include the increased installation of automatic change-making machines, vending machines, and other types of automatic and electronic equipment. Job opportunities will be available to those experienced in bookkeeping, typing, business machine operation, and general office skills. Many part-time jobs should also be available. Although the majority of cashiers employed are 24 years of age or younger, many businesses have started hiring the elderly to fill some job openings.

FOR MORE INFORMATION

For additional information about a career as a cashier, contact:

National Retail Federation
325 7th Street, NW, Suite 1000
Washington, DC 20004
Tel: 202-783-7971
Web: http://www.nrf.com

CATERERS

SCHOOL SUBJECTS:
BUSINESS, FAMILY AND CONSUMER SCIENCE

PERSONAL SKILLS:
ARTISTIC, HELPING/TEACHING

MINIMUM EDUCATION LEVEL:
HIGH SCHOOL DIPLOMA

OUTLOOK:
FASTER THAN THE AVERAGE

OTHER ARTICLES TO LOOK AT:

Cooks, Chefs, and Bakers
Dietetic Technicians
Food Service Workers
Nutritionists
Purchasing Agents
Waiters

WHAT CATERERS DO

Caterers plan, prepare, and serve meals to large groups of people. They coordinate parties, formal dinners, wedding receptions, and a variety of other gatherings. They may be involved with all aspects of a celebration, such as planning the menu, buying the food and drinks, preparing the food, and supervising the food service.

In addition to preparing food, caterers must also be able to make a room look special. They use flowers, wall-hangings, and other decorations to make an area attractive. Caterers also set up the tables and chairs and provide the necessary linen, silverware, and dishes. A large catering company may organize as many as 50 or more events a month.

If handling a large banquet in a hotel or other location, the caterer will usually prepare the food at the hotel. The caterer might also work in a customer's kitchen if the affair is going to be at the customer's home. In both of these instances, it is important that the caterer visit the site of the function well before the actual event to determine how and where the food will be prepared. Caterers may also prepare the food in their own kitchens or in a mobile kitchen. In all cases, frequent phone contact is often necessary to coordinate events.

The caterer and customer will usually work together within a budget to develop a menu and atmosphere the customer can enjoy. Customers always want their affairs to be special, and the caterer's ability to accomplish that will contribute to his or her success.

Caterers hire all of the wait staff that will work an event, and they are responsible for making sure enough people show up to work all the tables and assist at the bar.

EDUCATION AND TRAINING

Caterers must be outgoing, friendly people. They must be able to greet guests, comfort nervous customers, and supervise servers and other workers. They must be able to solve problems and keep minor disappointments from disturbing an event.

Although many caterers have college training in baking, cooking, or business management, other caterers may have picked up their training outside of school at a restaurant or another catering company. Persons who become caterers may start off by serving food or cleaning the dishes at an event. They may also work as a chef's assistant or as an assistant business manager for the catering department of a hotel. No matter how they start out, caterers must feel comfortable with planning and preparing an event, supervising workers, and advertising their services.

EARNINGS AND OUTLOOK

Earnings vary widely, depending on the size and location of the catering operation and the skill and motivation of the individual entrepreneur. Many caterers charge according to the number of guests attending a function. In many cases, the larger the event, the larger the profit. Earnings are also influenced by whether a caterer works full-time or only part-time. Even very successful caterers often work part-time, working full-time at another job either because they enjoy their other job or to protect themselves against a possible downturn in the economy.

Full-time caterers can earn between $15,000 and $60,000 per year, depending on skill, reputation, and experience. An extremely successful caterer can easily earn more than $75,000 annually. A part-time caterer may earn $7,000 to $15,000 per year, subject to the same variables as the full-time caterer. Because most caterers are self-employed, vacations and other benefits are usually not part of the wage structure.

A caterer who works as a manager for a company cafeteria or other industrial client may earn between $18,000 and $35,000 per year, with vacation, health insurance, and other benefits usually included.

Because the U.S. food service industry is strong, employment opportunities in catering should continue to grow through 2006. Business should be good for caterers who handle weddings, bar and bat mitzvahs, business functions, and other events.

Competition is keen as many hotels and restaurants branch out to offer catering services. Like all service industries, catering is sensitive to the economy, and a downturn in the economy may limit catering opportunities. Despite the competition and fluctuating economic conditions, highly skilled and motivated caterers should be in demand throughout the country, especially in and around large metropolitan areas.

A catering worker puts the finishing touches on a buffet.

FOR MORE INFORMATION

For more information about a career as a caterer, contact the following:

International Food Service Executives Association
1100 South State Road #7, Suite 103
Margate, FL 33068
Tel: 954-977-0767
Web: http://www.ifsea.org/

This trade association offers information on certification and other career information.

National Association of Catering Executives
60 Revere Drive, Suite 500
Northbrook, IL 60062
Tel: 847-480-9080
Web: http://www.nace.net/

CEMENT MASONS

SCHOOL SUBJECTS:
CHEMISTRY, MATHEMATICS, TECHNICAL/SHOP

PERSONAL SKILLS:
MECHANICAL/MANIPULATIVE, TECHNICAL/SCIENTIFIC

MINIMUM EDUCATION LEVEL:
HIGH SCHOOL DIPLOMA
APPRENTICESHIP

OUTLOOK:
LITTLE CHANGE OR MORE SLOWLY THAN THE AVERAGE

OTHER ARTICLES TO LOOK AT:

Bricklayers and Stonemasons

Construction Laborers

Marble Setters, Tile Setters, and Terrazzo Workers

Plasterers

WHAT CEMENT MASONS DO

Cement masons are skilled workers who smooth and finish surfaces of concrete on many different kinds of construction projects, ranging from floors and sidewalks to highways, dams, and airport runways. Cement masons are also known as cement finishers or concrete masons.

At a building site, a cement mason first sets up the forms that will hold the poured concrete until it hardens into the desired shape. After the forms are in place, the mason positions steel rods or mesh in the space where the concrete will be placed; this strengthens the concrete after it dries. Finally, the cement mason pours or directs the pouring of the concrete into the forms. The wet concrete is then spread, leveled, and compacted.

Using a large trowel called a float, cement masons smooth the surface. On driveways, pavements, and similar projects, they finish by brushing the concrete to produce the desired texture. On projects where curved edges are necessary, masons may use tools such as a curb edger. On walls and floors, they may remove rough or defective spots with a chisel and hammer.

Smaller projects, such as sidewalks, patios, and driveways, are usually done by hand. On large-scale projects such as highways, power-operated floats and finishing machines are used. Although such large equipment can perform many services, corners and other inaccessible areas usually require hand finishing.

EDUCATION AND TRAINING

For most jobs in this field, employers try to hire persons who are in good physical condition and who possess good manual skills. A high school diploma is not required, but a diploma will give you an advantage. Applicants must have completed at least the eighth grade and have some understanding of basic math. In any case, to qualify as a cement mason, you must also complete either an apprenticeship or an on-the-job training program.

The apprenticeship program consists of two or three years of planned and supervised work experience combined with classroom instruction. Apprentices learn proper use and handling of tools, equipment, and materials, plus blueprint reading, applied math, estimating procedures, building regulations, and other subjects.

On-the-job training usually requires more time to learn the necessary skills and knowledge. Trainees work under the guidance of experienced masons, often starting as cement helpers or laborers. As you learn job skills, you become eligible for higher positions.

EARNINGS AND OUTLOOK

In the late 1990s, most cement masons earned about $19,000 to $33,000 per year. About 10 percent earned over $40,000, while some made as little as $14,800 and less. Since the amount of time spent working is limited by weather conditions, many workers' earnings vary from these figures. Hourly wages in 1996 were $15 to $45. Apprentices start at wages that are approximately half of a fully qualified mason's wage; they receive periodic raises, so in the last phase of training, their wage is almost as much as the experienced worker's pay.

Employment opportunities for cement masons are expected to increase more slowly than the average for all occupations over the next seven years. Cement masons will be in demand to help build roads, bridges, buildings, subways, shopping malls, and many other structures. The productivity of cement masons will be improved considerably by the introduction of better equipment, tools, and materials; that is, fewer cement masons will be needed to do the same amount of work. Many new openings will arise every year as experienced workers move into other occupations or leave the labor force.

FOR MORE INFORMATION

This multinational union affiliated with the AFL-CIO offers a quarterly publication and has a Plasterers and Cement Masons Action Committee.

Operative Plasterers and Cement Masons International Association of the United States and Canada
14405 Laurel Place, Suite 300
Laurel, MD 20707
Tel: 301-470-4200

Cement masons put the finishing touches on the foundation for a new home.

For information on training and apprenticeship programs, contact:

Associated General Contractors of America
1957 E Street, NW
Washington, DC 20006
Tel: 202-393-2040
Web: http://www.agc.org

IMI is a labor-management cooperative that offers design and technical assistance as well as an annual masonry camp for chosen apprentices.

International Masonry Institute (IMI)
Training and Research Center
PO Box 755
Cascade, MD 21719
Tel: 301-241-5503
Email: cmuldoon@imiweb.org
Web: http://imiweb.org

For information on specialized education and research programs and apprenticeships, contact:

Mason Contractors Association of America
1550 Spring Road, Suite 320
Oak Brook, IL 60521-1363
Tel: 630-782-6767
Web: http://www.masoncontractors.com/

CERAMIC ARTISTS

SCHOOL SUBJECTS:
ART, HISTORY

PERSONAL SKILLS:
ARTISTIC, MECHANICAL/MANIPULATIVE

MINIMUM EDUCATION LEVEL:
SOME POSTSECONDARY TRAINING

OUTLOOK:
LITTLE CHANGE OR MORE SLOWLY THAN THE AVERAGE

OTHER ARTICLES TO LOOK AT:

Art Directors
Artists
Creative Arts Therapists
Glaziers
Pottery and Porcelainware Industry Workers

WHAT CERAMIC ARTISTS DO

Ceramic artists, also known as potters, ceramists, sculptors, and clay artists, work with clay to make art objects, such as sculptures, beads, and decorative tiles and functional objects, such as cups, lamps, and vases. They blend clay with water and other materials and form the mixture into shapes. Sometimes they use their hands to shape the forms. Sometimes they use a potter's wheel (this is called "throwing on the wheel").

Clay is found in the earth beneath rich topsoil and layers of rock. Weather conditions, such as rain, snow, and wind, wear down the earth's surface, causing it to break down. Different types of clay are dug from the earth and can then be used by the artist. If you hold a lump of wet clay in your hands, you can feel its softness and squeezability. To become hard after shaping, each type of clay needs to be heated, or fired, in an open fire or a kiln.

The term *production potter* usually refers to someone who makes a series of household wares, such as matching dinner plates, cups, and saucers. Production potters also make vases, bowls, and other pieces for display rather than for everyday use. These artists might work alone in a studio or with one or two helpers, or they might set up a large workshop that employs several people.

The *ceramic sculptor* creates works of art rather than functional pottery. These artists use their hands more than they use the potter's wheel to make their products. They build shapes with clay coils or slabs, or carve into a solid lump of clay to create sculptures or images.

EDUCATION AND TRAINING

If you want to be a ceramic artist, you have to be willing to get your hands dirty playing with mud. You're never too young or too old to work with clay. Pottery classes are usually offered for people of all ages. Like other types of artists, those who work with clay often learn the basics of their craft in formal art programs with experienced artists and then they practice their own styles. In class, you learn how to work with clay, how to build shapes with your hands and with a potter's wheel, and how to glaze and fire what you make. To become a professional ceramic artist, your goal should be to earn a bachelor's degree in fine arts, with a major in ceramic art and design.

EARNINGS AND OUTLOOK

For many artists, earnings come in a different form than money. Many artists would like to become successful by selling a lot of their pieces, but this doesn't happen with every artist. You might work hundreds of hours on one piece and then realize that you want to keep it for yourself, or you might sell it to the first person who comes to your studio.

If you decide that you want to earn steady pay, you can work for an established potter or a large ceramics manufacturing firm. This type of job might allow you to earn at least $15,000 to $25,000 per year.

It is very hard to predict whether ceramic artists will enjoy success and recognition in the near future. Within the broader art world—which includes painting, architecture, and sculpture—ceramic art and design is quite new. Ceramics instruction is widespread today, but as late as the 1930s ceramics wasn't really considered much of an art. People today still debate whether it is a craft or an art.

However, there are good signs that ceramics as an art form has the potential to become well recognized. The 1990s have produced many books, videos, and magazines on the subject, along with workshops, conferences, and competitions throughout the world. Ceramic artists gather to show their work, work together, and teach others. Many have made names for themselves in the art world and are valued as artists.

A ceramic artist shapes a decorative vase.

FOR MORE INFORMATION

For more information about a career as a ceramic artist, contact:

National Art Education Association
1916 Association Drive
Reston, VA 22091
Tel: 703-860-8000
Web: http://www.cedarnet.org/emig

This association supports established and emerging artists and arts organizations. For information on art programs, contact your state agency, or:

National Assembly of State Arts Agencies
1029 Vermont Avenue, NW, 2nd Floor
Washington, DC 20005
Tel: 202-347-6352
Email: nasaa@nasaa-arts.org
Web: http://www.nasaa-arts.org

For education information, contact:

National Council on Education for the Ceramic Arts
PO Box 1677
Bandon, OR 97411
Tel: 503-347-4394
Web: http://www2.tamucc.edu/nceca

CERAMIC ENGINEERS

SCHOOL SUBJECTS:
CHEMISTRY, PHYSICS

PERSONAL SKILLS:
MECHANICAL/MANIPULATIVE
TECHNICAL/SCIENTIFIC

MINIMUM EDUCATION LEVEL:
BACHELOR'S DEGREE

OUTLOOK:
LITTLE CHANGE OR MORE SLOWLY THAN THE AVERAGE

OTHER ARTICLES TO LOOK AT:

Mechanical Engineers
Metallurgical Technicians
Mining Engineers
Plastics Engineers
Pottery and Porcelainware Industry Workers

WHAT CERAMIC ENGINEERS DO

Ceramic engineers work with materials that have scientific names like nitride and zirconia, but simply speaking, they work with clay materials. Any product made by heating clay and other earth materials is called ceramic. Glass, brick, cement, and tile are all ceramic products. Ceramics are affected by what materials are used to make the clay and by the temperature at which they are fired (baked). How they are baked changes their ability to absorb water and resist heat. Various coatings also change the use of any ceramic object.

Because they can resist heat and do not corrode, ceramic products have many uses. For example, electricity doesn't melt ceramic circuit breakers; car exhaust fumes can't eat away at ceramic parts.

Some ceramic engineers do research; they work in laboratories testing new materials and trying out new combinations of minerals for ceramics and glazes. They also develop new products and figure out how to manufacture them. Ceramic research engineers have developed products such as thin glass fibers for communications equipment and the heat-resistant tile that protects the space shuttle.

Many ceramic engineers work in manufacturing plants. They design the equipment used to make ceramic products. They supervise those who use the equipment. They may also work with ceramic processes or materials in another industry. For example, the steel industry uses a special kind of heat-resistant ceramic brick to make huge furnaces, called blast furnaces. Steel plants need ceramic engineers to supervise the building and operation of these blast furnaces.

Other ceramic engineers test products to make sure they perform the way they are supposed to; some engineers sell the products to other industries. Ceramic engineers who work in testing or selling travel around to meet customers, check how they are using the product, and help with any problems. Some ceramic engineers teach at universities and colleges.

EDUCATION AND TRAINING

Ceramic engineering jobs require a college degree in engineering. Many jobs in ceramic engineering also require further, specialized study in graduate programs. To teach at the university level or to direct most research projects, an even higher degree is required.

Engineering programs look for high school students with strong backgrounds in math and science. Ceramic engineers must know a great deal about different materials and how they behave. They must also be able to apply their knowledge in practical situations. Whether ceramic engineers are writing research reports or directing workers in a factory, they must communicate well with others.

Any engineer whose work may affect the public welfare must be licensed. Most states require an engineering degree, four years' job experience, and passing a state exam for a license.

EARNINGS AND OUTLOOK

The average annual salary for a ceramics engineer just beginning a career is about $35,000. Those who have been working in the field for some years earn an average of about $59,000; those in senior managerial positions with years of experience can earn nearly $100,000 per year. Salaries for government workers are generally less than for those who work for private companies.

Although employment for ceramics engineers is expected to grow more slowly than the average through 2006, there won't be a lot of competition for jobs because of the low number of new graduates in ceramics engineering. And even though industries that need ceramics engineers (those specifically involved in stoneware, clay, and glass products; primary metals; fabricated metal products; and transportation equipment) are not expected to have much growth in the near future, some segments of the ceramics industry are expected to grow. These sections include research and testing, engineering, and architectural services.

FOR MORE INFORMATION

For information on the ceramics industry, contact:

American Ceramic Society
735 Ceramic Place
PO Box 6136
Westerville, OH 43086-6136
Web: http://www.acers.org

A ceramic engineer studies the computer reading of one phase of ceramic production.

JETS provides activities, events, competitions, programs, and materials that allow high school students to "try on" engineering. Visit the JETS homepage for a complete list of programs, including a broad range of guidance materials about the various engineering disciplines.

Junior Engineering Technical Society, Inc.
1420 King Street, Suite 405
Alexandria, VA 22314-2794
Tel: 703-548-5387
Web: http://www.asee.org/JETS

For information on a program for high school seniors that covers science material not traditionally offered in high school, contact:

Worcester Polytechnic Institute
Frontiers in Science, Mathematics, and Engineering
100 Institute Road
Worcester, MA 01609-2280
Tel: 508-831-5514
Web: http://www.wpi.edu

CERTIFIED NURSE-MIDWIVES

SCHOOL SUBJECTS:
HEALTH, PSYCHOLOGY, SOCIOLOGY

PERSONAL SKILLS:
COMMUNICATION/IDEAS
HELPING/TEACHING

MINIMUM EDUCATION LEVEL:
BACHELOR'S DEGREE

OUTLOOK:
FASTER THAN THE AVERAGE

OTHER ARTICLES TO LOOK AT:

Homeopaths
Naturopaths
Licensed Practical Nurses
Nurses
Osteopaths
Physicians

WHAT CERTIFIED NURSE MIDWIVES DO

Certified nurse-midwives are registered nurses who assist in family planning, pregnancy, and childbirth. They also provide routine health care for women. Certified nurse-midwives work in hospitals, with physicians in private practice, in freestanding birth centers or well-woman care centers, in women's clinics, and even in clients' homes.

Nurse-midwives examine pregnant women and monitor the growth and development of fetuses. Typically a nurse-midwife is responsible for all phases of a normal pregnancy, including prenatal care, assisting during labor, and providing follow-up care. A certified nurse-midwife always works in consultation with a physician, who can be called upon should complications arise during pregnancy or childbirth. Many nurse-midwives provide the full spectrum of women's health care, including regular gynecological exams and well-woman care.

An important part of a certified nurse-midwife's work is the education of patients. Nurse-midwives teach their patients about proper nutrition and fitness for healthy pregnancies and about different techniques for labor and delivery. Nurse-midwives also counsel their patients in the postpartum period about breast-feeding, parenting, and other areas concerning the health of mother and child.

Some nurse midwives also record patient information, file documents and patient charts, do research to find out why a woman is having a particular problem, and consult with physicians and other medical personnel.

Not all midwives are certified nurse-midwives. Most states recognize other categories of midwives, including direct-entry (or licensed) midwives, certified professional midwives (CPMs), and lay (or empirical) midwives. Direct-entry midwives are not required to be nurses in order to practice as midwives. Lay midwives usually train by apprenticing with professional midwives, although some may acquire formal education as well. Many lay midwives practice as part of religious communities or specific ethnic groups, and typically assist in home birth situations.

Nurse-midwives need to enjoy working with people. They need to be independent and able to accept responsibility for their actions and decisions. Strong observation skills are important, as nurse-midwives must be tuned into their patient's needs during pregnancy and labor. Nurse-midwives also need to listen well and respond appropriately. They must communicate effectively with patients, family members, physicians, and other hospital staff, as well as insurance company personnel. Nurse-midwives should be confident and composed, responding well in an emergency and keeping their patients calm.

Nurse-midwifery is a field dominated by women. Well over 98 percent of CNMs in the United States are female. Women have traditionally helped each other through pregnancy and delivery. Just as women who became doctors 100 years ago had to overcome many barriers, men considering entering midwifery should be prepared for hurdles of their own.

EDUCATION AND TRAINING

In high school, you should begin preparing for a career as a nurse-midwife by taking college preparatory courses, with a focus on science classes. Anatomy, biology, and chemistry will give you solid background information for what you will be studying in college. Additional classes in sociology and psychology will help you learn how to deal with a variety of patients from different ethnic and economic groups. Finally, you should consider learning foreign languages if you want to serve as a midwife to immigrant communities.

All certified nurse-midwives begin their careers as registered nurses. In order to become a registered nurse, you will need to graduate from either a four-year bachelor's degree program in nursing or a two-year associate's degree program in nursing. After receiving a degree, you can apply for admission into an accredited certificate program in nurse-midwifery.

EARNINGS AND OUTLOOK

Nurse-midwives earn about $70,100 per year. Starting salaries for beginning nurse-midwives range from $21,580 to around $45,000 per year, depending on the place of employment; those working for large hospitals tend to earn more that those working for small hospitals, clinics, and birthing centers.

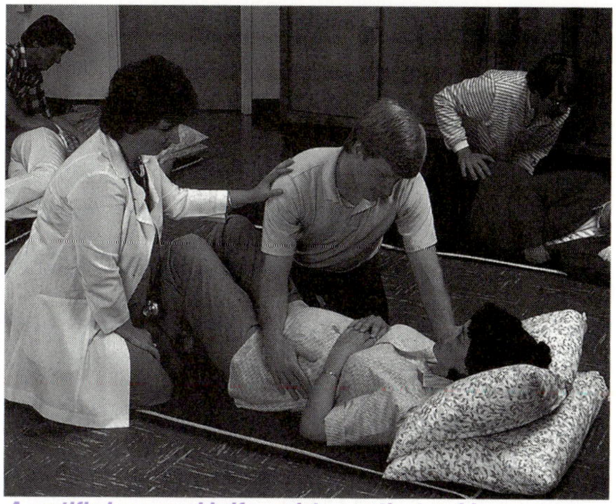

A certified nurse-midwife assists a patient and her partner during a prenatal class.

The number of nurse-midwifery jobs is expected to grow faster than the average for all occupations through 2006, as nurse-midwives gain a reputation as an integral part of the health care community. Currently, there are more positions than there are midwives to fill them.

FOR MORE INFORMATION

ACNM is the largest midwifery organization in the United States. For more information about the midwife certification process, contact:

American College of Nurse-Midwives
818 Connecticut Avenue, NW, Suite 900
Washington, DC 20006
Tel: 202-728-9860
Web: http://www.midwife.org/ or
http://www.acnm.org/

Midwives Alliance of North America
Tel: 888-923-MANA (6262)
Web: http://www.mana.org/

For a list of nursing programs, contact:

American Association of Colleges of Nursing
1 Dupont Circle, NW, Suite 530
Washington, DC 20036
Web: http://www.aacn.nche.edu/

CHEMICAL ENGINEERS

SCHOOL SUBJECTS:
CHEMISTRY, PHYSICS

PERSONAL SKILLS:
COMMUNICATION/IDEAS
TECHNICAL/SCIENTIFIC

MINIMUM EDUCATION LEVEL:
BACHELOR'S DEGREE

OUTLOOK:
ABOUT AS FAST AS THE AVERAGE

OTHER ARTICLES TO LOOK AT:

Chemical Technicians
Chemists
Industrial Chemicals Workers
Mechanical Engineers
Plastics Engineers

WHAT CHEMICAL ENGINEERS DO

Chemical engineers make life easier by converting research laboratory inventions, creations, and ideas into everyday reality. They work in chemical and petroleum industries where they are involved in the manufacture of all types of chemicals. Many do research at universities and government agencies and also consult for private engineering firms. Among the products that chemical engineers help bring to the market are plastics, detergents, synthetic rubber compounds, and pharmaceuticals.

There is hardly an aspect of modern life in which a chemical engineer has not been involved one way or another. These few examples will give you an idea of the important role chemical engineers play in our daily lives. Chemical engineers have figured out how to extract oxygen, the life sustaining gas representing 21 percent of our atmosphere, from the air to yield a pure 100 percent gas that is essential in hospitals, steelmaking, and the construction industries. All of us are acquainted with efforts to recycle glass, paper, metals, and plastics to save energy and our environment. Chemical engineers have determined how to convert the gathered materials into valuable resources instead of polluting the earth in garbage dumps. Today, a large percentage of our food is prepackaged in materials made by chemical engineers so that meals can be easily and rapidly prepared by busy people. Were it not for modern medicine, many of us would not live to be senior citizens. Diseases that used to be fatal and life threatening just a few years ago are easily cured today thanks to chemical engineers who pioneered synthetic processes to produce life-saving medicines. Years ago, the only available clothing was of natural origin, from cotton, linen, wool, silk, or leather. Today, the number and types of synthetic fabrics, many invented by chemical engineers, is staggering.

EDUCATION AND TRAINING

If you want to become a chemical engineer, you should take as many science and mathematics courses as you can in high school. You also should take college preparatory courses, as you will have to earn a bachelor's degree in chemical engineering to find a position as a chemical engineer. Many college programs begin with two years of basic sciences such as mathematics, physics, and chemistry; courses in English and writing, and other humanities subjects also will be helpful. The last two years are devoted to specific engineering courses with a specialization in chemical engineering subjects.

Some colleges offer five-year programs that combine classroom study with practical

The structure used for experiments is adjusted during the testing by the chemical engineer.

experience working for an engineering firm. In this way, students gain practical as well as theoretical experience.

To teach in a college or university and to obtain promotions within an engineering firm, a master's degree or even a doctoral may be required.

EARNINGS AND OUTLOOK

Median salaries for government chemical engineers are about $67,000 per year, while in private industry, the salaries average over $78,000 per year.

Employment of chemical engineers should increase about as fast as the average for all occupations as chemical companies research and develop new chemicals and increase the efficiency of their production. Chemical engineering graduates may face competition for engineering jobs in manufacturing as the number of these openings is projected to be lower than the number of graduates. Jobs that become available will result from the need to replace people either leaving the field or retiring. Pharmaceutical, plastics, and specialty chemicals industries will probably provide better opportunities than other sections of the chemical industry.

FOR MORE INFORMATION

American Chemical Society
Career Education
1155 16th Street, NW
Washington, DC 20036
Tel: 202-452-2113
Web: http://www.acs.org

American Institute of Chemical Engineers
Communications Department
345 East 47th Street
New York, NY 10017-2395
Tel: 212-705-7660 or 800-242-4363
Web: http://www.aiche.org

CHEMICAL TECHNICIANS

SCHOOL SUBJECTS:
CHEMISTRY, MATHEMATICS

PERSONAL SKILLS:
FOLLOWING INSTRUCTIONS
TECHNICAL/SCIENTIFIC

MINIMUM EDUCATION LEVEL:
ASSOCIATE'S DEGREE

OUTLOOK:
FASTER THAN THE AVERAGE

OTHER ARTICLES TO LOOK AT:

Chemical Engineers
Chemists
Mechanical Engineers
Metallurgical Technicians
Plastics Engineers
Quality Control Technicians

WHAT CHEMICAL TECHNICIANS DO

There are two types of chemical technicians: *chemical laboratory technicians* and *laboratory testing technicians*. Although the titles are similar, the jobs are different.

Most chemical technicians who work in the chemical industry are involved in the development, testing, and manufacturing of plastics, paints, detergents, synthetic fibers, industrial chemicals, and pharmaceuticals. Others work in the petroleum, aerospace, metals, electronics, automotive, and construction industries. Some chemical technicians work in universities and government laboratories.

Chemical technicians may work in any of the fields of chemistry, such as analytical, biochemistry, inorganic, organic, physical, or any of the many subbranches of chemistry. Within these subfields, chemical technicians work in research and development, design and production, and quality control. In research and development, chemical laboratory technicians often work with Ph.D. chemists and chemical engineers to set up and monitor laboratory equipment and instruments, prepare laboratory setups, and record data.

Laboratory testing technicians are employed by all kinds of laboratories in industries such as electronics, aerospace, oil, automobile, and construction companies. They are trained to conduct tests on countless substances and products to see that they meet specifications and performance standards.

Technicians usually work in clean, neat, and well-lighted places. However, if they have to go out into the field, they may encounter hot, rainy, damp, cold, snowy, or other unpleasant conditions. Working with dangerous, poisonous, flammable, or explosive materials is sometimes part of the job, but the chemical industry is now the safest industry in which to work because of rigidly enforced government safety regulations.

EDUCATION AND TRAINING

Students who want to be chemical technicians should take courses in mathematics, chemistry, physics, and computer science in high school. More mathematics and science may be required if you wish to enter a two-year chemical technology program available at many community colleges. In these programs, you will take courses such as general and organic chemistry. There is a strong emphasis on laboratory work and writing detailed reports. Other required subjects may include mathematics, physics, and industrial safety. Many employers only hire chemical technicians who have completed a two-year training program after high school and some even prefer chemists with a bachelor's degree in science.

A high school diploma is necessary for employment as a testing technician. Preparation for employment should include courses in science, mathematics, and computer courses. Shop experience is also valuable in acquiring mechanical skills. Only a few kinds of chemical technicians require a license. These include those who work with food products and radioactive materials.

Community colleges may offer help in finding employment to students who have completed their two-year courses. If you wish to apply directly to a company, college placement offices may have information on companies employing chemical technicians.

EARNINGS AND OUTLOOK

For chemical technicians in private companies who have completed a two-year training program, the starting salary is about $21,000 per year. Those with experience can earn from $32,000 to $42,000 annually. In general, inexperienced chemical laboratory technicians can expect to earn somewhat higher salaries than laboratory testing technicians, but much depends on educational background and the industry in which they work.

Job opportunities for chemical technicians vary from industry to industry. The pharmaceutical industry is expected to have the greatest need for chemical technicians. The consumer goods, metallurgical, and industrial products industries will continue to hire chemical testing technicians in good numbers. Overall, the number of opportunities for all technicians will be higher than the average.

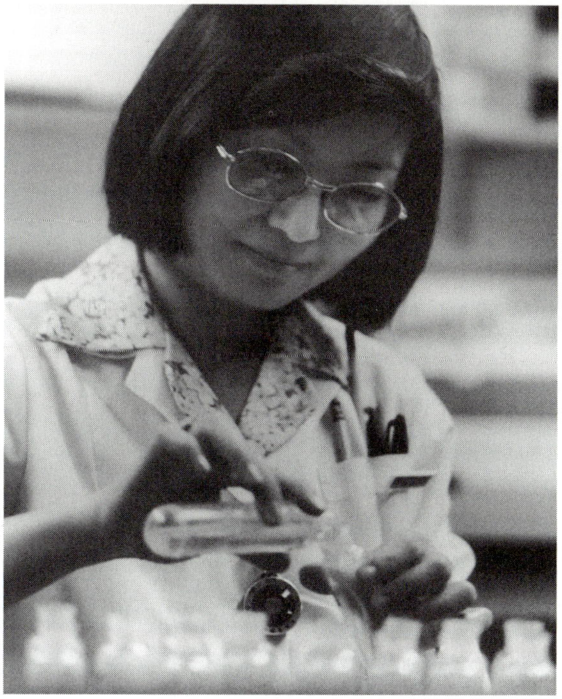

A chemical technician makes precise measurements.

FOR MORE INFORMATION

Young people interested in becoming chemical technicians may begin by doing experiments on a home chemistry set.

For further information about a career as a chemical technician, contact:

American Chemical Society
Department of Career Services
1155 16th Street, NW
Washington, DC 20036
Tel: 202-452-2113
Web: http://www.acs.org

American Institute of Chemists
515 King Street
Allexandria, VA 22914
Tel: 703-836-2090

Junior Engineering Technical Society
1420 King Street, Suite 405
Alexandria, VA 22314-2794
Tel: 703-548-5387
Web: http://www.jets.org

CHEMISTS

SCHOOL SUBJECTS:
CHEMISTRY, PHYSICS, MATHEMATICS

PERSONAL SKILLS:
COMMUNICATION/IDEAS
TECHNICAL/SCIENTIFIC

MINIMUM EDUCATION LEVEL:
BACHELOR'S DEGREE

OUTLOOK:
FASTER THAN THE AVERAGE

OTHER ARTICLES TO LOOK AT:

Biochemists
Biologists
Chemical Engineers
Pharmacists
Plastics Engineers
Toxicologists

WHAT CHEMISTS DO

Chemistry, a science concerned with the study of the physical and chemical properties of matter, began in ancient Egypt. The early Egyptian "scientists" developed alchemy, which is a mixture of chemistry, superstition, and myth. The alchemists' goal was to convert cheap metals such as lead into gold and precious gems, but they never succeeded. The era of modern chemistry dates from the late 1700s, when Antoine Lavoisier established the law of the conservation of matter. *Chemists* use the knowledge they acquire to improve products and create new ones. Examples of these products are pharmaceuticals, synthetic plastics and fabrics, rocket fuels for space travel, and the production process for obtaining light metals such as aluminum, magnesium, and titanium.

The five possible specializations within the field of chemistry are analytical, inorganic, organic, physical, and biological chemistry. Although there are many other branches, all are offshoots of these five. Food chemists develop new foods and try to improve their shelf lives. They determine how methods of cooking, canning, freezing, and packaging affect the taste, appearance, and quality of different food products. They test samples of meats, cereals, and dairy products to make sure that they meet government food standards. Irradiation is the latest technique developed to preserve meats and to eliminate bacterial contamination.

Analytical chemists study the composition of substances and establish methods of analysis for them. They set standards for safe levels of certain chemicals in drinking water and also examine wastewater effluents from industrial plants for pollutant levels. Physical chemists study the physical properties of atoms and molecules to predict how they will behave under a variety of reaction conditions. Chemists known as toxicologists study the by-products produced by paint, petroleum, leather, and pharmaceutical manufacturers. They design procedures to prevent harmful effects on users of the products and the environment.

While teaching or conducting research for the government, private industry, or universities, chemists often publish papers with their findings in technical and scientific journals to share their information with others.

EDUCATION AND TRAINING

Chemists are highly trained professionals. Although only a bachelor's degree is required for a beginner, higher level jobs often require additional education. To become a supervisory researcher in industry, a master's or a doctoral degree is necessary. Today, almost all college and university research and teaching positions require a doctoral degree.

High school students who want to become chemists must take at least three or four years of mathematics, including algebra, geometry, and calculus; three years of science, including biology, chemistry, and physics; and four years of English. These courses will provide an excellent foundation for becoming a chemistry major in college. Computer expertise is also highly recommended.

EARNINGS AND OUTLOOK

Chemists' salaries depend on factors such as ability, creativity, education, experience, the nature of the job, and the industry itself. In a 1998 survey, the average starting salary for a bachelor's degree chemist without experience in private industry was $29,500 a year. With a master's degree, the starting salary might be about $38,000. An experienced chemist with a Ph.D. and supervisory duties could earn $90,000 a year or more. A chemist accepting a government position or a beginning teacher would probably have to settle for a lower salary.

As highly trained, full-time professionals, most chemists receive health insurance, paid vacations, and sick leave.

Developing new products for private industry will provide the most opportunity for future jobs in the upcoming decade. The majority of openings will be in pharmaceuticals, biotechnology, and firms that produce specialty chemicals. Job opportunities are expected to decrease for chemists in industrial chemical and petroleum industries. At this time, few faculty openings are available in colleges and universities. However, that may change as the number of college-age students increases in the coming years.

A chemistry professor and her graduate student helper work on a research project at a university laboratory.

FOR MORE INFORMATION

Working under the supervision of an adult, interested young people can perform experiments with a junior chemistry set.

For more information about a career as a chemist, contact the following organizations:

American Chemical Society
Department of Career Services
1155 16th Street, NW
Washington, DC 20036
Web: http://www.acs.org

American Institute of Chemists
515 King Street, Suite 420
Alexandria, VA 22914
Web: http://www.theaic.org/

American Association for Clinical Chemistry
2101 L Street, NW, Suite 202
Washington, DC 20037-1526
Web: http://www.aacc.org

Chemical Institute of Canada
130 Slater Street, Suite 550
Ottawa, Ontario Canada K1P 6E2

CHILD CARE WORKERS

SCHOOL SUBJECTS:
FAMILY AND CONSUMER SCIENCE

PERSONAL SKILLS:
COMMUNICATION/IDEAS
HELPING/TEACHING

MINIMUM EDUCATION LEVEL:
HIGH SCHOOL DIPLOMA

OUTLOOK:
FASTER THAN THE AVERAGE

OTHER ARTICLES TO LOOK AT:

Adult and Vocational Education Teachers

Child Life Specialists

Elementary School Teachers

Secondary School Teachers

Teacher Aides

WHAT CHILD CARE WORKERS DO

As a *child care worker,* you'll be employed by day care centers, preschools, or other child care facilities to work with infants, toddlers, and preschool-aged children. While parents and guardians are at work, you'll watch children of various ages and help them develop skills through games and activities. You'll make sure that babies are fed, diapered, and held when awake. You'll instruct toddlers in how to tie their shoes and button their coats. You'll help preschoolers develop basic skills, such as recognizing letters, numbers, and colors.

You'll be assisting center owners, teachers, and directors in planning and directing activities. You may be working in a classroom with a specific age group or you may be working in small facility that involves you with all age groups. You'll read to the children, instruct them in arts and crafts projects, and teach them songs. In planning activities with the director, you must consider the abilities and interests of the children. You must also think about which skills children should be learning at a particular age. To teach children about the senses, telling time, writing the alphabet, and other basic things, you'll use finger-painting, puppets, music, and games. You'll encourage the children to think creatively and to express their feelings and ideas. You will help them develop social skills and work to build their confidence.

You'll help children get used to being in school with other children and introduce them to the concepts of sharing and playing in groups.

You must also supervise the children and guide them in their manners, hygiene, and interaction with other children and adults. You'll lead them in simple tasks, such as cleaning up after themselves, picking up toys, and washing their hands.

You may also get to know the children's parents, providing them with reports on progress and behavior. You might also invite parents along on field trips and into the classroom to observe.

EDUCATION AND TRAINING

In high school, you should take child development, home economics, and other classes that involve you with child care. You should also take courses in English, art, music, and theater to develop creative skills.

A high school diploma and some child care experience is usually all that's required to get a job as a child care worker, but requirements vary among employers. Some employers prefer to hire workers who have taken college courses in child development, or hold bachelor's degrees; they may also pay

A child care worker plays a game with her students using hand signals.

better wages to those with some college education. Certification isn't required of child care workers, but some organizations such as the Council for Early Childhood Professional Recognition and the National Child Care Association do offer credentialing.

EARNINGS AND OUTLOOK

Child care workers with high school diplomas have average annual earnings of $10,151. Workers with some college credits earn around $11,617 a year, and those holding college degrees earn an average of $14,506 a year.

There are more families in which both parents are working, so good day care centers are in high demand. One-third of all child-care workers leave their centers each year, most likely because of the low pay and lack of benefits. This will mean plenty of job openings for qualified child care workers.

FOR MORE INFORMATION

Preschools, day care centers, and other child-care programs often hire high school students for part-time positions as aides. There are also many volunteer opportunities that will give you experience in working with children—check with your library or local literacy program about tutoring children and reading to preschoolers.

National Association for the Education of Young Children
1509 16th Street, NW
Washington, DC 20036
Tel: 800-424-2460
Web: http://www.naeyc.org

Council for Early Childhood Professional Recognition
2460 16th Street, NW
Washington, DC 20009
Tel: 800-424-4310
Web: http://www.cdacouncil.org

CHILD LIFE SPECIALISTS

SCHOOL SUBJECTS:
HEALTH, PSYCHOLOGY

PERSONAL SKILLS:
COMMUNICATION/IDEAS
HELPING/TEACHING

MINIMUM EDUCATION LEVEL:
BACHELOR'S DEGREE

OUTLOOK:
ABOUT AS FAST AS THE AVERAGE

OTHER ARTICLES TO LOOK AT:

Child Care Workers
Creative Arts Therapists
Preschool Teachers
Psychologists
Social Workers
Teacher Aides

WHAT CHILD LIFE SPECIALISTS DO

A *child life specialist* helps ease the fears and concerns of children who are hospitalized. When children are in the hospital, they face all sorts of new and terrifying experiences. They may have blood tests or shots, procedures such as spinal taps (where fluid is taken from the base of the spine with a long, hollow needle), or chemotherapy (where they take strong drugs to get rid of cancer).

Children may not feel able to talk about their fears and concerns. They might need help to express their feelings and worries. The child life specialist helps them do this mainly through play, art, and fun recreational activities geared toward a child's needs. Child life specialists usually work with children in a hospital playroom, but they may also visit with patients in their rooms or in an outpatient waiting room. The child life specialist becomes a familiar, trusted individual who is there for support and can be counted on to visit at regularly scheduled times. The child life specialist is often the only professional staff person who is not there to perform some kind of uncomfortable test or procedure on the child.

One of the goals of child life specialists is to help children in the hospital understand what is happening to them and why. What may look to an outsider like ordinary play with dolls may actually be a child's way of acting out. The child life specialist may encourage children to use a doll and some medical instruments to talk about their fears or to answer their questions about an upcoming operation or medical procedure. For instance, children may practice giving a doll a shot before they are to receive one. Or they may take the doll and comfort it, saying that everything will be all right. The child life specialist watches and guides the children through these feelings to help them cope.

Because hospitalized children can feel as though they're missing out on fun times while they're in the hospital, child life specialists make a special effort to celebrate birthdays and other special occasions. Regularly scheduled meeting times are set up so that younger children, as well as older children and teenagers, can play or talk with others of the same age. They may do art projects, sing songs, or share their experiences.

The children's parents are also given support by meeting with the specialists and talking with other parents to better understand what is happening. The specialist may provide parents with books and tapes for further education. It is important for a child life specialist to work together with the parents.

With so much support needed by the children and their families, child life specialists should be emotionally stable. They should be mature enough to put their patients' needs ahead of their own at work. Because the work can be emotionally draining, especially when a patient dies, child life specialists should have a strong support network of family and friends to help prevent burnout.

EDUCATION AND TRAINING

High school students should try to take child development or psychology classes if they are available. To become a child life specialist, you must have at least a bachelor's degree in one of the following areas: child development, psychology, education, or social work. During the senior year of college, an internship is usually required in which you work in a child life center assisting and observing child life specialists.

Voluntary certification as a Certified Child Life Specialist (CCLS) is available through the Child Life Council's Child Life Certifying Committee.

EARNINGS AND OUTLOOK

Child life specialists can expect a starting salary of about $19,000 to $23,000 per year, depending on the location and size of the hospital. Salaries for child life specialists in large metropolitan hospitals are usually higher than in smaller community hospitals. Directors can earn $30,000 or more.

With more hospitals opening child life centers, the outlook for child life specialists is steady through the next decade, with most positions becoming available in larger teaching hospitals.

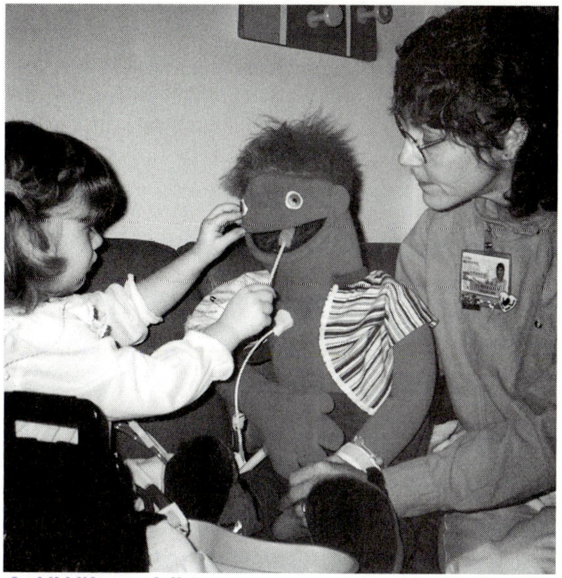

A child life specialist encourages a young patient to "prep" a puppet patient for surgery, as a way to prepare for her own upcoming surgery.

FOR MORE INFORMATION

This organization offers educational materials, a journal, Children's Health Care, *and a newsletter:*

Association for the Care of Children's Health
19 Mantua Road
Mt. Royal, NJ 08061
Tel: 609-224-1742
Web: http://www.acch.org

For career and certification information, contact:

Child Life Council
11820 Parklawn Drive, Suite 202
Rockville, MD 20852-2529
Tel: 301-881-7090
Web: http://www.childlife.org

CHIROPRACTORS

SCHOOL SUBJECTS
BIOLOGY, HEALTH

PERSONAL SKILLS
MECHANICAL/MANIPULATIVE
TECHNICAL/SCIENTIFIC

MINIMUM EDUCATION LEVEL
MEDICAL DEGREE

OUTLOOK
FASTER THAN THE AVERAGE

OTHER ARTICLES TO LOOK AT:

Acupuncturists
Aromatherapists
Holistic Physicians
Homeopaths
Naturopaths
Osteopaths

WHAT CHIROPRACTORS DO

Chiropractors are health care professionals who practice a healing art called chiropractic. Chiropractic is a complete system of health maintenance and disease prevention and treatment. It stresses proper nutrition, exercise, posture, stress management, and care of the spine and the nervous system. Chiropractors believe the body has a natural ability to remain healthy if it has the proper ingredients.

Chiropractic teaches that a person's health is affected by the nervous system. The core of the central nervous system is the spinal cord. It is protected by the bones of the backbone or spine. Problems in the spinal cord affect the body's natural defense mechanisms. This can be the underlying cause of disease. Chiropractors move the bones of the spine by gentle manipulation (called spinal adjustment) to relieve pain and restore the spine to its natural, healthy state.

Chiropractors treat common ailments, such as headaches, respiratory disorders, digestive problems, allergies, and other illnesses. They most often treat backaches, lower back pain, and whiplash.

On the first visit, chiropractors meet with the patient and take a full medical history before beginning treatment. They ask many questions about the patient's eating habits, sleeping habits, stress, and exercise. Next they perform a careful physical examination. They rely on skillful touch to locate any source of pain in the spine or joints. This examination may include laboratory tests and X rays if needed.

Chiropractors use many natural approaches to help restore health. The best-known chiropractic treatment is the spinal adjustment. Chiropractors also use massage, light, water, heat, cold, and ultrasound. Sometimes one treatment is enough. Usually the patient needs to come back several times. To help with the healing process, chiropractors may suggest lifestyle changes such as more exercise, more sleep, less stress, or a better diet. With the patient's cooperation, the chiropractor can often resolve the problem permanently. Chiropractors only use natural healing methods. They do not prescribe medicine or perform surgery. If their patients need medication or surgery, chiropractors refer them to other health care professionals.

Most chiropractors are self-employed. They work in their own offices, in hospitals or health clinics. Others teach or do research at chiropractic colleges.

EDUCATION AND TRAINING

Training to become a chiropractor can begin in high school. Classes that will help prepare for a career as a chiropractor include biology, chemistry, physics, and mathematics. Chiropractors also need a good general foundation in English, business, and computer courses.

After graduation from high school, at least two years of college are necessary. Courses in English, the social sciences, chemistry, anatomy, biology, physics, and mathematics provide a solid, general education. After two years, many chiropractic colleges will accept transfer students. Increasingly, chiropractic students are first completing four years of undergraduate education before they enter a chiropractic college. Chiropractic studies last four years. They emphasize classes in manipulation and spinal adjustments.

In most chiropractic colleges, the first two years are spent in the classroom or laboratory studying the human body. During the last two years, students begin working with patients. After completing chiropractic training, students are awarded a Doctor of Chiropractic (D.C.) degree.

Before they may practice, chiropractors are required to obtain a license. To do this, they must either pass a state board examination or the National Board of Chiropractic Examiners' test. Most states require chiropractors to continue taking a certain number of class hours each year to ensure that chiropractors stay up to date with the latest advances in their field.

EARNINGS AND OUTLOOK

Newly licensed chiropractors often begin working in a clinic or in an office with an experienced chiropractor. As they gain more experience, many open their own offices or become partners in larger, more successful practices. Incomes for chiropractors range from $39,000 to $102,500 a year. The average income for experienced chiropractors is $88,500 per year.

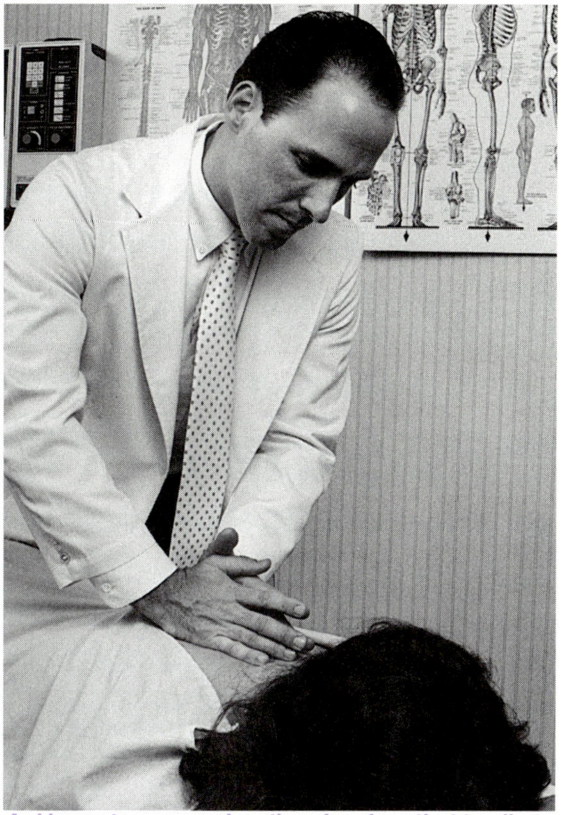

A chiropractor presses along the spine of a patient to adjust the bones.

With the increased interest in alternative health care, the field of chiropractic is growing rapidly. Because of chiropractic's preventive approach, more and more insurers are covering their services. Therefore, employment for chiropractors is expected to increase faster than the average for all other occupations into the next decade.

FOR MORE INFORMATION

American Chiropractic Association
1701 Clarendon Boulevard
Arlington, VA 22209
Web: http://www.amerchiro.org

International Chiropractors Association
1110 North Glebe Road, Suite 1000
Arlington, VA 22201
Web: http//www.chiropractic.org

CHOREOGRAPHERS

SCHOOL SUBJECTS:
MUSIC, THEATER/DANCE

PERSONAL SKILLS:
ARTISTIC, COMMUNICATION/IDEAS

MINIMUM EDUCATION LEVEL:
SOME POSTSECONDARY TRAINING

OUTLOOK:
FASTER THAN THE AVERAGE

OTHER ARTICLES TO LOOK AT:

Actors
Athletes
Circus Performers
Composers
Dancers
Musicians

WHAT CHOREOGRAPHERS DO

Choreographers create original dance routines for dancers to perform. Choreographers must have a thorough understanding of dance and music, as well as costume, lighting, and dramatics. Besides inventing new dance routines, choreographers teach their dances to performers and sometimes direct and stage the presentation of their works.

There are several basic types of dance with which choreographers work: ballet, modern, jazz, acrobatic, and tap. Some choreographers work strictly in ballet, modern, or jazz dance theaters; others focus on dances to complement operas, musical comedies, and television productions.

To develop the many skills they will need, choreographers must have a solid background in dance and know all the movements and positions of the dance form in which they are working. A strong knowledge of music is important, as is the creativity and inspiration to think up new dance ideas. Choreographers must have the expertise to put their ideas into physical form. Patience, perseverance, and dedication are also important ingredients for a successful choreographer.

EDUCATION AND TRAINING

Many choreographers begin their careers as dancers. There are no formal educational requirements, but an early start (around eight years old for ballet, slightly older for jazz, tap, modern, folk, or acrobatic dance) and years of practice are essential. Talented students begin serious training with regional or national dance schools in their early teens, and many dancers have professional auditions by the time they are 17 or 18 years old.

A dancer may begin choreographing after mastering the basics of his or her chosen dance form. Generally speaking, however, dancers spend years performing in other people's dances before attempting to create their own.

A college degree is not necessarily an advantage for professional choreographers. Colleges that offer degrees in dance with extensive emphasis on practice are a good place to train.

EARNINGS AND OUTLOOK

Very few dancers and choreographers work year round and, like other artists, they often take other jobs to make extra money. And, while opportunities exist in regional dance companies and in television and film work, more than half the dance companies in the United States are located in New York City, which means the majority of choreographers live there, too.

A choreographer teaches a group of dancers a new routine.

Salaries vary tremendously, depending on the size of the theater and earnings from performance royalties and fees. In small professional theaters, choreographers may earn approximately $1,000 per week, and as much as $30,000 for a Broadway production requiring eight to ten weeks of rehearsal time. When working for big-budget motion pictures, choreographers can earn an average of $3,000 per week, while those working in television can earn up to $10,000 in a 14-day period.

Employment for choreographers is expected to grow faster than the average through the next decade, but only the most talented choreographers will find jobs. Cuts in funding for the National Endowment for the Arts may limit opportunities for choreographers.

FOR MORE INFORMATION

A directory of dance companies and related organizations and other information on professional dance is available from:

Dance USA
1156 15th Street, NW, Suite 820
Washington, DC 20005-1704
Tel: 202-833-1717
Web: http://www.danceusa.org

Information on purchasing directories about colleges and universities that teach dance, including details on types of courses offered and scholarships, is available from:

National Dance Association
1900 Association Drive
Reston, VA 22091
Tel: 800-321-0789

CINEMATOGRAPHERS

SCHOOL SUBJECTS:
ART, ENGLISH

PERSONAL SKILLS:
ARTISTIC, TECHNICAL/SCIENTIFIC

MINIMUM EDUCATION LEVEL:
BACHELOR'S DEGREE

OUTLOOK:
LITTLE CHANGE OR MORE SLOWLY THAN THE AVERAGE

OTHER ARTICLES TO LOOK AT:

Film and Television Directors
Film Editors
Lighting Technicians
Photographers
Stage Production Workers

WHAT CINEMATOGRAPHERS DO

As a *cinematographer*, you'll run the cameras during the production of a film or video. You'll follow the director's instructions to ensure that the actions of the actors and actresses are recorded on film or videotape. Cinematographers may work on feature films in Hollywood or elsewhere, or they may work on educational films, documentaries, or commercials. Specific job responsibilities depend on the size of the production crew. On a documentary with a small crew, for example, you may be responsible for setting up the lighting and directing the movements of the actors. On larger productions, you will concentrate solely on running the camera, while a team of assistants helps out with loading and unloading film and setting up the equipment.

You'll work both indoors and outdoors, depending on the requirements of the movie. You may spend several months on location, but often you can live at home during the filming of a motion picture and commute to the location. Although the life of a cinematographer can be glamorous, there is also a lot of routine work, such as loading and unloading film from the camera, setting up tripods, and carrying the camera long distances. There are hours of rehearsal before a scene is actually filmed. The work can be physically demanding, although most of the heavy lifting is done by other crew members. It is important to remember that camera operators always are behind the scenes. Actors, actresses, and directors enjoy most of the credit for a production, although cinematographers play a significant role in the final product.

EDUCATION AND TRAINING

In high school, you should follow your guidance counselor's college preparatory program. Art and photography courses can help you understand the basics of lighting and composition. A broadcast journalism or media course may give you some hands-on experience in camera operation and video production.

A college degree is not always necessary to find a position as a cinematographer. Those with the right experience and the proper connections have better opportunities for finding employment. Although many colleges and film schools offer valuable training in camera operation, there is no substitute for experience in this field.

You'll need to become familiar with all aspects of camera operations and be able to handle lighting assignments, if that is required. You should also be able to work closely with other members of a film crew. You must be able to follow directions quickly and accurately. Since films and videos often are produced under stressful conditions, cine-

A cinematographer films a winter scene.

matographers must be able to work well under pressure.

EARNINGS AND OUTLOOK

Wages for cinematographers vary widely. When starting out, apprentice filmmakers may make nothing; they may even be spending their own money to finance their own projects. Since they generally are hired one film at a time, there may be periods of unpaid time between assignments. On the other end of the scale, well-established cinematographers working on big-budget productions can make well over a million dollars a year. For union members, the minimum pay is $523 a day for a feature film.

A large number of people are excited by the chance to work in motion pictures. This means that there are far more qualified cinematographers than there are job openings. Of course, those with a high degree of skill and training should find positions, but it could take a long time before finding work in Los Angeles or New York.

FOR MORE INFORMATION

American Society of Cinematographers
1782 North Orange Drive
Hollywood, CA 90028
Tel: 323-969-4333
Web: http://www.cinematographer.com

For information about colleges with film and television programs of study, and to read interviews with filmmakers, visit the AFI Web site.

American Film Institute (AFI)
2021 North Western Avenue
Los Angeles, CA 90027
Tel: 323-856-7600
Web: http://www.afionline.org

CIRCUS PERFORMERS

SCHOOL SUBJECTS:
PHYSICAL EDUCATION, THEATER/DANCE

PERSONAL SKILLS:
ARTISTIC, MECHANICAL/MANIPULATIVE

MINIMUM EDUCATION LEVEL:
HIGH SCHOOL DIPLOMA
APPRENTICESHIP

OUTLOOK:
LITTLE CHANGE OR MORE SLOWLY THAN AVERAGE

OTHER ARTICLES TO LOOK AT:

Actors
Animal Trainers
Clowns
Comedians
Magicians
Stunt Performers

WHAT CIRCUS PERFORMERS DO

Circus performers are entertainers. Like many other entertainers, such as *actors*, they perform for audiences. The difference is that many of these entertainers make their living performing daring and dangerous physical acts. *Trapeze artists* leap from one trapeze to another, or do somersaults in midair. *Highwire* or *wire walkers* may walk, ride bicycles, or even ride unicycles on a wire suspended high above the ground. *Acrobats* perform gymnastic routines of many varieties. *Animal trainers* show off the strength or abilities of their animals while often appearing to risk their own lives. The elephants they have trained sit on chairs or stand on their heads. Bears ride bicycles, and lions roar fiercely before being coaxed to jump through hoops. *Aerialists* perform various athletic feats in the air such as flips and spins. *Jugglers* can keep many objects in the air at once, even if the objects are dangerous ones like fiery rings or knives. *Aquatic performers* do most of their circus work in the water. Only very large circuses can accommodate their specialized performances. Most circuses also have a circus band whose members keep the action exciting with their musical accompaniment. Show *horse riders* perform fast-paced routines on elegantly dressed horses. Sometimes they ride bareback, and sometimes their horses leap over large barriers.

Most circuses have several circus performers working at once in different rings. These simultaneous performances are usually introduced by an announcer, known as the *ringmaster*, who calls the audience's attention to one or more rings. Although most circuses at one time were held in outdoor tents, known as big tops, most today are held in large indoor arenas.

EDUCATION AND TRAINING

Many full-time circus performers were born into circus families. Without coming from a circus family, becoming a circus performer can be difficult. Many acrobats, riders, and other circus performers learn their craft from more experienced performers.

For high school students who hope to become circus performers, skills can be developed in physical education classes in school and in community athletic games and competitions. Knowledge of foreign languages will be helpful for performers hoping to travel overseas. Athletic training that develops coordination, strength, and balance is necessary for almost all circus performers and should be developed at a young age. Other training includes acting, music, dance and, for those interested in animals, veterinary care. You can develop confidence and ease with animals by volunteering at your local zoo. No diploma is required by most circuses. A high school or college education, however, will give you an advantage because you will be better able to manage your business affairs and communicate with others.

EARNINGS AND OUTLOOK

According to the Circus World Museum, those just starting out usually do not earn much more than the minimum wage, and sometimes even lower, perhaps $200 to$400 per week. Generally, however, you are provided with food and lodging. Less-skilled performers, such as showgirls and clowns may earn $600 to $700 per week, while those whose acts involve animals may earn from several thousand per week and up to $100,000 or more for the circus season. Earnings depend on a number of factors, but performers who develop highly unusual and distinctive acts and achieve a degree of fame or recognition stand the best chance of higher earnings.

Few jobs as circus performers provide permanent full-time work. The outlook for circus performers does not seem to be improving. Those who work in a resident company of a circus can become well known and have greater job security. There are more opportunities for circus performers outside the circus, and there is always an interest for new, unusual, never-been-seen acts. The private party business is growing, and circus performers may be used in television and music videos. Even with the changes, the popularity of circuses has remained steady and should remain so for the next 10 years.

But the number of circus performers far outnumbers the number of job openings.

It may look easy, but this circus performer has spent hours practicing riding gracefully atop an elephant.

FOR MORE INFORMATION

Doing business as National Circus Project, this organization provides arts and education programs to schools. It also operates Circus Information Referral Center.

Circus Education Specialists
56 Lion Lane
Westbury, NY 11590
Tel: 516-334-2123

This library and research center documents the history of the circus in America. It offers referrals to camps and schools that provide training, as well as to producers and circuses.

Circus World Museum
426 Water Street
Baraboo, WI 53913-2597
Tel: 608-356-8341

CITY MANAGERS

SCHOOL SUBJECTS:
GOVERNMENT, MATHEMATICS

PERSONAL SKILLS:
LEADERSHIP/MANAGEMENT

MINIMUM EDUCATION LEVEL:
BACHELOR'S DEGREE

OUTLOOK:
LITTLE CHANGE OR MORE SLOWLY THAN THE AVERAGE

OTHER ARTICLES TO LOOK AT:

Ambassadors
Campaign Workers
Congressional Aides
Lobbyists
Political Scientists
Urban and Regional Planners

WHAT CITY MANAGERS DO

If you work as a *city manager*, you'll direct the day-to-day operations of a city. You'll determine what the city needs, such as the improvement of air quality of the city and its buildings, better public transportation, promotion of the diverse cultures of a community, and creating a new park. You'll make long-range plans for the city's needs as it grows larger. One important job of a city manager is to prepare a yearly budget for the city. The budget outlines the amount of money the city plans to spend on law enforcement, public health, recreation, economic development, and other services, such as garbage pickup and street improvements. You'll keep up to date on the needs and interests of the members of the community, and you'll keep them informed of city projects and proposals.

A *mayor* is elected, but you are appointed to your position as a city manager by the city council. The mayor makes the decisions on policies and programs, approves them, and meets with the public and news media to discuss the issues. You will work behind the scenes, using your managerial experience and skills, to put these programs in place.

You may be responsible for appointing department heads and a staff to coordinate the various activities of the government. These people have supervisory duties over tax collection, public health, public buildings, law enforcement, and all the other details of keeping a city or town working smoothly. In addition, you will coordinate and compile reports received from the department heads and distribute them to the city council.

City managers need to be decisive problem-solvers with a knack for communicating with a variety of people and groups.

EDUCATION AND TRAINING

In high school, take government and social studies classes to learn about the nature of cities and counties. Math courses are important, because you'll be working with budgets and statistics, and preparing financial reports. To work as a city manager, you must have a bachelor's degree. With a master's degree in public administration, you'll have more job opportunities. Some city managers have a master's or other advanced degree in political science, urban planning, or law. To be eligible for city management jobs, you are usually required to take a civil service examination. Recent college graduates may begin as assistants in a city manager's office. There you learn to solve various city management problems. After about five years' experience, you may become qualified to be a city manager yourself.

EARNINGS AND OUTLOOK

City managers earn an average of $70,541 a year. This is down just slightly from the previous year's survey results of $70,597 a year. The International City/County Management Association found that the average county manager's annual salary is $88,929. Individual earnings, of course, vary depending on the person's education and experience, as well as on the size of the city. The survey also found that salaries are highest in the Pacific Coast region of the United States.

In a city with a population over one million, an experienced city manager may earn up to $130,000 a year. In towns of 2,500 or less, salaries for city managers average $33,000 a year. Salaries are set by the city council, and good city managers are sometimes given higher than average pay as an incentive to keep them from seeking more lucrative opportunities. Benefits for city managers include paid vacations, health insurance, sick leave, and retirement plans. Cities may also pay travel and moving expenses and provide a city car or a car allowance.

Although city management is a growing profession, the field is still relatively small. Few job openings are predicted, and applicants with only a bachelor's degree will have difficulty finding employment. Even an entry-level job often requires an advanced degree. ICMA provides funds to those cities wanting to establish the county-manager form of government, as well as to cities where the form is threatened.

The issues that affect a city are constantly changing. Future city managers will need to focus on clean air regulations, promoting diversity, providing affordable housing, new policing methods, and revitalizing old downtown areas.

The city manager works closely with the mayor so that they can better plan the city's future.

FOR MORE INFORMATION

Young people interested in becoming city managers can take part in their school's student government.

For more information about the county-manager form of government, and the issues effecting today's cities, visit these Web sites, or contact:

International City/County Management Association.
777 North Capitol Street, NE, Suite 500
Washington, DC 20002-4201
Tel: 202-289-4262
Web: http://www.icma.org

National League of Cities
1301 Pennsylvania Avenue, NW
Washington, DC 20004
Tel: 202-626-3000
Web: http://www.nlc.org

CITY PLANNERS

SCHOOL SUBJECTS:
BUSINESS, GOVERNMENT, ENGLISH

PERSONAL SKILLS:
COMMUNICATION/IDEAS
FOLLOWING INSTRUCTIONS

MINIMUM EDUCATION LEVEL:
BACHELOR'S DEGREE

OUTLOOK:
MORE SLOWLY THAN THE AVERAGE

OTHER ARTICLES TO LOOK AT:

Architects
City Managers
Civil Engineers
Congressional Aides
Real Estate Developers

WHAT CITY PLANNERS DO

City planners develop plans for making cities as efficient and attractive as possible. When you work as an urban planner, you're concerned with the economic life of the city, its cultural life, and with environmental factors such as water pollution and trash disposal. You work closely with city officials and citizens.

You'll begin your work by becoming familiar with the existing buildings, transportation routes such as bus, subway and railroad lines, geographical features such as hills and rivers, and other important elements of the city, including schools, parks and airports. You'll pay special attention to stores and factories, studying their needs for services such as water and electric power, and how people can travel to and from them. Churches, recreational areas, residential districts, and other parts of the city are also studied. In addition, you are involved in figuring out how and where to provide shelters for the homeless, space and facilities for drug treatment centers, and low-cost housing and nursing homes for senior citizens.

Once you understand the needs and goals of the city, you draw up a plan showing how land could be used for housing, business, and other purposes. The plan should provide information about the types of industry that can be expected, their location, and how these industries will benefit the city as well as the problems they may create in terms of water, sewage, and transportation. To do your job well, you'll have to think about what's best for the city as well as what's best for the businesses and industries the city wants to attract.

The plan will also include ideas about zoning to regulate the use of land. If redevelopment of rundown areas is required, the plan will suggest ideas for remodeling or replacing old buildings. You are also responsible for determining the cost of a specific project as well as ways it might be paid for.

EDUCATION AND TRAINING

In high school, you should take classes in government and social studies to learn about the structure of cities and counties. You'll need good communication skills for working with people in a variety of professions, so take courses in English composition and journalism. A college education, with a major in planning, architecture, landscape architecture, civil engineering, or public administration, is the minimum requirement for a trainee job involved with city planning. Courses in economics, demography, and health administration are also highly recommended. For a career in city planning, however, a master's degree in city or regional plan-

City planners in Rocky Mount, North Carolina, discuss development plans.

ning is essential. The last part of the master's program usually includes a period of practical experience called an internship.

EARNINGS AND OUTLOOK

Salaries received by city planners vary depending on who employs them, how much education and experience they have, and their level of responsibility. The overall average is about $45,000 a year. Planners with more than ten years of experience can make from $52,000 to over $63,000, with those working in heavily populated areas making the most. Qualified job seekers who are flexible about where they can live and who are willing to work in small towns or rural areas will have the best prospects.

The employment outlook for city planners is expected to be slower than the average through 2006. Cities will continue to face important concerns having to do with economic development, environmental problems, transportation needs, and energy production. Also, planners will be needed to help determine how undeveloped land along coastal and rural areas should be zoned and used.

FOR MORE INFORMATION

American Planning Association
122 South Michigan Avenue, Suite 1600
Chicago, IL 60603
Tel: 312-786-6344
Web: http://www.planning.org

International City/County Management Association
777 North Capitol Street, NE, Suite 500
Washington, DC 20002
Tel: 202-289-4262
Web: http://www.icma.org

CIVIL ENGINEERING TECHNICIANS

SCHOOL SUBJECTS:
MATHEMATICS, PHYSICS

PERSONAL SKILLS:
MECHANICAL/MANIPULATIVE
TECHNICAL/SCIENTIFIC

MINIMUM EDUCATION LEVEL:
ASSOCIATE'S DEGREE

OUTLOOK:
FASTER THAN THE AVERAGE

OTHER ARTICLES TO LOOK AT:

Architects
City Managers
City Planners
Construction Inspectors
Operating Engineers
Surveyors

WHAT CIVIL ENGINEERING TECHNICIANS DO

Civil engineering technicians help *civil engineers* design, plan, and build highways, airports, tunnels, bridges, and other structures. They help engineers in all areas of work, from estimating costs of a construction project to assisting in the preparation of drawings, maps, and charts. Technicians also often order the building materials that will be used on a project. Some technicians may inspect water treatment systems to make sure that they are not polluting the environment.

Civil engineering technicians work under the direction of civil engineers and carry out different jobs depending on what is needed at the time. One of their responsibilities is to make sure that each step of the construction process is completed before the next stage is started. The variety of job responsibilities requires that a technician have a basic knowledge of civil engineering and be able to do work at the construction site.

Although civil engineering technicians participate in all stages of the construction process, some may specialize. Some technicians, for instance, focus their work primarily on building materials. They run tests on rock, soil, cement, steel, and other substances and then report back to the engineers on which materials would be best suited to a particular building site. Other specialists within the field include *research engineering technicians,* who test and develop new construction equipment, and *sales engineering technicians,* who sell building materials and construction equipment.

EDUCATION AND TRAINING

Civil engineering technicians must be able to draw and understand blueprints and sketches and follow directions carefully and completely. They must be good at organizing projects and paying close attention to details; a small error could completely stop a building project and cost thousands of dollars to fix.

The best way to become a civil engineering technician is to complete a two-year civil engineering technology program at a technical or vocational school. To be accepted into one of these programs, high school graduates should have a strong background in mathematics (algebra and geometry), physics, and the other sciences. These programs will include courses in mechanical drawing, advanced physics and mathematics, surveying, and computer programming. Students will also take courses in such specialty areas as heavy construction, construction technology, and bridge construction. Some technicians may get their training at a four-year college while majoring in engineering.

EARNINGS AND OUTLOOK

Civil engineering technicians usually begin their first jobs at a salary range of $16,500 to $29,000 a year, with the higher paying jobs going to those with advanced education. Most experienced technicians earn between $33,000 to $49,390 or more annually. Some senior technicians earn as much as $71,500 a year or more. The incomes of many civil engineering technicians who operate their own construction, surveying, or equipment businesses are excellent. Some of these companies can earn millions of dollars each year.

Paid vacations, pension plans, and insurance are normal parts of the benefits paid to civil engineering technicians. Many companies pay a bonus if a job is completed ahead of schedule or if the job is completed for less than the estimated cost. These bonuses sometimes amount to more than the employee's regular annual salary.

The outlook for civil engineering technicians is generally favorable. As in most industries, those with certification and the most education will have the best outlook. Construction is, however, one of the industries most likely to feel the effects of economic recessions, so civil engineering technicians must be prepared for slowdowns in business.

FOR MORE INFORMATION

For information on careers and scholarships, send a self-addressed, stamped envelope to the following:

American Society of Certified Engineering Technicians
PO Box 1348
Flowery Branch, GA 30542
Tel: 404-967-9173
Web: http://www.nmsu.edu/~ascet/ASCET

This civil engineering technician uses his computer to finalize the plans for building a bridge.

This organization offers the brochure "Engineering: Your Future" online:

American Society for Engineering Education
11 Dupont Circle, Suite 200
Washington, DC 20036
Tel: 202-331-3500
Web: http://www.asee.org

American Society of Civil Engineers
345 East 47th Street
New York, NY 10017
Tel: 212-705-7496
Web: http://www.asce.org

American Congress on Surveying and Mapping
5410 Grosvenor Lane
Bethesda, MD 20814-2122
Tel: 301-493-0200

CIVIL ENGINEERS

SCHOOL SUBJECTS:
MATHEMATICS, PHYSICS

PERSONAL SKILLS:
MECHANICAL/MANIPULATIVE

MINIMUM EDUCATION LEVEL:
BACHELOR'S DEGREE

OUTLOOK:
FASTER THAN THE AVERAGE

OTHER ARTICLES TO LOOK AT:

City Planners
Civil Engineering Technicians
Construction Inspectors
Environmental Engineers
Mechanical Engineers
Plastics Engineers

WHAT CIVIL ENGINEERS DO

Civil engineers design and supervise the construction of a variety of structures, including bridges, dams, tunnels, buildings, highways, airstrips, and water-supply and sewage systems. Some civil engineers specialize in a particular category, such as railroads, irrigation, sanitation or public health, airports, transportation, waterworks, and even forests.

Like all engineers, civil engineers apply scientific knowledge to practical, everyday problems. In designing structures, they often must do a great deal of research and testing. They may have to change a design many times before it is considered acceptable.

Once a design has been completed, civil engineers supervise the building of the structure. They purchase materials, choose the equipment that is to be used, and assign the work crews. They must consider the time and cost involved in completing each part of the project. They must also try to solve any problems that occur. Civil engineers spend a lot of their time on construction sites. Many of these are in or near major cities and commercial developments, while others may be in very remote areas. Some engineers travel from place to place to work on different projects, spending two or three years at one site and then moving on to the next.

More than 40 percent of civil engineers work for government agencies—federal, state, county, and city. About 35 percent work for companies that provide engineering consulting services, such as developing designs for new construction projects. Others work for construction firms, public utilities, railroads, and manufacturers.

EDUCATION AND TRAINING

Most civil engineering jobs require a bachelor's degree in engineering. A large number of schools offer this degree, as well as master's degrees and doctorates. While a bachelor's degree is sufficient for an entry-level engineering job, students who wish to teach engineering or learn a new technology will improve their chances for promotion by getting an advanced degree. Since there are many other related types of engineers—petroleum, mining, nuclear, industrial, aeronautical, metallurgical, and chemical, to name a few—it is sometimes possible to switch to another field of engineering without having to start at the beginning.

Students interested in becoming civil engineers should begin preparing while in high school. Important courses include algebra, geometry, physics, and chemistry. Courses in mechanical drawing are valuable. Because civil engineers must be able to communicate well with others, both in speech and in writing, English is also important.

The work of civil engineers often affects the public health and welfare. In such cases, many states require that they be licensed or registered.

EARNINGS AND OUTLOOK

Civil engineers are among the lowest paid in the engineering field. However, starting salaries are usually higher than for other occupations. Entry-level civil engineers with a bachelor's degree earn approximately $33,000 per year in private industry; those with a master's degree, about $35,000; and those with a doctorate, about $47,000. Those working in government jobs earn less than civil engineers at private companies.

Civil engineers working for the federal government earn slightly less. The salaries of all civil engineers increase with experience. The average salary for a mid-level engineer is $46,000 in private industry and $42,000 in the government. Senior-level engineers who manage others may earn $100,000 or more.

The employment outlook for civil engineers looks good through the year 2006. Their skills will be needed for the design and building of new transportation systems, factories, and office buildings. They will also be needed to help repair or replace roads, bridges, and public buildings.

FOR MORE INFORMATION

Schools and public libraries have many books on engineering and construction. Ask a librarian to help select a group of books. In high school, you can join a group such as the Junior Engineering Technical Society or attend a summer camp such as the Worcester Polytechnic Institute's 12-day program.

A civil engineer inspects plans at a highway construction site.

American Society of Civil Engineers
345 East 47th Street
New York, NY 10017
Tel: 212-705-7496

Institute of Transportation Engineers
525 School Street, SW, Suite 410
Washington, DC 20024
Tel: 202-554-8050
Web: http://www.io.com/

Junior Engineering Technical Society
1420 King Street, Suite 405
Alexandria, VA 22314
Tel: 703-548-5387
Web: http://www.asee.org/external/jets

Frontiers in Science, Mathematics and Engineering
Worcester Polytechnic Institute
100 Institute Road
Worcester, MA 01609
Tel: 508-831-5000
Web: http://cs.wpi.edu

CLERKS

SCHOOL SUBJECTS:
BUSINESS, ENGLISH, MATHEMATICS

PERSONAL SKILLS:
COMMUNICATION/IDEAS
FOLLOWING INSTRUCTIONS

MINIMUM EDUCATION LEVEL:
HIGH SCHOOL DIPLOMA

OUTLOOK:
LITTLE CHANGE OR MORE SLOWLY THAN THE AVERAGE

OTHER ARTICLES TO LOOK AT:

Bank Services Occupations
Bookkeepers
Medical Secretaries
Receptionists
Retail Sales Workers
Secretaries

WHAT CLERKS DO

Clerks are the support workers found in offices, businesses, and stores. They perform a wide variety of tasks, from greeting customers and seeing to their needs, to typing and filing, to operating computers, phones, cash registers and other machinery.

There are many types of clerks. *Billing clerks* keep track of a company's business transactions. They send out bills and check for payments received by the company. *Car rental agents* are clerks who act as salespersons. When a customer needs to rent a car from the airport or the company's local office, the agent writes a rental contract and answers questions about such things as the size of the car, air-conditioning, mileage, and extra insurance the client may need. *Counter and retail clerks* also work directly with customers in supermarkets, department stores, laundries, bicycle repair shops, and any business that sells goods and is open to the public. They receive payments and answer customer questions. *Data entry clerks* work in stores, insurance and manufacturing companies, hospitals, schools, banks, government agencies, and utility companies. They enter information into a computer system, which the computer then processes to produce such documents as bills and mailing lists. *File clerks* are responsible for keeping business records accurate, up to date, and properly stored, either in folders inside file cabinets or on computers. *General office clerks* perform a variety of tasks to help an office run smoothly, including typing, filing, answering telephones, delivering messages, and operating office machines.

Hotel clerks are employed by hotels, motels, and inns to greet and register guests, assign rooms, issue keys, answer questions about the hotel and the area, and take care of guests' bills when they check out. *Railroad clerks* keep track of all transactions of a railroad company. Their duties include selling tickets, keeping books, and recording the time each train arrives or leaves a station. *Shipping and receiving clerks* make sure that their company's products are shipped properly and that the products they receive from other companies arrive in good condition.

Statistical clerks collect and organize information that businesses and governments need to make smart decisions. *Stock clerks* receive, sort, store, and give out supplies used by businesses, industries, and institutions. They work in stockrooms and warehouses. *Traffic agents* are concerned with the movement of cargo (goods) by air, water, truck, or rail. They handle the booking, billing, claims, and related paperwork for the movement of goods.

EDUCATION AND TRAINING

Some businesses hire high school students as counter and retail clerks and as stock clerks. Most other clerk jobs require a minimum of a high school diploma. Courses in English, business, mathematics, typing, and bookkeeping are helpful. Some car rental agencies, especially in Florida and the Southwest, prefer agents who speak Spanish as well as English. Companies looking for traffic agents prefer candidates with one or two years of college, and many hotels prefer clerks with a college degree. In hotels where foreign travelers stay, clerks may be required to speak a foreign language.

EARNINGS AND OUTLOOK

The average salary for full-time clerks ranges from about $15,300 per year to $26,700, though starting wages may be lower and will depend on the employee's skills as well as the size and location of the company. Experienced clerks average between $21,800 and $29,000 per year. Wages tend to be highest in public utilities and mining companies, and they tend to be lower in companies involved in construction, finance, insurance, and real estate.

As is the case with most office workers, office clerks work an average 37- to 40-hour week. Full-time workers generally also receive paid vacations, health insurance, sick leave, and other benefits.

About 3,111,000 people held jobs as office workers in the late 1990s. Although employment of office clerks is expected to grow more slowly than the average through 2006, there will still be many jobs available due to the vastness of this field, along with a high turnover rate. With the increased use of data processing equipment and other types of automated office machinery, more and more employers are hiring people proficient in a variety of office tasks.

A billing clerk reviews her calculations before sending the bill to a customer.

FOR MORE INFORMATION

Students who wish to learn more about a clerk's job may seek a part-time or summer job in a local office or business, store, or car rental agency.

For further information, write to the following:

Office Team
2884 Sand Hill Road
Menlo Park, CA 94025

CLINICAL CHEMISTS

SCHOOL SUBJECTS:
BIOLOGY, CHEMISTRY

PERSONAL SKILLS:
HELPING TEACHING
TECHNICAL/SCIENTIFIC

MINIMUM EDUCATION LEVEL:
BACHELOR'S DEGREE

OUTLOOK:
ABOUT AS FAST AS THE AVERAGE

OTHER ARTICLES TO LOOK AT:

Biochemists
Biologists
Biomedical Engineers
Chemical Engineers
Chemists
Medical Technologists

WHAT CLINICAL CHEMISTS DO

Clinical chemists perform laboratory tests. These tests are an important way for physicians and patients to detect, diagnose, and treat disease. For example, tests can determine the level of medication in the blood to see whether a patient is taking the proper dosage, and whether the body is responding to the treatment.

Clinical chemists are specialized lab technologists who prepare specimens and analyze the chemicals and hormones found in body fluids (blood, urine, spinal fluid, and gastric juices). The clinical chemist's exact duties depend on the test being performed. If the test is automated, the chemist is responsible for calibrating (setting), loading specimens into, and monitoring the instruments to make sure all goes correctly. After the results are ready, the chemist verifies their accuracy and sends them out or reports them to the attending physician. A test that is more involved, such as identifying cell types in leukemia, requires very different procedures, including special stains and chromosome studies. Because of their advanced education and training, clinical chemists handle more sophisticated equipment and testing. They may be responsible for ordering, purchasing, maintaining, and repairing the specialized equipment and instruments required for the laboratory tests. They design new laboratory procedures, and establish or continue training and supervision of other employees in laboratory procedures and skills.

Clinical chemists work most often in hospitals, clinics, and commercial laboratories. They also work for pharmaceutical companies developing new products.

EDUCATION AND TRAINING

Clinical chemists need at least a bachelor's degree with a major in medical technology or one of the life sciences, but most have advanced degrees—a master's, Ph.D. or even an M.D. degree. Although the emphasis is placed on courses in chemistry, biological sciences, microbiology, and mathematics, the curriculum may also include courses in management, business, and computers.

Most states require clinical chemists to be licensed or registered. In addition, most employers require certification by such organizations as the American Medical Technologists and the Credentialing Commission of the International Society for Clinical Laboratory Technology.

EARNINGS AND OUTLOOK

Those entering the career earn about $26,500 a year. Clinical chemists with a master's degree and experience can earn over $40,000 a year. Senior administrators earn still more.

As highly trained, full-time professionals, most chemists receive health insurance, paid vacations, and sick leave. The specifics of these benefits vary from employer to employer.

Because of the increased volume of medical testing, the outlook for clinical chemistry jobs is good through the year 2006. However, greater use of automation and specialized instruments may eliminate some jobs for clinical chemists.

Usually, openings occur when clinical chemists leave the field. Career advancement means becoming a sales representative, consultant, or teacher, or moving into administrative positions.

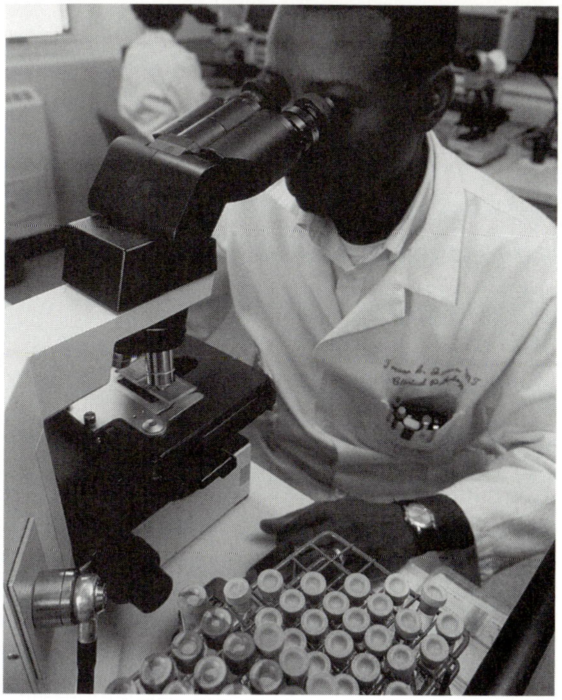

This clinical chemist uses his microscope to view a tissue sample.

FOR MORE INFORMATION

For more information on careers in clinical chemistry, contact the following organization:

American Association for Clinical Chemistry
2101 L St. NW, Suite 202
Washington, DC 20037-1526
Tel: 202-857-0717
Web: http://www.aacc.org

For general information about chemistry careers and a list of colleges and universities with accredited programs in chemistry, contact:

American Chemical Society
Department of Career Services
1155 16th Street, NW
Washington, DC 20036
Tel: 202-872-4600 (list) or
202-452-2113 (general information)
Web: http://www.acs.org

American Society for Clinical Laboratory Science
7910 Woodmont Avenue, Suite 530
Bethesda, MD 20814
Tel: 301-657-2768
Web: http://www.ascls.org

American Medical Technologists
710 Higgins Road
Park Ridge, IL 60068
Tel: 847-823-5169
Web: http://www.amtl.com

International Society for Clinical Laboratory Technology
917 Locust Street, Suite 1100
St. Louis, MO 63101
Tel: 314-241-1445

CLOWNS

SCHOOL SUBJECTS:
PHYSICAL EDUCATION, THEATER/DANCE

PERSONAL SKILLS:
ARTISTIC

MINIMUM EDUCATION LEVEL:
HIGH SCHOOL DIPLOMA

OUTLOOK:
LITTLE CHANGE OR MORE SLOWLY THAN THE AVERAGE

OTHER ARTICLES TO LOOK AT:
Actors
Circus Performers
Comedians
Magicians
Stunt Performers

WHAT CLOWNS DO

Clowns work in circuses, in movies, on television, in musical plays, at birthday parties and other events, or in fairgrounds or amusement parks. Their job is to divert and entertain audiences. They perform comical routines often while wearing unusual makeup and costumes. They juggle, dance, or display other technical skills, and make people laugh.

Some clowns perform in large groups. Circus clowns often perform routines while the rings are being prepared for other acts. They might sing songs, tell jokes, or do acrobatic stunts. Some of the routines they perform are written specifically for particular clowns. Others are stock comedy routines. Clowns must have a good sense of timing and balance and must be able to adjust their performance to the audience.

The makeup and costumes vary for different kinds of clowns. *Whiteface clowns* wear white makeup and caps that make them appear to be bald. They are the elegant clowns and are usually in charge of a routine. *Auguste clowns* wear baggy clothes and seem clumsy or silly. They trip over objects on the stage or drop things other clowns were juggling. *Tramp clowns* look unshaven and wear tattered clothes. They often appear sad or forlorn. *Character clowns,* like Charlie Chaplin, have unique routines, and usually perform alone. In some performances, different kinds of clowns work together to create a more balanced or entertaining show.

Clowns must be willing to travel to find work. The work is performed under many different kinds of conditions. They work outdoors or indoors depending on the job. If they get a circus job, they must be willing to travel for much of the year. Circus clowns may perform in a large tent outdoors or in a large indoor arena.

EDUCATION AND TRAINING

Training in dance and pantomime is helpful for would-be clowns. Clowns who can move well and use their bodies to communicate with an audience will have more success. Dance academies, schools for dramatic arts, and colleges and universities offer classes in pantomime and dance. Many high schools also have drama or dance classes for students. Experience acting or performing in plays is important. Shows are put on regularly by high schools and community centers.

Clowns should be able to project their voices. Any debate or public speaking clubs can help develop this skill. Clowns need to have good voice control as well as poise before an audience. Like other actors, clowns benefit from a solid education. A high school diploma is not required by most circuses, but a diploma and a college education certainly help a clown's job prospects. Employers in the motion-picture and television industry also prefer to hire performers who have diplomas.

EARNINGS AND OUTLOOK

Because the job market for clowns is unpredictable, and because of the freelance nature of clowning, there are no set salaries. Circus clowns generally earn $400 to $500 per week, while those working in nightclubs, casinos, or on Broadway can make as much as $10,000, according to the American Guild of Variety Artists. A clown's weekly income can vary widely—they may earn $300 one week, $1,000 the next, and nothing the week after that. For a child's birthday party, a clown may earn $50 to $500 depending on the length of the party and the performer's popularity.

The outlook for people who want to work as clowns is not very promising. There is a tremendous amount of competition, and the field is overcrowded, as it is in other careers in the entertainment industry. It can take more than a year to find a job working as a clown. Wages are often controlled by unions. Like most performing artists, most clowns are not permanently employed and must repeatedly audition for positions.

FOR MORE INFORMATION

This labor union serves singers, dancers, variety performers, circus performers, ice skaters, and theme park performers.

American Guild of Variety Artists
184 Fifth Avenue
New York, NY 10019

Clowns often entertain at children's birthday parties.

Doing business as National Circus Project, this organization provides arts and education programs to schools. It also operates Circus Information Referral Center.

Circus Education Specialists
56 Lion Lane
Westbury, NY 11590
Tel: 516-334-2123

For techniques and information for serious-minded amateurs, semiprofessionals, and professionals, including a magazine, clown alleys, and annual convention and competitions, contact:

Clowns of America International
PO Box 6468
Lee's Summit, MO 64064
Tel: 888-52CLOWN
Web: http://www.clown.org

COAL MINING TECHNICIANS

SCHOOL SUBJECTS:
CHEMISTRY, EARTH SCIENCE

PERSONAL SKILLS:
MECHANICAL/MANIPULATIVE
TECHNICAL/SCIENTIFIC

MINIMUM EDUCATION LEVEL:
SOME POSTSECONDARY TRAINING

OUTLOOK:
DECLINE

OTHER ARTICLES TO LOOK AT:

Energy Conservation and Use Technicians

Geologists

Mining Engineers

Surveying and Mapping Technicians

Surveyors

WHAT COAL MINING TECHNICIANS DO

Coal mining technicians assist other mining workers in digging, preparing, and transporting of coal. They help survey, map, and plan the mining of a coal field; drill test holes and analyze samples; and prepare reports on how mining for coal will affect the environment. Once a coal mine or field is established, the technicians manage safe mining operations and train other workers in safety techniques. They plan the most economical and efficient way of removing the coal, and test for coal quality and air impurities. Technicians dispose of mine waste; select, operate, and maintain the special machinery used; and figure out how to reclaim strip mining areas after the coal has been removed.

Coal mining can be hazardous work, and coal mining technicians work under unusual and often harsh conditions. Those employed at surface mines work outdoors for long hours and are exposed to all kinds of weather. In underground mines, technicians work in tunnels that may be cramped, dark, dusty, wet, and cold. All mining jobs are physically demanding, and they almost always involve getting dirty; however, technological advances have reduced many of the health hazards.

EDUCATION AND TRAINING

Students interested in becoming coal mining technicians should begin preparing in high school. Your studies should include mathematics, physics, and chemistry, as well as English, with special attention to reading, writing, and communication skills. Courses in computers and mechanical drawing or drafting would also prove helpful.

After high school, you should enroll in one of the 20 or so schools around the country that offer two-year coal mining technology programs. Many of these schools offer summer intern programs which allow you to work in actual coal mines. This gives you a clear picture of the coal mining industry in general, and helps you choose the work area that best fits your abilities.

Coal mining technicians are usually hired by company recruiters before you complete your last year of technical or vocational school. After a few years of experience, you may advance to such positions as supervisor, production superintendent, or mine manager, or possibly even go into business for yourself as a private consultant or contractor.

EARNINGS AND OUTLOOK

It is hard to determine what coal mining technicians earn because they do such a

Masks and other safety devices help protect coal mining technicians as they do their work.

wide variety of jobs. Within five years, technicians' salary's increase quite a bit, while those who become successful managers or private consultants earn considerably more. The average salary for coal mining workers is $857 per week.

Employment levels for coal mining technicians will depend on the demand for coal, which may decrease or increase according to how much oil and natural gas are available. Also, safety regulations and environmental quality controls may lead to lower employment levels for the mining industry in general. Still, jobs will be available for people who are prepared to meet the challenge of producing more coal more efficiently, while at the same time protecting the environment and making sure of mine safety.

FOR MORE INFORMATION

This nonprofit educational organization has free materials (booklets, brochures, posters) for students on coal, electricity, and land reclamation.

American Coal Foundation
1130 17th Street, NW, Suite 220
Washington, DC 20036
Tel: 202-466-8630
Web: http://ket.org/trips/coal/ACE.html

For career information, contact:

American Institute of Mining, Metallurgical, and Petroleum Engineers
3 Park Avenue
New York, NY 10016-5998
Tel: 212-419-7676
Web: http://www.idis.com/aime

COLLECTION WORKERS

SCHOOL SUBJECTS:
COMPUTER SCIENCE, PSYCHOLOGY, SPEECH

PERSONAL SKILLS:
FOLLOWING INSTRUCTIONS

MINIMUM EDUCATION LEVEL:
HIGH SCHOOL DIPLOMA

OUTLOOK:
MUCH FASTER THAN THE AVERAGE

OTHER ARTICLES TO LOOK AT:

Bank Services Occupations

Clerks

Insurance Claims Representatives

Insurance Policy Processing Occupations

Telemarketers

WHAT COLLECTION WORKERS DO

Collection workers try to persuade people to pay their overdue bills. They are sometimes called *bill collectors*, *collection correspondents*, or *collection agents*. When a customer fails to pay a bill, the collection worker is given a bad-debt file. This file contains information about the customer, the amount of the unpaid bill, and the date of the last payment. The collection worker then calls or writes to the customer to find out why the bill has not been paid. The worker tries to encourage the customer to pay all or part of the bill. If the customer has moved and left no forwarding address, the collector tries to find him or her by checking with the post office, telephone company, credit bureaus, or former neighbors of the customer. The collector also may use online computer databases to track down a customer.

Sometimes the customer will say that the bill has not been paid because it is incorrect or because the item purchased was faulty. In such cases the collection worker suggests that the customer contact the seller of the item. If the problem remains unresolved after these steps are taken, the collector tries again to encourage payment by the customer.

Some customers are unable to pay a bill because of a financial emergency, such as unemployment or illness. Others have fallen into debt because they have not managed their money properly. In such cases the collection worker may arrange a new payment schedule. If a customer simply refuses to pay a bill, the worker might suggest that the matter be turned over to an attorney.

When all efforts to collect a bill fail, the account is given to a *repossessor*. This collection worker takes back, or repossesses, the item that has not been paid for and returns it to the seller. Items such as furniture or appliances are picked up in a truck. Vehicles are driven to the seller's place of business. If the buyer will not give the key to the repossessor, he or she might use special tools to enter and start the vehicle.

In small offices collection workers sometimes perform clerical duties. They might read and answer mail, file papers, and record amounts paid.

Collectors are employed by banks, finance companies, credit unions, hospitals, department stores, and collection agencies. They also work for wholesale businesses and utility companies.

Collection workers usually work at desks in offices. Most of their work is done by telephone. Customers sometimes become angry and insult the collector or the company. Workers must be able to deal calmly with these insults. At the same time, they must try to persuade customers to pay their bills. Good communication and people skills are required for this line of work.

EDUCATION AND TRAINING

A high school education is usually sufficient for this job. In high school, students should concentrate on courses in speech, psychology, and English. Collection workers are usually trained on the job. This training typically lasts about two months. During the training course workers will learn the company's strategy, what language to use, and how to communicate with particularly difficult customers. They also will learn how to use the company's computer and telephone systems. Special courses on becoming a collection worker are also available through the American Collectors Association.

EARNINGS AND OUTLOOK

Collection workers may receive a flat salary or a salary plus a bonus on the amounts they collect. The average yearly salary of a full-time collector is about $21,300. Those at the low end of the pay scale might make only $15,000. Workers with experience could earn as much as $34,300 a year.

The employment outlook for collection workers is very good. More and more people are buying items on credit, an indication that they might not have enough money to pay for them. Thus, more collection workers will be needed to deal with those who do not pay their bills. Many collection workers will leave their jobs because they find the work stressful or because they do not make enough money. This will create additional job openings.

A collection worker talks to a client on a telephone headset.

FOR MORE INFORMATION

For more information about a career as a collection worker, contact:

American Collectors Association
PO Box 39106
Minneapolis, MN 55439
Tel: 612-926-6547
Web: http://www.collector.com

American Association of Credit Management
8815 Centre Park Drive, Suite 200
Columbia, MD 21045-2158
Tel: 410-740-5560
Web: http://www.nacm.org

National Association of Credit Management
8815 Centre Park Drive, Suite 200
Columbia, MD 21045-2158
Tel: 410-740-5560
Email: info@nacm.org
Web: http://www.nacm.org

COLLEGE ADMINISTRATORS

SCHOOL SUBJECTS:
BUSINESS, ENGLISH

PERSONAL SKILLS:
LEADERSHIP/MANAGEMENT
HELPING/TEACHING

MINIMUM EDUCATION LEVEL:
BACHELOR'S DEGREE

OUTLOOK:
LITTLE CHANGE OR MORE SLOWLY THAN THE AVERAGE

OTHER ARTICLES TO LOOK AT:

Adult and Vocational Education Teachers

College Professors

Guidance Counselors

Office Administrators

School Administrators

WHAT COLLEGE ADMINISTRATORS DO

College administrators develop and manage services for students in colleges and universities. When working as an administrator, you are responsible for arranging housing, special services for veterans and minority students, and social, cultural, and recreational activities. Specific job titles vary, but the most common are *dean*, *registrar*, and *director of student activities*.

The *dean of students* heads the entire student-affairs program. *Associate or assistant deans* in this department may be in charge of specific aspects of student life such as housing. *Academic deans* are concerned with such issues as the courses offered or faculty hired in a specific academic division such as the college of nursing. *Registrars* prepare class schedules, make room assignments, keep records of students and their grades, and assemble data for government and educational agencies. The *director of student activities* assists student groups in planning and arranging social, cultural, and recreational events.

Other student-affairs workers are concerned with particular areas of college life. The *director of housing* is responsible for such matters as room assignments and the upkeep of dormitory buildings. *Residence counselors* live in the dormitories and try to help the students live in harmony. Often, these are older students who help new students who may be having problems. The director of religious activities coordinates the activities of the various religious groups.

Foreign-student advisors work with foreign students and give special help with admissions, housing, financial aid, and English as a second language. The director of the student health program hires staff, manages the facilities and equipment, and develops programs and services to meet the students' health care needs. *Athletic directors* are in charge of all intercollegiate athletic activities. They hire coaches, schedule sports events, and direct publicity efforts.

EDUCATION AND TRAINING

To prepare for a job in college administration, take accounting and math courses in high school, as you may be dealing with financial records and statistics. Courses in English literature and composition will help you develop communication skills.

A bachelor's degree is the minimum requirement for college administrators. Because of the wide range of duties involved with college student affairs, the education and background required varies considerably. In many cases, a master's degree in education, psychology, or divinity may be preferred. In order to become a college dean,

A college dean discusses problems with an associate on his staff.

you'll need a doctorate and many years experience with a college or university.

EARNINGS AND OUTLOOK

Salaries vary greatly for college deans and related workers and depend to a great extent on the part of the country and the size of the institution. Most of the jobs described above pay salaries that average from $32,000 to $45,000 a year. University presidents make the higest salaries, followed by deans of students or athletic directors. Dean positions pay from $70,000 a year to well over $200,000 a year, depending on the school and the department.

The number of college-age students is expected to increase by the year 2006, so more jobs may open in the field. However, leaner budgets are currently making the job market in college administration competitive. Most job openings will be to replace workers who are retiring or leaving their jobs.

FOR MORE INFORMATION

For more information about a career as a college administrator, visit the Web sites of these organizations:

College & University Personnel Association
1233 20th Street, NW
Washington, DC 20036
Tel: 202-429-0311
Web: http://www.cupa.org

American Association of University Administrators
PO Box 696
Heflin, AL 36264
Tel: 256-463-2682
Web: http://www.aaua.org

COLLEGE PROFESSORS

SCHOOL SUBJECTS:
ENGLISH, HISTORY

PERSONAL SKILLS:
COMMUNICATION/IDEAS
HELPING/TEACHING

MINIMUM EDUCATION LEVEL:
MASTER'S DEGREE

OUTLOOK:
ABOUT AS FAST AS THE AVERAGE

OTHER ARTICLES TO LOOK AT:
College Administrators
Elementary School Teachers
School Administrators
Special Education Teachers
Teacher Aides

WHAT COLLEGE PROFESSORS DO

College and university faculty instruct students in specific areas of learning. They teach at junior colleges or at four-year colleges and universities. As a college professor, you'll have three main responsibilities: teaching, advising, and conducting research. Teaching is the most important. In the classroom, you'll lecture, lead discussions, administer exams, and assign text book reading and term papers. Though you may spend fewer than ten hours a week in the actual classroom, you'll spend many hours preparing lectures and lesson plans, grading papers and exams, and preparing grade reports. You'll also meet with students individually outside of the classroom to help guide them in the course, and to keep them updated as to their progress. To supplement your work, you might also teach classes in the evenings and on weekends, or in places away from the college, as part of an extension program of your university.

Some faculty members become student advisers, helping students decide which courses to take, informing them of requirements, and directing them toward scholarships and other financial aid. You may also help students adjust to college life, and guide them through difficult problems.

Another aspect of your work involves research. You will conduct research in your field of study and publish the results in textbooks and journals. You'll attend conferences and present your research findings to professors from other universities. You'll also direct graduate students who assist you in research.

Eventually, you may advance to become head of your department and take charge of many department activities such as creating new courses, hiring faculty members, and overseeing student activities.

EDUCATION AND TRAINING

You should follow your guidance counselor's college preparatory plan in high school, taking courses in English, science, foreign language, history, math, and government. You should also take speech courses to prepare for speaking effectively in front of large groups.

To teach in a college or university, you must have at least a master's degree. A doctorate will be necessary to advance beyond the rank of instructor.

Assistant professor is the entry-level job title for college faculty members with doctorates. Faculty members usually spend no more than six years as assistant professors. During this time, the college will decide whether or not the faculty members' abilities are strong enough for the school. If they are, the teach-

Professors may lecture in small classrooms or large auditoria, depending upon the size of the university and the popularity of their courses.

ers will be granted tenure, which is a type of job security, and promoted to *associate professor*. An associate professor may eventually be promoted to *full professor*.

EARNINGS AND OUTLOOK

Full professors at public universities earn an average of about $70,000 a year, while professors at private universities receive about $85,000 a year. Associate professors earn an average of $50,000 annually at public universities, and $56,000 at private.

To meet budget demands, colleges are hiring more part-time faculty than full-time faculty. These part-time instructors must often work for low pay with no benefits. Competition will continue to be heavy for the few full-time positions available; but an expected increase in student enrollment may result in more opportunities for college professors.

FOR MORE INFORMATION

To read about the issues affecting college professors, visit the Web sites of these organizations:

American Federation of Teachers
555 New Jersey Avenue, NW
Washington, DC 20001
Tel: 202-879-4400
Web: http://www.aft.org

American Association of University Professors
1012 Fourteenth Street, NW Suite 500
Washington, DC 20005
Tel: 202-737-5900
Web: http://www.aaup.org

COLUMNISTS

SCHOOL SUBJECTS:
ENGLISH, FOREIGN LANGUAGE

PERSONAL SKILLS:
COMMUNICATION/IDEAS
HELPING/TEACHING

MINIMUM EDUCATION LEVEL:
BACHELOR'S DEGREE

OUTLOOK:
ABOUT AS FAST AS THE AVERAGE

OTHER ARTICLES TO LOOK AT:

Book Editors
Foreign Correspondents
Magazine Editors
Newspaper Editors
Reporters
Writers

WHAT COLUMNISTS DO

Columnists write their opinions for newspapers, magazines, or places called syndicates that sell stories to many publications at once. Some columnists write about personal experience. Others write about current events.

Columns are written on a schedule, perhaps every day, week, or month, depending on how often the newspaper or magazine comes out. Like other journalists, columnists must complete their work by strict deadlines.

Columnists choose what they want to write about within their area of specialty. Some may write humor columns, while others write in a more serious tone about government and politics, health, or business.

Most columnists work in newsrooms or magazine offices. But some work out of their homes or private offices. Many well-known columnists work in Washington, DC.

Some columnists become famous after their columns run in newspapers across the country. For example, the late Mike Royko started writing his column in Chicago. Soon his work was syndicated, and his name became familiar to newspaper readers in many cities and towns.

The majority of columnists start out as reporters first. After they gain experience, they may be offered a columnist's job.

Columns are different than regular news stories in that columns usually take a side on an issue. A columnist must hold strong opinions and not be afraid to express them. Columns usually start out and end strong, and have middle sections filled with facts.

EDUCATION AND TRAINING

In high school you should take English, journalism, social studies, speech, computer science, and typing. It is a good idea to try to write for your high school's yearbook or for the high school newspaper. Joining your school's debate team also would be helpful.

Going to a university and earning at least a bachelor's degree is essential. Most editors prefer that their employees hold a degree in journalism. Others prefer applicants with a bachelor's in liberal arts and a master's in journalism.

Many colleges and universities have student newspapers that are excellent for providing reporting and column-writing experience. During the summers, another great place to gain experience is at newspapers or magazines that offer internships.

Much training will come on the job as a reporter, where journalists can learn the key parts of being a columnist: interviewing, research, and people skills. Also, reporters learn how to manage their time, write quickly and to the point, and finish before deadline.

Abby (Abigail) Van Buren (left) and Ann Landers (right) are famous for their daily advice columns.

EARNINGS AND OUTLOOK

Writers, including columnists, start out making an average of about $20,000, according to the Dow Jones Newspaper Fund. Experienced columnists can earn top salaries of $60,000 or more.

Employment of columnists is expected to stay about the same in coming years. Newspaper jobs could decrease but magazine writer jobs could increase. It is likely that the number of columnists, small to begin with, will remain constant.

There will be strong competition for such jobs. The best place to start is at smaller publications, where newspaper reporters and magazine editorial assistants take on many tasks, but they also get promoted faster. However, the pay is less than at bigger publications.

FOR MORE INFORMATION

For information on careers in newspaper reporting, contact:

American Society of Journalists and Authors
1501 Broadway, Suite 302
New York, NY 10036
Web: http://www.asja.org/cw950615.htm

For general educational information on all areas of journalism (newspapers, magazines, television, and radio), contact:

Association for Education in Journalism and Mass Communication
121 LaConte College
University of South Carolina
Columbia, SC 29208-0251
Web: http://www.aejmc.sc.edu/online/home.html

COMEDIANS

SCHOOL SUBJECTS:
ENGLISH, THEATER/DANCE

PERSONAL SKILLS:
ARTISTIC, COMMUNICATION/IDEAS

MINIMUM EDUCATION LEVEL:
HIGH SCHOOL DIPLOMA

OUTLOOK:
ABOUT AS FAST AS THE AVERAGE

OTHER ARTICLES TO LOOK AT:

Actors
Circus Performers
Clowns
Radio and Television Announcers
Writers

WHAT COMEDIANS DO

Comedians try to make people laugh. Some entertain audiences in nightclubs and at concerts. Some perform in comedy shows on television. Some even write jokes for other comedians.

Comedians who work in nightclubs are called *stand-up comedians*. They try to entertain audiences with stories, jokes, one-liners, and impressions. In comedy clubs in large cities, comedians may do more than one show a night, and perform either before or after another comedian. Depending on whether they are the opening act or the main act, they perform sets of material that are anywhere from 10 minutes to an hour long.

Stand-up comedians spend much of their time traveling from city to city entertaining different types of audiences and sharpening their acts in the process. To book these out-of-town performances, the comedians may call the club owners themselves or go through a booking agent. In medium- and small-sized cities they perform only one night and then drive or fly to the next city. Stand-up comedians entertain at conventions, concerts, hotels, parties, and outdoor festivals—anywhere they can be paid to entertain an audience.

After comedians have sharpened their acts, they may be asked to appear on a television talk show or a comedy special. Some comedians do comedy concerts that are videotaped and broadcast. Only a few comedians become so well known that they appear in a television series developed especially for them.

EDUCATION AND TRAINING

There is no way to become a comedian except to step on a stage and perform. People from all walks of life have become comedians. It takes a great deal of work and practice to become a good comedian. It takes many hours on stage to know how to deliver a joke, structure the pace of a show, and read an audience to determine what type of comedy they would enjoy.

While there are no schools for comedians, certain school subjects can be very helpful. English and composition are necessary to write jokes well. Speech and drama classes will help to build a strong presence on stage. The most important thing a comedian needs to know is something that cannot be taught: to be funny and be able to make others laugh. While this skill can be improved through practice and hard work, it is most often a skill that a person either has or does not have.

EARNINGS AND OUTLOOK

The pay scale for comedians varies widely. Stand-up comedians only earn money when

Actor/comedian Billy Crystal serenades Tonight Show host Jay Leno.

they are working. They are paid either per show or for a week of performances. Comedians who are starting out may earn as little as $20 for a 20-minute show. Those who perform at colleges earn about $500 per show. A headline comedian in a comedy club in a large city can earn from $1,000 to $20,000, while the comedians that open the evening's show can earn from $125 to $350 per week. In smaller clubs, headline comedians make between $300 to $800 per show. Those who are just starting out earn very little but can make valuable contacts with club owners, agents, and other comedians. The comedy club usually pays for the comedian's lodging.

Those who write jokes for famous comedians usually get paid around $50 for every joke used. The writers of a network comedy show can be paid anywhere from $50,000 to $150,000 or more a year.

There are hundreds of comedy clubs across the country (usually in larger cities) and each club needs performers to get their audiences laughing. The spread of legalized gambling across the United States, and the opening of many resorts and theme parks, continue to add new opportunities for comedians. Thousands of comedians will continue to find work into the next decade.

FOR MORE INFORMATION

Contact the following organizations for more information on professional comedy careers.

The Association of Comedy Artists
PO Box 1796
New York, NY 10025
Tel: 212-864-6620

National Comedians Association
581 Ninth Avenue, Suite 3C
New York, NY 10036
Tel: 212-875-7705

COMMUNICATIONS EQUIPMENT MECHANICS

SCHOOL SUBJECTS:
MATHEMATICS, TECHNICAL/SHOP

PERSONAL SKILLS:
FOLLOWING INSTRUCTIONS
MECHANICAL/MANIPULATIVE

MINIMUM EDUCATION LEVEL:
HIGH SCHOOL DIPLOMA

OUTLOOK:
DECLINE

OTHER ARTICLES TO LOOK AT:

Electrical and Electronics Engineers

Electronics Engineering Technicians

Telephone Installers and Repairers

Wireless Technicians

WHAT COMMUNICATIONS EQUIPMENT MECHANICS DO

Communicating is sharing information. Today, much of the communication between individuals, businesses, and governments takes place electronically over standard telephone wires. Telephone wires transmit more than just phone calls. Telegrams are sent over phone wires, as is the information shared by computers located in different cities. Thanks to the fax machine, an architect in Chicago can send copies of drawings to a client in New York, using telephone lines. The telephone system plays a very important role in our ability to communicate with one another. *Communications equipment mechanics* install, maintain, test, and repair telephone communications systems. These mechanics usually work in telephone company offices or in phone company customers' offices.

There are several kinds of communications equipment mechanics. *Central office equipment installers* work in a telephone company's central office, assembling, installing, and replacing the complex switching and dialing equipment that is headquartered there. Sometimes they will assemble a whole new central office. At other times, they might install equipment to expand a central office or to replace outdated equipment. They also adjust and test the equipment. These installers must be able to read blueprints and use a variety of hand and power tools.

Central office repairers test and repair switches and relays used in telephone circuits. They use switching equipment, hand tools, and electronic testing meters to locate problems and make repairs. *Maintenance administrators* test a customer's lines at the central office to discover where and why problems are occurring. When a problem is found, they direct outside maintenance crews in making repairs. In addition, these workers may contact customers to arrange service calls and then send over repair crews. They must understand the causes of any equipment failure.

PBX systems technicians work on private branch exchanges, which are special telephone systems set up in businesses that bypass phone company lines. *PBX installers* install these systems, which may include customized switchboards. *PBX repairers* maintain and repair these systems. They also may work on mobile radiophones and microwave transmission devices.

EDUCATION AND TRAINING

The training needed to become a communications equipment mechanic begins in high school or vocational school. Useful high school classes include computer courses, algebra, geometry, English, physics, and shop. Knowledge of the major principles of electricity is important. In addition, most telephone companies conduct their own training programs for new employees who have high school or vocational school diplomas.

Many telecommunications companies prefer to hire graduates of two-year technical schools. Programs in telecommunications technology, electronics, or even computer maintenance teach many of the basic skills required for these workers.

A communications equipment technician checks some telephone switching equipment.

EARNINGS AND OUTLOOK

The Bureau of Labor Statistics estimates that communications equipment mechanics earn an average salary of $36,260. Some make less than $18,000 a year, while some make over $50,000. Most workers in this group who are employed by telephone companies are union members, and their earnings are set by contracts between the union and the company. Benefits vary, but generally include paid vacations, paid holidays, sick leaves, and health insurance. In addition, some companies offer pension and retirement plans.

There will be fewer jobs for communications equipment mechanics in the future because of continuing automation and equipment advances. New equipment has fewer mechanical parts that break, wear out, or need to be periodically cleaned and lubricated. In addition, computers can detect problems in equipment automatically and route operations around trouble spots until repairs can be made. Many telephone companies are laying off employees, and it will be hard for new workers to enter this field.

FOR MORE INFORMATION

A good way to explore the work done by communications equipment mechanics is to take electrical shop classes in high school.

To learn about issues affecting jobs in telecommunications, visit the CWA Web site.

Communications Workers of America (CWA)
501 Third Street, NW
Washington, DC 20001
Web: http://www.cwa-union.org

For more information, contact:

The National Association of Radio and Telecommunications Engineers
PO Box 678
Medway, MA 02053
Web: http://www.narte.org/

International Brotherhood of Electrical Workers
1125 15th Street, NW
Washington, DC 20005
Web: http://ibew.org/

COMPOSERS

SCHOOL SUBJECTS:
MUSIC, THEATER/DANCE

PERSONAL SKILLS:
ARTISTIC, COMMUNICATION/IDEAS

MINIMUM EDUCATION LEVEL:
HIGH SCHOOL DIPLOMA

OUTLOOK:
LITTLE CHANGE OR MORE SLOWLY THAN THE AVERAGE

OTHER ARTICLES TO LOOK AT:

Music Teachers
Musicians
Orchestra Conductors
Singers
Songwriters

WHAT COMPOSERS DO

Composers write music for musical stage shows, television commercials, movies, ballet and opera companies, orchestras, and other musical performing groups. Composers work in many different ways. Often they begin with a musical idea and write it down using standard music notation. They use their music training and their own personal sense of melody, harmony, rhythm, and structure. Some compose music as they play an instrument and may or may not write it down.

Most composers specialize in one style of music, such as classical, jazz, country, rock, or blues. Some combine features from several styles. Composers who work on commission or on assignment meet with their clients to discuss their wishes. They will talk about the composition's theme, length, style, and the number and types of performers. After the piece is completed, the composer usually takes part in rehearsals and works with the performers. Composers work at home, in offices, or in music studios. Some need to work alone to plan and build their musical ideas. Others work with fellow musicians to help create a piece of music. Composing can take many long hours of work, and composing jobs may be irregular and low-paying. However, it is extremely satisfying for composers to hear their music performed, and successful commercial music composers can earn a lot of money.

EDUCATION AND TRAINING

Young people interested in becoming composers should study music and learn to play an instrument, such as piano. You may join or form your own musical group and try your hand at writing music for the group to perform. While in high school, students interested in musical composition should take as many courses in music as are available. These may include vocal technique, choral singing, music theory, and orchestra.

There are different requirements for composers of different types of music. All composers need to have a good ear, and almost all composers must be able to notate, or write down, their music. Composers of musicals, symphonies, and other large works must have years of study in a college, conservatory, or other school of music. Composers of popular songs do not need as much training. However, studying music enables composers to develop and express their musical ideas better. Music school courses for those who wish to be composers include music theory, musical form, music history, composition, conducting, and arranging. Composers also play at least one musical instrument, usually piano, and some play several instruments. Most composers of classical music know how to speak, read, and write at least one foreign language, often Italian or German.

EARNINGS AND OUTLOOK

The average earnings of a composer are difficult to determine. Most earn very little and work only part-time, while others may earn a great deal. Some composers work on commission. When a piece of music is commissioned, the composer is paid a lump sum for writing it. Other composers work under contract with a music publishing or recording company. Their compositions become the property of the company. Some composers receive royalties, or payments for each performance or sale of the piece.

A composer's pay for music written for the theater is based on the size and type of the theater company or play. A regional theater company may pay a composer between $3,000 to $8,000, an off-Broadway show pays from $3,000 to $6,000, and a Broadway show pays $5,000 to $12,000.

Opera companies commission works for one-act operas and full-length operas. A small company may pay in the range of $10,000 to $20,000 for a one-act opera and $30,000 to $70,000 for a full-length opera. Large opera companies pay from $15,000 to $40,000 for a one-act opera, and from $75,000 to $150,000 for a full-length opera.

A film for a major studio may pay a composer $50,000 to $200,000 or more for a musical score.

A composer may be paid per episode for a television program or series, ranging from $1,000 to $8,000, depending on the length of the episode, and whether for a network, cable or an independent television company.

As long as there are commercials, movies, operas, and orchestras, there will be a need for composers to write music.

A composer practices an arrangement for a musical piece he has written.

FOR MORE INFORMATION

Contact the following organizations for information on career opportunities for composers.

American Composers Alliance
170 West 74th Street
New York, NY 10023
Tel: 212-362-8900

American Federation of Musicians of the United States and Canada
1501 Broadway, Suite 600
New York, NY 10036
Tel: 212-869-1330
Web: http://www.afm.org

American Society of Composers, Authors, and Publishers
One Lincoln Plaza
New York, NY 10023
Web: http://www.ascap.com

American Women Composers, Inc.
c/o George Washington University
Department of Music
B-144 The Academic Center
Washington, DC 20052

COMPUTER AIDED DESIGN TECHNICIANS

SCHOOL SUBJECTS:
COMPUTER SCIENCE, MATHEMATICS, TECHNICAL/SHOP

PERSONAL SKILLS:
MECHANICAL/MANIPULATIVE
TECHNICAL/SCIENTIFIC

MINIMUM EDUCATION LEVEL:
HIGH SCHOOL DIPLOMA

OUTLOOK:
ABOUT AS FAST AS THE AVERAGE

OTHER ARTICLES TO LOOK AT:

Computer Operators
Computer Programmers
Computer Systems Analysts
Drafters
Graphic Designers
Industrial Designers

WHAT COMPUTER AIDED DESIGN TECHNICIANS DO

Computer aided design technicians, also known as *CAD technicians*, use computers to help design, improve, change, or produce manufactured items and manufacturing systems. Although CAD usually stands for computer aided design, it can also mean computer aided drafting. CAD technicians are involved in all parts of the manufacturing process. CAD technicians work under the direction of CAD engineers and designers, who are experts in applying computer technology to industrial design and manufacturing.

CAD technicians help to design and develop new products. These technicians need both drafting and computer skills. CAD technicians usually work at specially designed computer workstations. They call up computer data files that contain information about a new product. Then, they use computer programs to change that information into diagrams and drawings of the product. These are displayed on a video-display screen, which acts as an electronic drawing board.

Under the direction of a CAD engineer or designer, the CAD technician can make changes in diagrams and drawings. These changes can either be typed into the computer or touched onto the screen with a stylus, or light pen.

Once the changes have been made, technicians use computer programs to display the new diagrams or drawings. After the design of the product has been approved, CAD technicians may have more work to do. They may use the computer to make detailed drawings of the parts to be manufactured, as well as the tools that will be needed.

CAD technicians work in a variety of fields including architecture; electronics; the manufacturing of automobiles, aircraft, computers, and missiles; and design organizations.

EDUCATION AND TRAINING

CAD technicians must have at least a high school diploma. Most have completed a two-year program at a technical school. Such a program includes courses in basic drafting, machine drawing, architecture, civil drafting (with an emphasis on highways), process piping, electrical, electrical instrumentation, and plumbing. It should also include courses in data processing and in computer programming, systems, and equipment. Some companies have their own training programs.

EARNINGS AND OUTLOOK

Apprentice CAD technicians can expect to earn an average of $17,316 per year. Experienced technicians make an average of

$33,410 annually, with the most experienced earning around $49,500. Some technicians with special skills, extensive experience, or additional responsibilities can earn even more.

The U.S. Department of Labor predicts that the employment outlook for CAD technicians will be about as fast as average for all other occupations through 2006. Many companies in the near future will feel pressures to increase productivity in design and manufacturing activities, and CAD technology provides some of the best opportunities to improve that productivity. By some estimates, there will be as many as a million jobs available for technically trained personnel in the field of CAD/CAM technology in the next few years.

Any economic downturn could adversely affect CAD technicians because many of the industries that they serve—such as auto manufacturing or construction—fluctuate greatly with economic swings. In any event, the best opportunities will be for drafters and technicians proficient in CAD technology who continue to learn, both in school and on the job.

FOR MORE INFORMATION

It is hard to get a part-time or summer job that deals directly with CAD technology. But part-time jobs in drafting or engineering fields will give you a glimpse of a similar work atmosphere. If you are in high school and interested in a career in CAD technology, join the science club (especially computer and electronics clubs), participate in science fairs, or pursue hobbies that involve computers, drafting, electronics, or mechanical equipment.

CAD technicians spend most of their time in front of a computer, creating plans for everything from buildings to cars.

For more information about the career of computer aided design technician, contact the following organizations:

American Design and Drafting Association
PO Box 11937
Columbia, SC 29211
Tel: 803-771-0008
Email: national@adda.org
Web: http://www.adda.org

Institute of Electrical and Electronics Engineers (IEEE)
1828 L Street, NW, Suite 1202
Washington, DC 20036-5104
Tel: 202-785-0017
Web: http://www.ieee.org/usab

Society of Manufacturing Engineers
One SME Drive
Dearborn, MI 48121
Tel: 800-733-4763
Web: http://www.sme.org

COMPUTER AND ELECTRONICS SALES REPRESENTATIVES

SCHOOL SUBJECTS
BUSINESS, COMPUTER SCIENCE

PERSONAL SKILLS
COMMUNICATION/IDEAS
TECHNICAL/SCIENTIFIC

MINIMUM EDUCATION LEVEL
BACHELOR'S DEGREE

OUTLOOK
ABOUT AS FAST AS THE AVERAGE

OTHER ARTICLES TO LOOK AT:

Customer Service Representatives

Real Estate Agents and Brokers

Retail Sales Workers

Services Sales Representatives

Wireless Sales Workers

WHAT COMPUTER AND ELECTRONICS SALES REPRESENTATIVES DO

Computer and electronics sales representatives sell hardware, software, peripheral computer equipment, and electronics equipment to customers and businesses of all sizes. Sometimes they follow up sales with installation of systems, maintenance, or training of the client's staff. They are employed in all aspects of businesses. Sales representatives that work for retail stores deal with consumers. Representatives that specialize in a particular piece of hardware, certain software program, or electronic component may do business with banks, insurance companies, or accounting firms, among others.

The first step in the selling process, no matter the sale environment—retail or corporate—is client consultation. Sales representatives determine the client's current technological needs, as well as those of the future. During consultation, reps explain the technology's value and how well it will perform. Often, customers do not have expertise in computer or electronics technology, so the rep must explain and translate complicated computer tech-talk, as well as answer numerous questions. In retail computer sales, the customer decides what system, peripheral, or software to purchase and then brings it home or arranges for its delivery.

To stay abreast of technological advances, sales representatives must attend training sessions or continuing education classes. It also helps to know the essence of each client's field and the nature of their work.

EDUCATION AND TRAINING

Classes in speech and writing will help you learn how to communicate your product to large groups of people. Computer science and electronics classes will give you a basic overview of the field. General business and math classes will also be helpful.

Prepare yourself for a career in this field by developing your computer knowledge—take computer and math classes, as well as business classes to help develop a sound business sense. Excellent communications skills are a must. Hone yours by taking courses in English, speech, and technical writing and communication.

For computer sales representatives specializing in a specific industry, say health care or banking, training in the basics and current issues of that field is needed. Such training can be obtained through special work training seminars, adult education classes, or courses at a technical school. Many companies require their sales staff to complete a training program where they will learn the technologies and work tools needed for the job.

Electronics sales workers demonstrate televisions to customers.

EARNINGS AND OUTLOOK

According to a recent WetFeet.com Industry study, sales associates specializing in hardware components averaged between $45,000 and $60,000 a year (including commissions). Experienced account representatives in the computer/information field earned an annual salary of about $52,000; sales managers earned about $75,000; and marketing managers earned $104,125.

Employment opportunities should remain healthy for computer and electronics related sales careers through the year 2006. Increased retail sales will warrant competent and knowledgeable sales representatives. Employment opportunities will also be found with computer specialty stores or consulting companies that deal directly with businesses and their corporate computer and application needs. Computers have become an almost indispensable tool for running a successful business.

FOR MORE INFORMATION

National Association of Retail Dealers of America
10 East 22nd Street
Lombard, IL 60148-4915
Tel: 630-953-8950
Web: http://www.Narda.com

Association for Computing Machinery
1515 Broadway
New York, NY 10036-5701
Tel: 212-869-7440
Web: http://www.acm.org

The Electronics Representatives Association
444 North Michigan Avenue, Suite 1960
Chicago, IL 60611
Tel: 312-527-3050
Web: http://www.era.org

COMPUTER AND OFFICE MACHINE TECHNICIANS

SCHOOL SUBJECTS:
COMPUTER SCIENCE, TECHNICAL/SHOP

PERSONAL INTERESTS:
TECHNICAL/SCIENTIFIC

MINIMUM EDUCATION LEVEL:
SOME POSTSECONDARY TRAINING

OUTLOOK:
MUCH FASTER THAN THE AVERAGE

OTHER ARTICLES TO LOOK AT:

Computer Operators
Computer Programmers
Electrical and Electronics Engineers
Electromechanical Technicians
Electronics Engineering Technicians

WHAT COMPUTER AND OFFICE MACHINE TECHNICIANS DO

Businesses use computers and office machines to do a variety of daily tasks. Since the 1960s, computers have played an important role in business, research, and government. Today, computers are a part of everyone's lives.

Although computers and office machines have gotten smaller, they are still incredibly complex machines. Highly skilled electronics technicians are needed to keep computers and office machines operating properly and efficiently. *Computer and office machine technicians* service, install, calibrate, operate, maintain, and repair computers, peripherals, and other office machines.

Computer and office machine technicians may work for a computer manufacturer, a large corporation, or a repair shop. Technicians who work for a manufacturer learn how their company's products work and how to repair them when they break. Sometimes, technicians employed by a computer manufacturer may be headquartered at a customer's workplace where they help to plan and install new computer systems. They also perform regular maintenance to make sure the equipment continues to operate properly. If the equipment breaks down, technicians will work together with the customers to fix it.

Some technicians work in the maintenance or service department of large corporations. They work with many different types of machines, both mechanical and electronic.

Some computer and office machine technicians work for companies or repair shops that specialize in providing maintenance services to computer and office machine users. When equipment breaks down or needs regular maintenance, technicians are sent to the customer's offices to provide the necessary services.

EDUCATION AND TRAINING

Because computers and office machines are such complex electronic devices, the technicians who work on them must have excellent engineering, electrical, and mechanical skills. They should know basic mathematics, including algebra and trigonometry. Knowledge of computer programming is also important. Technicians must be able to follow written and spoken instructions and be able to communicate well. The best way to prepare for this career is to attend a special two-year program after high school. These programs are offered by technical institutes and some community colleges. In high school, students should take two years of mathematics, including algebra. They should also take at least three years of language and communication courses, and at least one year of physics or chemistry. Any computer electronics/automotive/engine repair courses offered at the high school level will also be helpful.

EARNINGS AND OUTLOOK

According to the *Occupational Outlook Handbook*, in 1996, service technicians specializing in communications and industrial electronic equipment earned an average annual salary of $31,304, while computer equipment service technicians earned an average of $30,264 a year. Technicians with extensive work experience and certification earn more.

Opportunities for employment in the computer and office machine field are excellent for those with good computer skills. These opportunities are expected to grow in the coming years.

FOR MORE INFORMATION

A great way to explore a career as a computer and office machine technician is to join one of the many computer user groups that have sprung up throughout the country. Many schools also have computer or shop clubs in which students can participate.

For industry information or details on their certification program, contact:

International Society of Certified Electronics Technicians
2708 West Berry Street
Fort Worth, TX 76109-2356
Tel: 817-921-9101
Web: http://www.iscet.org

An office machine service technician repairs a photocopy machine.

Contact ACM for information on internships, student membership, and the ACM magazine, Crossroads. *ACM also offers a student Web site at http://www.acm.org/membership/student/.*

Association for Computing Machinery (ACM)
1515 Broadway, 17th Floor
New York, NY 10036-5701
Tel: 212-869-7440
Web: http://www.acm.org

For certification, career, and placement information, contact:

Electronics Technicians Association and Satellite Dealers Association
602 North Jackson
Greencastle, IN 46135
Tel: 765-653-4301
Web: http://www.eta-sda.com

COMPUTER AND VIDEO GAME DESIGNERS

SCHOOL SUBJECTS:
ART, COMPUTER SCIENCE

PERSONAL SKILLS:
COMMUNICATION/IDEAS
TECHNICAL/SCIENTIFIC

MINIMUM EDUCATION LEVEL:
BACHELOR'S DEGREE

OUTLOOK:
FASTER THAN THE AVERAGE

OTHER ARTICLES TO LOOK AT:

Computer Operators
Computer Programmers
Graphics Programmers
Software Designers
Toy Industry Workers

WHAT COMPUTER AND VIDEO GAME DESIGNERS DO

Computer and video game designers create the games played on computers and through online Internet subscriptions. They generate ideas for new game concepts, including sound effects, characters, story lines, and graphics. Designers work either for the companies that make the games, or create the games on their own and then sell their ideas and programs to companies that produce them. Computer and video game design is a relatively new type of employment.

Designing computer games involves computer programming as well as creating stories, graphics, and sound effects. It is a creative process, requiring imagination and computer and communication skills to develop games that are interactive and entertaining. Whether you work alone or for a company, your aim is to create games that get players involved.

Each game must have a story as well as graphics and sound that will entertain and engage the players. Designers develop a plan for combining the story or concept, music or other sound effects, and graphics. They design rules to make the game fun, challenging, or educational, and they create characters for stories or circumstances, worlds in which these characters live, and problems or situations these characters face.

Designers need to understand games and their various forms, create new ideas, and experiment with and evaluate new designs. They assemble the separate elements (text, art, sound, video) of a game into a complete form, and follow through with careful planning and preparation, such as writing scripts, designing storyboards, and other documents. The average time it takes to design a game can be from about six to 18 months.

As designing computer games has become more complicated, design teams have begun to include not only programmers, but also artists, musicians, writers, and animators. Designers make such breakthroughs as using more entertaining graphics, creating more complicated games, using virtual reality in computer games, and using more realistic graphics in many games.

EDUCATION AND TRAINING:

If you want to be a computer and video game designer, you will need to learn many different computer skills. In high school, learn as much as you can about how to program computers, including learning as many computer languages that you can. Because designers must be creative, you should take courses in art, literature, and music as well. To become a computer and video game designer, you need to develop a variety of skills, including writing stories, programming, and designing sound effects. You also need to continually keep up with technology, which changes quickly.

Although you don't necessarily need to have a college degree to be a game designer, most companies are looking for creative people who have earned their bachelor's degree.

The major requirement for game design is that you must love to play computer games.

EARNINGS AND OUTLOOK:

Computer and video game designers earn between $30,000 and $75,000 per year. Earnings depend on how much experience you have, where you live, the size of the company you work for, and possible bonuses and royalties (the percentage of profit you receive from each game that is sold).

The computer and video game industry is growing quickly, with more and more companies hiring skilled people at many levels. Because the industry is fairly new, it is difficult to estimate exactly how many people work as game designers. About 90,000 people work within the video game industry as a whole.

Game development is popular—it is estimated that 15 million people in the United States have grown up playing computer and video games and that this number could go beyond 100 million by the year 2010. People in the industry expect more and more integration of interactive entertainment into mainstream society. Online development tools like engines, graphic and sound libraries, as well as programming languages like Java will probably create opportunities for new types of products that can feature game components.

A team of computer and video game designers ham it up.

FOR MORE INFORMATION:

This organization fosters information exchange and communication among professionals in the computer game and interactive development industry.

Computer Game Developers Association
Email: info@cdga.org
Web: http://www.cdga.org

This institute offers the world's first-ever bachelor of science degree in Real Time Interactive Simulation.

DigiPen Institute of Technology
5001 150th Avenue, NE
Redmond, WA 98052
Web: http://www.digipen.edu

This university lab trains students as game designers and programmers.

The Laboratory for Recreational Computing
University of North Texas
Department of Computer Science
PO Box 311366
Denton, TX 76203-1366
Web: http://hercule.csci.unt.edu/larc/info.html

COMPUTER NETWORK SPECIALISTS

SCHOOL SUBJECTS:
COMPUTER SCIENCE, MATHEMATICS

PERSONAL SKILLS:
HELPING/TEACHING
TECHNICAL/SCIENTIFIC

MINIMUM EDUCATION LEVEL:
BACHELOR'S DEGREE

OUTLOOK:
FASTER THAN THE AVERAGE

OTHER ARTICLES TO LOOK AT:

Computer Operators
Computer Programmers
Computer Systems Analysts
Computer Trainers
Database Specialists
Technical Support Specialists

WHAT COMPUTER NETWORK SPECIALISTS DO

A computer network is a system of computer hardware, such as computers, terminals, printers, modems, and other equipment, which is linked together electronically. Networks allow many users to share computer equipment and software at the same time. Networks also allow busy workers to share files, view each other's schedules, and send email.

Computer network specialists make sure computer networks run properly at all times. They install, maintain, update, and repair network equipment and files. They also help train network users on how to use the network. Sometimes, they help their supervisors decide which computer system to buy and help change existing software to better meet the needs of the business. There are many kinds of network specialists, and the responsibilities of a specific position depend on the nature and size of the company.

Computer network administrators manage the network. They work with the files and directories on the network's central computer, called the server. The server holds important files, including software applications, databases, and electronic mail services, all of which must be updated regularly. Some networks have separate servers for specific operations, such as communications or printing or databases.

Network security specialists concentrate most of their efforts on ensuring that the computer system is safe from internal and external tampering. Security is very important because most companies store highly confidential information on their computers. Network security specialists can tell when unauthorized changes are made in the files and who makes them. They report these problems to a supervisor and devise better ways to eliminate such errors in the future. For example, one important school database that must be protected by security specialists involves student grades; only authorized personnel have access to these files.

Data recovery operators are responsible for setting up emergency computer sites in case the main computers experience major problems. Business emergencies can be caused by natural catastrophes, such as power outages, floods, and earthquakes. Data recovery operators choose alternative locations, decide which hardware and software should be stored there, and designate how often files should be backed up.

EDUCATION AND TRAINING

All computer network specialists have bachelor's degrees in computer science or computer engineering. Many also earn official certification from a commercial educational center. The certification process is difficult and proves to employers that the individual has reached a high level of understanding in the field. Most computer professionals have taken a lot of classes in mathematics, science, and computers during high school.

EARNINGS AND OUTLOOK

Computer network specialists start at about $46,000 per year. After some experience and more training, average salaries rise to $58,000 per year. The best-paid network specialists can earn up to $72,000 or more per year. Most employers of network specialists offer full benefits, including health insurance, sick leave, and paid vacation.

Because so many businesses are using computer networks, this field is growing very quickly. Many companies will be looking for well-qualified computer network specialists for a long time to come.

FOR MORE INFORMATION

Contact ACM for information on internships, student membership, and the ACM student magazine, Crossroads. *ACM also offers a student Web site at http://www.acm.org/membership/student/.*

Association for Computing Machinery (ACM)
1515 Broadway
New York, NY 10036-5701
Tel: 212-869-7440
Email: SIGS@acm.org
Web: http://www.acm.org

Computer network administrators must attend training seminars to keep them up to date.

For information on certification and education, contact:

Network Professional Association
710 East Ogden Avenue, Suite 600
Naperville, IL 60563
Tel: 630-579-3282
Email: npa@b-online.com
Web: http://www.npa.org

For information on scholarships, student membership, and the student newsletter, looking.forward, *contact:*

IEEE Computer Society
1730 Massachusetts Avenue, NW
Washington, DC 20036
Tel: 202-371-0101
Web: http://www.computer.org

COMPUTER OPERATORS

SCHOOL SUBJECTS:
BUSINESS, ENGLISH

PERSONAL SKILLS:
TECHNICAL/SCIENTIFIC

MINIMUM EDUCATION LEVEL:
HIGH SCHOOL DIPLOMA

OUTLOOK:
DECLINE

OTHER ARTICLES TO LOOK AT:

Computer Network Specialists
Computer Programmers
Computer Trainers
Instrumentation Technicians
Secretaries
Stenographers

WHAT COMPUTER OPERATORS DO

Computers use various types of information to solve complicated problems. For a computer to operate correctly, it needs to be fed information in a form that it can understand. *Computer operators* prepare this information to be entered (input) into a computer and then load the information into the machine. They read information from checks, bills, and other forms and type it into the computer using a regular keyboard or numbers only keypad. They check the accuracy of their work regularly.

While *computer programmers* develop the operating instructions for a particular computer system, computer operators actually follow through with these instructions. They use keyboards to enter commands into the computer so that the computer can operate correctly. Their tasks may include setting controls on the computer, loading tapes, disks, and paper, and watching the screen for any messages or abnormalities. Some computer operators prepare printouts for all the people in a company who will be using the computer, and they keep a log of all malfunctions in the system.

As computers become more and more sophisticated, computer operators have to keep up with new technologies. Some companies now have computers, for instance, that can perform some of an operator's easier tasks automatically, such as scanning information for direct input, which frees up some operators to take on the more challenging responsibilities. These responsibilities include investigating and reporting complicated mistakes or glitches that occur in the system to appropriate supervisors. Most jobs for computer operators are in companies, industries, or organizations that process a large amount of information. These include banks, insurance companies, government agencies, accounting firms, utilities, and other industries.

EDUCATION AND TRAINING

Most people working as computer operators in large companies are high school graduates. Some have college or technical school education. A large company seeking a computer operator usually looks for applicants who are fast and accurate at typing. They also prefer applicants who are familiar with their machines. So the wider the range of experience an applicant has, the more likely he or she is to find a good job. In smaller companies, requirements for entry-level jobs as computer operators are the same, but might also include typical secretarial skills. Most companies provide on-the-job training courses lasting several days or weeks.

A computer operator at the National Oceanic and Atmospheric Administration enters data into his computer.

EARNINGS AND OUTLOOK

Computer operators earn average salaries of about $22,400 per year. Computer operators working for the federal government start at about $14,000 a year if they have a high school diploma, and $16,000 if they have one year of college. Those with more experience are paid higher starting salaries.

Most computer operators receive medical and dental insurance, paid vacations, sick days, and yearly bonuses.

The use of computers has grown tremendously in the past few years, and this growth should continue. But as the ability to input information automatically grows, the need for computer operators will decrease sharply. Experienced operators will be needed, however, to supervise the running of the system and check for accuracy.

FOR MORE INFORMATION

Taking computer courses in high school is a good way to experience the work of a computer operator while learning skills that are valuable after graduation.

Contact ACM for information on internships, student membership, and the ACM student magazine, Crossroads. *ACM also offers a student Web site at http://www.acm.org/membership/student/.*

Association for Computing Machinery (ACM)
1515 Broadway
New York, NY 10036-5701
Tel: 212-869-7440
Email: SIGS@acm.org
Web: http://www.acm.org

COMPUTER PROGRAMMERS

SCHOOL SUBJECTS:
COMPUTER SCIENCE, MATHEMATICS

PERSONAL SKILLS:
COMMUNICATION/IDEAS
TECHNICAL/SCIENTIFIC

MINIMUM EDUCATION LEVEL:
ASSOCIATE'S DEGREE

OUTLOOK:
FASTER THAN THE AVERAGE

OTHER ARTICLES TO LOOK AT:

Computer and Office Machine Technicians

Computer Operators

Computer Programmers

Computer Systems Analysts

Database Specialists

WHAT COMPUTER PROGRAMMERS DO

Computer programmers write and code the instructions that control the work of a computer. Computers perform work by following these carefully prepared instructions.

Computer programmers work for companies that create and sell computer hardware and software. They also work for all kinds of businesses, from manufacturers of office machines to distributors of machinery and equipment, as well as banks, hospitals, educational systems, and the federal government.

To do their work, programmers have to break down each step of a desired task into a logical series of instructions that the computer can understand. Then programmers translate the instructions into a specific computer language, such as COBOL or FORTRAN. Then they test each part of the program to make sure it works, correcting any errors or debugging the program. Finally, they write the instructions for the operators who will use the program. Some programs can be created in a matter of hours, while others may take more than a year of work. It is not uncommon for programmers to work together on teams for a large project.

There are two basic kinds of computer programmers: *systems programmers* and *applications programmers*. Systems programmers must understand and care for an entire computer system, including its software, its memory, and all of its related equipment, such as terminals, printers, and disk drives. Applications programmers write the actual programs that do particular tasks—word processing, accounting, databases, and games. They tend to specialize in a field such as business, engineering, or science. Systems programmers often will help applications programmers with complicated tasks.

EDUCATION AND TRAINING

Many colleges offer courses and degree programs in computer science, and most employers prefer to hire college graduates. A number of two-year programs in data processing, and junior-level programming are available in junior and community colleges. Employers whose work is highly technical may want their programmers to be trained in their specific area—for example, a computer programmer for an engineering firm might need an engineering degree. Most employers look for candidates who are patient, persistent, very logical in their thinking, and who can work under pressure without making mistakes.

Because programmers work in so many different industries, there is no standard way to begin as a computer programmer. After learning the basics of computer programming, young people should choose a field that interests them and then seek out programming opportunities within that field. It generally takes up to a year to master all aspects of a programming job, and opportunities for advancement are great.

EARNINGS AND OUTLOOK

The average earnings for full-time programmers are about $40,100 a year, some programmers earning more than $65,200. Entry positions pay about $35,000 in private business and $19,500 in government.

Programmers in the West and the North are generally paid more than those in the South. This is because most big computer companies are located in the Silicon Valley in northern California or in the state of Washington, where Microsoft, a major employer of programmers, has its headquarters. Also, some industries, like public utilities and data processing service firms, tend to pay their programmers higher wages than do other types of employers.

As our society continues to rely more and more on computers to store and analyze data, employment opportunities for computer programmers should increase faster than the average through 2006. The best jobs will go to college graduates who know several programming languages and who are trained in a specific field, such as accounting, science, engineering, or management.

FOR MORE INFORMATION

The best way to learn about computers is to use one—either at home surfing the Internet or at school. Join a school computer club and ask a librarian for books on the history, use, and programming of computers.

A software writer checks data from the computer screen against a printout of the same information.

For more information, contact the following organizations:

Association for Computing Machinery
One Astor Plaza
1515 Broadway
New York, NY 10036
Tel: 212-869-7440
Email: ACMHELP@acm.org
Web: http://www.acm.org

Association of Information Technology Professionals
315 South Northwest Highway, Suite 200
Park Ridge, IL 60068-4278
Tel: 800-224-9371
Web: http://www.aitp/org

For information on certification, contact:

Institute for Certification of Computing Professionals
2200 East Devon Avenue, Suite 247
Des Plaines, IL 60018
Tel: 800-843-8422
Web: http://www.iccp.org

COMPUTER SECURITY SPECIALISTS

SCHOOL SUBJECTS:
COMPUTER SCIENCE, ENGLISH, MATHEMATICS

PERSONAL SKILLS:
COMMUNICATION/IDEAS
TECHNICAL/SCIENTIFIC

MINIMUM EDUCATION LEVEL:
HIGH SCHOOL DIPLOMA

OUTLOOK:
MUCH FASTER THAN THE AVERAGE

OTHER ARTICLES TO LOOK AT:

Computer Network Administrators

Computer Programmers

Computer Systems Analysts

Graphics Programmers

Hardware Engineers

WHAT COMPUTER SECURITY SPECIALISTS DO

A *computer security specialist* is responsible for protecting a company's network, which can be accessed through the Internet, from intrusion by outsiders. These intruders are called *hackers* (or *crackers*), and the process of breaking into a system is called *hacking* (or *cracking*). Internet security specialists are sometimes known as *Internet security specialists*, *Internet security administrators*, *Internet security engineers*, *information security technicians*, or *network security consultants*. A computer security specialist may work as a consultant—someone brought in from outside the company to work on a project—or as an in-house employee—someone who works full time for that company.

When a company connects to the Internet, a system known as a firewall is set up to act as a barrier of protection between the outside world of the Internet and the company. The computer security specialist creates the firewall to limit access or permit access to users.

Computer security specialists who work in-house are in charge of watching the flow of information through the firewall. They must be able to write code and configure the software to alert them when certain kinds of activities occur. Logs are kept of all access to the network. Security specialists monitor the logs and watch for anything out of the ordinary. If they see something strange, they must investigate, perhaps even tracking down the user who initiated the unusual action. Sometimes the specialists then create a new program to prevent that action from happening again.

The computer security specialist may also be in charge of virus protection. Viruses are programs written with the express purpose of harming a hard drive and can enter a network through email attachments or infected floppy disks. Another duty of the specialist may be to create the security policies for the company and educate employees on those policies.

Computer security specialists working as consultants are primarily in charge of designing and implementing solutions to a company's security problems. They must be able to understand the needs of the company and meet those needs. They determine if there are insecurities within the company's network and, if there are, find ways to correct them.

EDUCATION AND TRAINING

If you are thinking of becoming a computer security specialist, first you need to get involved with computers. In high school take as many computer science/programming classes as possible. Spend time in the school

A computer security specialist consults with a colleague about a new virus he has detected.

computer lab, learn how computers work, and play with the latest technologies.

Many colleges offer computer science, networking, and programming-related degrees, which are highly recommended. Programming also requires an understanding of mathematics.

EARNINGS AND OUTLOOK

The majority of computer security specialists make between $50,000 and $75,000 a year. If you have a lot of experience and an excellent reputation in the industry, you can earn as much as $120,000 a year.

The outlook for Internet security is much faster than the average. The number of companies on the Internet is growing rapidly. As these companies connect their private networks to the public Internet, they will need to protect their confidential information. Currently, the demand for computer security specialists is greater than the supply, and this trend is expected to continue as the number of businesses connecting to the Internet increases.

FOR MORE INFORMATION

CERT Coordination Center
Software Engineering Institute
Carnegie Mellon University
Pittsburgh, PA 15213-3890
Tel: 412-268-7090

A professional organization for information security professionals, CSI provides education and training for its members.

Computer Security Institute (CSI)
600 Harrison Street
San Francisco, CA 94107
Tel: 415-905-2626
Web: http://www.gocsi.com

COMPUTER SYSTEMS ANALYSTS

SCHOOL SUBJECTS:
COMPUTER SCIENCE, MATHEMATICS

PERSONAL SKILLS:
MECHANICAL/MANIPULATIVE
TECHNICAL/SCIENTIFIC

MINIMUM EDUCATION LEVEL:
BACHELOR'S DEGREE

OUTLOOK:
MUCH FASTER THAN THE AVERAGE

OTHER ARTICLES TO LOOK AT:

Computer Network Specialists
Computer Operators
Computer Programmers
Database Specialists
Software Engineers

WHAT COMPUTER SYSTEMS ANALYSTS DO

Computer systems analysts help banks, government offices, and businesses of all kinds understand their computer systems. As more and more offices change from keeping records by hand to storing data in computers, analysts who can tailor computer systems and programs to the needs of a business, or even to the needs of just one department within a business, have become very important to many organizations.

Computer systems analysts work with both the hardware and software parts of computer systems. The hardware includes the large items such as the computer itself, the monitor, and the keyboard; the software includes the computer programs, which are written and stored on diskettes, and the documentation (the manuals or guidebooks) that goes with the programs. Analysts design the best mix of hardware and software for the needs of the organization that employs them.

A computer systems analyst for the personnel department of a large company, for example, would first talk with the manager about which areas of the business could be aided by computer technology. The manager might be interested in knowing about how a new policy of giving employees longer paid vacations at Christmas has affected company profits for the month of December, for example. The analyst can show the manager what computer program to use, what data to enter, and how to read the charts or graphs that the computer produces. The work of the analyst thus frees the manager to review the raw data—in this case, the numbers that show company profits were the same as in the previous Decembers—and decide how this information should affect company policy.

Once analysts have the computer system set up and operating, they advise on equipment and programming changes. Often, two or more people in a department each have their own computer, but they must be able to connect with and use information from each others' computers. Analysts must then work with all the different computers in a department or an organization so the computers can connect with each other; this system of computers connecting with each other is called networking.

EDUCATION AND TRAINING

Computer systems analysts need to have at least a bachelor's degree in computer science. Analysts in specialized areas (aeronautics, for example) usually have graduate degrees as well. Also, proficiency in mathematics, engineering, accounting, or business will be helpful in some instances.

In addition to a college degree, job expe-

Two computer systems analysts discuss the best method for solving a technical problem.

rience as a computer programmer is very helpful.

The Institute for Certification of Computer Professionals offers voluntary certification to computer systems analysts. Analysts take classes and exams to become a Certified Systems Professional (CSP). Certification is an added credential for job hunters.

EARNINGS AND OUTLOOK

Starting salaries for computer systems analysts average about $46,300. With several years of experience analysts can earn as much as $59,000. Computer systems analysts with many years of experience and a master's degree can earn salaries of $63,000 per year and higher.

This field is one of the three fastest growing careers, and companies are always looking for qualified analysts, especially those with graduate degrees in computer science. As more businesses automate, more analysts will be needed to make the right decisions concerning new software and other technology and to keep current systems running smoothly.

FOR MORE INFORMATION

For more information about the career of computer systems analyst, contact:

Association for Systems Management
1433 West Bagley Road
PO Box 38370
Cleveland, OH 44138
Tel: 216-234-2930

Institute for Certification of Computing Professionals
2200 East Devon Avenue, Suite 246
Des Plaines, IL 60018
Tel: 800-843-8422
Web: http://www.iccp.org

COMPUTER TRAINERS

SCHOOL SUBJECTS:
COMPUTER SCIENCE, SPEECH

PERSONAL SKILLS:
HELPING/TEACHING
TECHNICAL/SCIENTIFIC

MINIMUM EDUCATION LEVEL:
BACHELOR'S DEGREE

OUTLOOK:
MUCH FASTER THAN THE AVERAGE

OTHER ARTICLES TO LOOK AT:

Adult and Vocational Education Teachers
Computer Network Specialists
Computer Operators
Computer Programmers
Technical Support Specialists

WHAT COMPUTER TRAINERS DO

Today's employees and students need to know how to send email, how to use the Internet, and how to use word processing programs. However, many people become frustrated when faced with a blank computer screen and a thick instruction manual. Sometimes, too, the computers and programs are too complex to be explained fully and clearly by a manual. *Computer trainers* teach people how to use computers, software, and other new technology. When a business installs new hardware and software, computer trainers work one-on-one with the employees, or they lead seminars. They may also offer instruction over the Internet. With technology changing every day, computer trainers are called upon often for support and instruction.

Computer trainers teach people how to use computer programs. For example a company's accounting department may need a computer trainer to teach its accounting clerks how to use a spreadsheet program, which is used to make graphs and charts, and to calculate sums. Other common business programs include database programs, which keep track of such things as customer names, addresses, and phone numbers, and word processing programs, which are used to create documents, letters, and reports. Some computer trainers may also teach computer programming languages such as C or Visual Basic.

Many magazines, corporations, advertisers, and individuals have set up home pages on the Internet. A computer trainer can help them use the language needed to design a page, and teach them how to update the page. Desktop publishing programs and laser printers allow individuals and businesses to create interesting graphics and full-color pages for brochures and newsletters. Computer trainers can help users get started in these programs. Some computer trainers may also help offices set up their own office network. With a network, all the computers in an office can be linked. Employees then share programs and files, conference with other employees, and send electronic mail.

Computer trainers may be self-employed and work on a freelance basis, or they may work for a computer training school or computer service company.

EDUCATION AND TRAINING

Most community colleges, universities, and vocational schools offer computer courses. Computer service companies and training schools also offer courses in specific software programs. Though college courses and training will make you an attractive candidate for a job with a computer service company, the most important quality is excellent computer knowledge. Some people gain this knowledge simply by working with computers on a regular basis, either at home, or in the work place. Computer experience can come from working in the sales department of a computer store or software company. Teaching experience can be gained by leading courses within the community or in a computer store. Education requirements vary at computer training schools and computer services companies, but to work as a teacher in the computer department of a community college, a bachelor's degree is the minimum requirement.

EARNINGS AND OUTLOOK

The average training specialist earned $40,300 in 1996. Senior training specialists averaged $47,400 per year, and training managers earned $57,000. In general, salaries in the area of computer trainers increased with the level of education. The average salary for managers with postgraduate degrees was significantly larger than average, totaling $52,111.

Most computer trainers who are employed by corporations receive medical and dental insurance, paid vacations, sick days, and yearly bonuses. Bonuses for training specialists averaged $1,600. Senior training specialists received $2,500, and training managers were awarded $5,200 on average in 1996.

The outlook for computer trainers is excellent through 2006 because more people are using computers than ever before. Most people do not have the time to teach themselves through trial and error and thick computer books, so they need an experienced computer trainer to teach them quickly.

Computer trainers must know their subject backwards and forwards in anticipation of questions from students at both beginning and advanced levels.

FOR MORE INFORMATION

There are a number of computer magazines available at your local newsstand or library. Some of these magazines publish articles written specifically for people unfamiliar with computers. The Internet is also a great resource for information on the latest software and technology. You can even download some software from the Internet for free. Also, people on the Internet usually are eager to answer your questions about computers and software; literally thousands of sites are devoted to computers and computer training.

For more information on a career as a computer trainer, contact the following organizations:

The American Society for Training and Development
1640 King Street, Box 1443
Alexandria, VA 22313-2043
Web: http://www.astd.org

International Association of Information Technology Trainers
9810 Patuxent Woods Drive
Columbia, MD 21046-1561
Web: http://www.itrain.org

CONGRESSIONAL AIDES

SCHOOL SUBJECTS:
GOVERNMENT, HISTORY

PERSONAL SKILLS:
LEADERSHIP/MANAGEMENT

MINIMUM EDUCATION LEVEL:
BACHELOR'S DEGREE

OUTLOOK:
LITTLE CHANGE OR MORE SLOWLY THAN THE AVERAGE

OTHER ARTICLES TO LOOK AT:

Ambassadors
City Managers
Foreign Service Officers
Lobbyists
Political Scientists
Press Secretaries

WHAT CONGRESSIONAL AIDES DO

Congressional aides are the men and women behind the scenes whose work makes it possible for senators and representatives to do their jobs. Congress consists of two branches, the Senate and the House of Representatives. Senators and representatives appoint aides to serve on their staffs. These staffs usually include an administrative assistant, a press secretary, an office manager, a legislative correspondent, and a state, or district director. As a congressional aide, you can play an important role in helping senators and representatives get elected and reelected. You'll organize fund-raising campaigns and stuff envelopes with information about the Congress member's qualifications and opinions. Since the main responsibility of Congress is to make federal laws, members of Congress spend six months of each year in Washington, DC, where they meet from January until the end of July. This means that they have two offices: one in the nation's capital and the other in their home state. Their aides help business run smoothly in both offices.

Aides work on either a personal or committee staff. The committee staff focuses primarily on the construction and passage of legislation, while the personal staff deals with matters concerning the home district or state. Aides assist the Congress members in a variety of ways: they sort mail, keep files in order, type letters, answer the telephone, maintain a computer base of constituents (voters from the home state), conduct opinion polls, do research about pending bills, and receive drop-in visitors. They often serve as a sounding board for their Congress member's ideas. Some even write speeches and position papers that describe how a senator or representative feels about a certain issue.

EDUCATION AND TRAINING

A college degree is required of a personal congressional aide, while most committee aides have an advanced degree in law or journalism. They attend committees with the Congress member and meet with lobbyists and special interest groups. Many aides are appointed through personal friendship or by contacts made when serving as a volunteer in an election campaign, for instance.

You should have good communications skills—both written and spoken—to work as an aide. You must be courteous and efficient. You need to be able to analyze information and do research. You must also be able to organize the enormous amount of paperwork and information that comes into a Congress member's office. In school, you should learn secretarial skills and take classes in public

Good communication skills are vital to congressional aides, who must listen carefully to their employers and articulate their own ideas as well.

speaking, math, English, bookkeeping, history, economics, and political science. Volunteer to help a candidate in an election campaign and learn the ins and outs of fund-raising.

EARNINGS AND OUTLOOK

Wages for most positions are higher in the Senate than they are in the House. Average salaries for the various positions range from $23,000 for those performing clerical duties, to $47,000 for those working as personal secretaries, to $110,000 for the chiefs of staff.

The number of congressional staff members working on Capitol Hill grew throughout the 20th century, but leveled off in the mid-1980s. Some members of Congress became concerned that too many aides kept a Congress member distanced from the voters and the work at hand. This concern, along with budget cuts, will effect the future hiring practices of Congress members.

FOR MORE INFORMATION

Visit the Senate and House Web pages for extensive information about Congress. You can also contact your state's Congress members by writing to them.

United States Senate
Washington, DC 20510
Tel: 202-224-3121
Web: http://www.senate.gov

House of Representatives
Washington, DC 20515
Tel: 202-224-3121
Web: http://www.house.gov

For information about ordering books about congressional aides and internships, contact:

The Congressional Management Foundation
513 Capitol Court, NE, Suite 300
Washington, DC 20002
Web: http://www.cmfweb.org

CONSERVATORS AND CONSERVATION TECHNICIANS

SCHOOL SUBJECTS:
ART, CHEMISTRY

PERSONAL SKILLS:
MECHANICAL/MANIPULATIVE
TECHNICAL/SCIENTIFIC

MINIMUM EDUCATION LEVEL:
SOME POSTSECONDARY TRAINING

OUTLOOK:
ABOUT AS FAST AS THE AVERAGE

OTHER ARTICLES TO LOOK AT:

Anthropologists
Archaeologists
Archivists
Artists
Assessors and Appraisers
Museum Curators

WHAT CONSERVATORS AND CONSERVATION TECHNICIANS DO

Conservators and conservation technicians are specially trained professionals who analyze and assess the condition of artifacts and art objects. These objects may include natural objects, such as bones and fossils, or man-made objects such as paintings, sculpture, metal, and paper. Conservation workers need a working knowledge of chemistry and scientific technique in order to plan and carry out conservation treatment and projects. They may work in private practice or in museums, historical societies, or state institutions.

Conservation workers usually specialize in a particular area of work, such as the preservation of books and paper, photographs, paintings, textiles, or wooden objects. Other conservators specialize in archaeological or ethnographical (human culture) materials. The main job of conservators is to conserve or preserve items so that they can be enjoyed and further studied in the future. They may study an object, such as a Native American ceremonial headdress, to determine its condition and stabilize its structure. They attempt to establish the best environment where the artifact can be preserved. Areas that are too hot or too cold, or that are high in humidity can cause the item to become damaged or to further deteriorate. Conservators' responsibilities may also include documenting the condition of the structure using written and visual recording. They design programs for preventive care and oversee conservation treatments. A conservator's tools can include microscopes and cameras, including equipment for specialized processes such as infra-red and ultra-violet photography, and X-ray processes.

Conservation technicians help conservators preserve and restore artifacts and art objects. To do this, they study descriptions and other information about the object. They may perform physical and chemical tests. If an object is metal, a technician may be instructed to clean it by gently rubbing it with a cloth or by applying chemical solvents. Statues can sometimes be washed with soap solutions, while silver and some types of furniture can be polished. If an object is damaged, conservation technicians may reassemble the broken pieces using solder or glue. They may repaint an object if the original paint is missing or faded, using paint of the same color and chemical make-up as the original. Technicians also build and repair picture frames and remount paintings in frames.

EDUCATION AND TRAINING

In the past, most conservation workers learned their craft through an apprenticeship with an established conservator. Nowadays, graduate training is the most recognized route into the conservation field. Graduate schools are highly selective, so it is important to carefully plan your academic path. Undergraduate course work should include classes in science, including inorganic and organic chemistry, the humanities (art, history, archaeology, and anthropology), and studio art. Some graduate schools consider work experience and internships as comparable to course work. Conservation technicians will need at least some education beyond high school to get a job in this field. High school students should study art, science, and social sciences, such as history and geography.

EARNINGS AND OUTLOOK

Salaries for conservation staff vary greatly by experience, specialty, region, job description, and employer. The average salary for a chief art museum conservator is $58,000. Senior conservators earn $40,000 to $61,000 a year. Associate conservators average $42,000 annually. These positions and their salaries are comparable to other university, museum, and library positions. Conservation technicians may earn starting salaries of $18,000 to $25,000 per year.

Increasing interest in cultural material of all forms has created a greater need for qualified conservation workers. This interest is offset by recent decreases in government funding of educational and arts programs. Museums may be forced to limit their conservation staffs, and instead rely on small staffs assisted by private conservation companies. As a result, private industry and for-profit companies will grow, while museum staffs and nonprofit organizations may experience reductions in employment.

The work of the conservator is painstakingly slow because the objects on which they work are usually priceless and irreplaceable.

FOR MORE INFORMATION

For information on conservation training, contact the following organizations:

The American Institute for Conservation of Historic and Artistic Works
1717 K Street, NW, Suite 301
Washington, DC 20006
Tel: 202-452-9545
Email: infoaic@aol.com
Web: http://aic.stanford.edu/

The International Institute for Conservation of Historic and Artistic Works
6 Buckingham Street
London WC2N 6BA UK
Tel: 01-44171-839-5975

Arizona Studio of Art Conservation
1640 East Lind Road
Tucson, AZ 85719
Tel: 520-323-6306

CONSTRUCTION INSPECTORS

SCHOOL SUBJECTS:
MATHEMATICS, TECHNICAL/SHOP

PERSONAL SKILLS:
MECHANICAL/MANIPULATIVE
TECHNICAL/SCIENTIFIC

MINIMUM EDUCATION LEVEL:
HIGH SCHOOL DIPLOMA

OUTLOOK:
FASTER THAN THE AVERAGE

OTHER ARTICLES TO LOOK AT:

Carpenters
Civil Engineers
Construction Laborers
Electricians
Mechanical Engineers
Plumbers

WHAT CONSTRUCTION INSPECTORS DO

Construction inspectors make sure that all new structures of any kind—hospitals, schools, housing projects, administrative buildings, bridges, highways, dams, sewer and water systems, military installations, and so on—are built legally, properly, safely, and at a reasonable cost. Construction inspectors work for local, federal, and state governments as well as for private industries, such as engineering and architectural firms. They are hired to visit construction sites, test for defects, and take photographs. They use tape measures, survey instruments, metering devices and equipment that measures the strength of concrete. They keep logs of their work and write reports that tell whether or not the structures are built soundly and meet all the necessary codes and contract specifications. Where special natural hazards exist, such as the danger of hurricanes or earthquakes, inspectors have to check to make sure extra regulations are followed.

The seven categories of construction inspectors are: building, electrical, elevator, home, mechanical, plumbing, and public works.

Building inspectors check for structural quality. They look at plans, visit the work site, and make a final inspection when the building is completed.

Electrical inspectors check out all the components of a structure's electrical system, including wiring, lighting, sound and security systems, and generators.

Elevator inspectors examine not only elevators, but escalators, moving sidewalks in airports, amusement park rides, and ski lifts.

Home inspectors work for people interested in buying a home; they look at the roof, the pipes, the electrical system, and the plumbing.

Mechanical inspectors inspect the mechanical parts of gas pipes, gas tanks, and big kitchen appliances.

Plumbing inspectors check plumbing systems, including how water is supplied to a structure and how waste is removed from it.

Public works inspectors check all government-built facilities, including water and sewer systems, highways, bridges, dams, and streets to make sure they will function safely.

EDUCATION AND TRAINING

Government construction inspectors must be high school graduates with a working knowledge of the materials used in construction. Those who have studied engineering or architecture for at least two years in college or those who have attended a community or junior college with courses in construction technology and building inspection will have a distinct advantage in obtaining jobs.

Construction inspectors receive most of

An architect talks on a mobile phone at a construction site.

their training on the job and most have proven themselves with several years' experience in private industry, either as a construction contractor or as a trade worker such as carpenter, electrician, plumber, or pipefitter.

EARNINGS AND OUTLOOK

Most inspectors earn between $26,500 and $46,000 a year, with building inspectors making the most. The average salary for inspectors working for the federal government is about $27,000 a year, a little higher than the average for all other inspectors.

As the concern for public safety continues to rise, the demand for inspectors should grow about as fast as average even if construction activity does not increase. Applicants who have some college education, are already certified inspectors, or who have experience as carpenters, electricians, or plumbers will have the best opportunities.

FOR MORE INFORMATION

For more information, contact:

Building Officials and Code Administrators International
4051 West Flossmoor Road
Country Club Hills, IL 60477
Tel: 708-799-2300

Southern Building Code Congress International
900 Montclair Road
Birmingham, AL 35213
Tel: 205-591-1853

Association of Construction Inspectors
8383 East Evans Road
Scottsdale, AZ 85260
Web: http://www.jami.org/aci.iam

American Construction Inspectors Association
12995 6th Street, Suite 69
Yucaipa, CA 92399-2549
Tel: 909-795-3039

CONSTRUCTION LABORERS

SCHOOL SUBJECTS:
MATHEMATICS, TECHNICAL/SHOP

PERSONAL SKILLS:
FOLLOWING INSTRUCTIONS
MECHANICAL/MANIPULATIVE

MINIMUM EDUCATION LEVEL:
HIGH SCHOOL DIPLOMA

OUTLOOK:
FASTER THAN THE AVERAGE

OTHER ARTICLES TO LOOK AT:

Bricklayers and Stonemasons
Carpenters
Plasterers
Plumbers
Roofers
Roustabouts

WHAT CONSTRUCTION LABORERS DO

Construction laborers are part of the team that builds homes, offices, highways, bridges, apartment buildings, and other structures. They load and unload bricks and other materials, clean up rubble, and pour and spread concrete. They bring tools, materials, and equipment to other workers at a construction site. They may set up scaffolding, dig trenches, and build braces to support the sides of excavations. They work alongside carpenters, electricians, plumbers, and bricklayers and stonemasons, carrying their equipment and assisting in other ways, helping out wherever they are needed. They may hold a ladder so a carpenter can work on a ceiling, or they may stack bricks in a corner for later use. They may sweep up loose stones or help connect plumbing pipes. But they also operate heavy machinery, such as jackhammers, cement mixers, front-end loaders, hoists, and laser beam equipment used to align and grade ditches and tunnels.

The tasks facing construction laborers are physically demanding and repetitive. Not only do they have to lift and carry heavy objects, they also have to kneel, crouch, crawl, and squeeze into awkward positions. Sometimes they have to work high up off the ground, and, because they most often work outdoors, they must be prepared to work in all kinds of weather conditions.

Laborers are trained in the methods, materials, and operations used in all kinds of construction work. They must be aware of safety considerations at all times and in all situations. They sometimes are exposed to harmful chemicals, fumes, and odors, or to dangerous machinery, and they must wear special safety clothing and helmets. This is especially true of those whose work involves potentially very hazardous assignments, such as those who work with the explosives used to blast rocks away before construction can begin. They must be aware of the effects of different explosives under varying rock conditions.

Construction work can involve travel to remote or isolated areas to build pipelines or shipping terminals, for instance, although the contractors who hire laborers often employ local workers.

EDUCATION AND TRAINING

The best way to become a construction laborer is to apply directly to local contractors who undertake all types of construction work. Contractors normally hire people who are at least 18 years old, in good physical condition, and show a willingness and ability to learn. Laborers then are given on-the-job training.

Apprenticeships give you the opportunity to acquire specialized skills. Apprenticeships usually last two to three years and are sponsored by local unions and contractors.

Although no formal education is needed to become a laborer, only those with at least a high school education are likely to have a chance to become supervisors or advanced workers (such as carpenters, bricklayers, and stonemasons).

Construction laborers clean up a work site.

EARNINGS AND OUTLOOK

Construction laborers ordinarily earn between $9 and $13 per hour, but because they don't work every day, yearly earnings are hard to estimate. Overall in 1997, the most recent period for which data is available, the federal Bureau of Labor Statistics estimates full-time laborers earned between $16,000 and $33,000.

In addition, laborers receive benefits like paid vacations and health insurance. In general, laborers who belong to the Laborers' International Union of North America tend to receive better benefits than non-union workers.

This is a large field, and turnover is high among laborers. For these reasons, every year there will be jobs available, mainly in connection with large projects, because employers need to replace those workers who have changed jobs or left the labor force. In addition, the level of construction activity always is affected by local economic conditions. Regions that are prosperous will offer better job possibilities for construction laborers than areas where the economy is not expanding.

Nationwide, the construction industry currently is experiencing a severe labor shortage expected to last several years. Job opportunities are plentiful. Jobs for laborers may not rise quite as fast as for other construction-related occupations, since technological developments, like more efficient grading machinery and mechanical lifting devices, may affect the need for these workers somewhat. In general, however, the outlook is very good, and faster than the average.

FOR MORE INFORMATION

The Associated General Contractors of America is a trade association which can give you more information about the building industry and life at a construction site.

Associated General Contractors of America
1957 E Street, NW
Washington, DC 20006
Tel: 202-393-2040
Web: http://www.agc.org

The Laborers' International Union can provide you with materials describing union benefits.

Laborers' International Union of North America
905 16th Street, NW
Washington, DC 20006
Tel: 202-737-8320
Web: http://www.liuna.org

COOKS, CHEFS, AND BAKERS

SCHOOL SUBJECTS:
FAMILY AND CONSUMER SCIENCE, MATHEMATICS

PERSONAL SKILLS:
ARTISTIC

MINIMUM EDUCATION LEVEL:
HIGH SCHOOL DIPLOMA

OUTLOOK:
FASTER THAN THE AVERAGE

OTHER ARTICLES TO LOOK AT:

Caterers
Dietitians
Food Service Workers
Nutritionists
Restaurant Managers
Waiters

WHAT COOKS, CHEFS, AND BAKERS DO

Cooks, *chefs*, and *bakers* prepare and cook food in restaurants, hotels, cafeterias, and other eating places. They plan menus, order food, measure and mix ingredients, cook and test the food, and arrange it on plates. Some specialize in a certain area, such as cutting meat, boning fish, fixing sauces, or making salads, soups, or desserts. Chefs may do many of these things, but their major job is to oversee all the activities in the kitchen. They also create recipes, train cooks, and keep track of work schedules. Some chefs specialize in a particular cooking style, such as French or Italian.

Bakers prepare cakes, pastries, cookies, rolls, muffins, biscuits, and breads for bakeries, hotels, restaurants, cafeterias, and large food-chain stores. Alhough cooks and chefs sometimes also bake, bakers specialize in preparing only baked goods. A baker's responsibilities include coordinating the baked goods that are to appear on restaurant menus, ordering supplies, creating recipes, measuring and mixing ingredients, and testing the results. Some bakers specialize in one particular kind of baked good, such as cakes or cookies.

Cooks and chefs may work a long week of 48 hours or more. This usually includes evening and weekend work because that is when many people eat in restaurants. Bakers who own their own businesses can determine their own hours, but bakers often start work very early in the morning to have freshly baked goods ready for breakfast time.

EDUCATION AND TRAINING

Many cooks, chefs, and bakers enter the profession through on-the-job training in restaurants or hotels. Although a high school education is not always required, it is vital for those who wish to move up to better jobs. The best job opportunities are available to those who graduate from a special cooking school or culinary institute. These schools have classes in menu planning, food costs, purchasing, food storage, sanitation, health standards, and cooking and baking techniques. Graduates may have to serve as an apprentice or work in a supporting role before being hired as a head chef or baker in a top restaurant or hotel.

In high school, students can prepare for a career as a cook, chef, or baker by taking classes in family and consumer science. Since many cooking terms are derived from the French language, foreign languages courses should also be helpful.

EARNINGS AND OUTLOOK

Cooks' and chefs' salaries depend on skill level, what type of food they prepare, and where they work. Salaries usually are higher in restaurants that serve higher-priced meals. Cooks and chefs in famous restaurants and hotels earn the highest salaries, generally between $40,000 and $80,000. A few famous chefs can earn much more. The average hourly wage of a chef is $9.80 per hour (about $20,380 per year). Most cooks earn between $6 and $10 an hour, and most chefs earn between $18,000 and $40,000 per year. A baker's salary depends on his or her specialty, experience, skill, and reputation, as well as the establishment in which he or she works. Bakers earn anywhere from $10,000 to $50,000 a year or more.

Job opportunities for cooks, chefs, and bakers should be quite good through 2006, as people with high- and medium-range incomes will continue to dine at restaurants.

This baker must be especially skilled in breadmaking techniques in order to prepare so many loaves at once.

FOR MORE INFORMATION

For information on careers in baking and cooking, contact these organizations:

American Culinary Federation, Inc.
10 San Bartola Drive
St. Augustine, FL 32086
Tel: 904-824-4468
Email: acf@aug.com
Web: http://www.acfchefs.org

American Institute of Baking
PO Box 3999
Manhattan, KS 66502-3999
Tel: 785-537-4758
Email: information@aibonline.org
Web: http://www.aibonline.org

Culinary Institute of America
433 Albany Post Road
Hyde Park, NY 12538-1499
Tel: 800-285-4627 (CULINARY), or 914-452-9600
Web: http://www.ciachef.edu

National Restaurant Association Educational Foundation
250 South Wacker Drive, Suite 1400
Chicago, IL 60606
Tel: 312-715-1010
Web: http://www.edfound.org

Educational Institute of the American Hotel & Motel Association
800 North Magnolia Avenue, Suite 1800
Orlando, FL 32803
Tel: 407-999-8100
Email: info@ei-ahma.org
Web: http://www.ei-ahma.org

COREMAKERS

SCHOOL SUBJECTS:
MATHEMATICS, TECHNICAL/SHOP

PERSONAL SKILLS:
MECHANICAL/MANIPULATIVE
TECHNICAL/SCIENTIFIC

MINIMUM EDUCATION LEVEL:
APPRENTICESHIP

OUTLOOK:
DECLINE

OTHER ARTICLES TO LOOK AT:

Forge Shop Workers
Iron and Steel Industry Workers
Machinists
Molders
Precision Machinists
Precision Metalworkers

WHAT COREMAKERS DO

In the foundry industry, *coremakers* prepare cores used in making metal castings with hollow centers, such as pipes and tubes. In the casting process, molten metal is poured around the core, where it solidifies. When the core is removed, the desired cavity or shape remains in the metal. Cores are made in different sizes and shapes depending upon the size and shape of the metal object to be cast.

Coremakers begin their work by cleaning the core box, which is a block of wood or metal hollowed out to the shape of the desired core. The box is then partially filled with sand, and the sand is compacted in the box by hand, mallet, or other tool. The core box is then put on a machine that packs the sand into the box even more tightly. When the sand has been compacted as much as possible, it is taken out of the box and baked until it is solid. It is then ready to be used in a metal mold.

There are several specialized jobs that coremakers may have. A machine coremaker, for example, makes cores with machines rather than by hand. They generally set up, adjust, and operate machines that make sand cores by forcing sand into specially shaped hollow forms. They are usually employed in large factories where a large number of identical parts must be made.

A core-blower operator runs machines that blow sand into a core box to make a core. A core checker uses various tools to make sure that the cores that have been produced are the correct size and shape. A core-oven tender puts cores into the oven and raises the heat to the proper temperature to harden and strengthen the cores. Coreroom foundry workers assist coremakers in various ways, such as hauling sand, fastening sections of cores together, and transporting cores to and from the ovens.

Coremakers sometimes face potentially dangerous conditions on the job. Older foundries may be noisy, hot, or smoky. Many foundry operations produce irritating fumes, but newer plants have improved working conditions.

Coremakers must have mathematical aptitude and be able to visualize three-dimensional objects by reading blueprints and drawings. They must be good with details and meeting deadlines. Because the work can be strenuous, coremakers should be in good physical health.

EDUCATION AND TRAINING

High school classes in mathematics, computer science, drafting, and machine shop will provide a good background to coremaking. Learning to read blueprints and how to use tools, in particular, would be helpful.

Most employers today prefer to hire entry-level workers with high school diplomas. New workers usually learn the basics of coremaking by working closely with a skilled coremaker in a planned program that teaches them all phases of coremaking.

In some cases, coremakers enter an apprenticeship program. These programs last four years and combine on-the-job training with classroom instruction. Opportunities for apprenticeship programs, however, can be very difficult to find.

EARNINGS AND OUTLOOK

On average, coremakers earn about $25,000 a year, according the U.S. Bureau of Labor Statistics. Apprentices generally start at a lower pay rate than a skilled coremaker, with incremental raises as they become proficient in different skills. Most coremakers belong to unions, so their work hours, overtime pay, and fringe benefits are established by contract between the unions and employers.

During recent years, more of the work involved in coremaking is being done by machines. As production in foundries has become increasingly automated, the demand for coremakers has decreased. In addition, production of some kinds of metal castings has decreased. For example, plastic is being used in place of metal for some car parts, thus reducing the overall need for coremakers and related workers.

FOR MORE INFORMATION

A young person interested in coremaking may be able to arrange a visit to a foundry through a teacher or school counselor. Additionally, jewelry-making is a hobby that gives good experience in casting and shaping metals.

This coremaker is busy assembling small, intricate cores that will be used in casting for aerospace equipment.

For more information about the metal fabricating industry, contact:

American Foundrymen's Society
505 State Street
Des Plaines, IL 60016-8399
Web: http://www.afsinc.org

For information about apprentice programs, contact:

Glass, Molders, Pottery, Plastics and Allied Workers International Union
608 East Baltimore Pike
Media, PA 19063-0607
Web: http://www.GMPIU.org

CORRECTIONS OFFICERS

SCHOOL SUBJECTS:
GOVERNMENT, PSYCHOLOGY

PERSONAL SKILLS:
COMMUNICATION/IDEAS
HELPING/TEACHING

MINIMUM EDUCATION LEVEL:
HIGH SCHOOL DIPLOMA

OUTLOOK:
MUCH FASTER THAN THE AVERAGE

OTHER ARTICLES TO LOOK AT:

FBI Agents
Parole Officers
Police Officers
Polygraph Examiners
Private Investigators
Security Guards

WHAT CORRECTIONS OFFICERS DO

Corrections officers guard persons who have been arrested and are awaiting trial. They also guard those who have been tried, found guilty, and sentenced to serve time in prison. They search prisoners and their cells for weapons and drugs and check locks, bars on windows and doors, and gates for signs of tampering. Prisoners must be under guard at all times—while eating, sleeping, exercising, and working. Corrections officers count prisoners from time to time to make sure they are all present. Some officers are stationed at gates and on towers to prevent escapes. Corrections officers carefully observe the attitude and behavior of prison inmates and remain alert for potential conflicts. Often, the officers attempt to settle disputes before they erupt into violence. When a disturbance or crime occurs at the prison, officers are responsible for stopping it and helping to investigate the cause.

Corrections officers are also responsible for giving work assignments to prisoners and supervising them as they carry out their tasks. Officers check prisoners' cells for unclean conditions and fire hazards. Sometimes they may check prisoners' mail for forbidden items. If a prisoner is injured, they give first aid. When visitors come to the prison, officers check their identification before taking them to the visiting area.

These workers may give help and advice to prisoners and help them adjust to prison life. They may also suggest where to look for a job after release from prison. Sometimes officers help prisoners contact their families. They may try to help prisoners with their personal problems.

Corrections officers usually keep a daily record of their activities. They make regular reports to their supervisors, the *head corrections officers*.

In small towns, corrections officers sometimes are called *jailers*. These officers may act as deputy sheriffs or police officers when they are not performing guard duties.

Many corrections officers work at prisons, prison camps, and reform schools run by state governments. Others work at city and county jails. Still others work at prisons run by the federal government. Many correctional facilities are run by private companies that employ corrections officers.

EDUCATION AND TRAINING

Corrections officers generally must be at least 18 to 21 years old and have completed high school, although many positions require some postsecondary education or related work experience. Most states and some local governments train corrections officers on the job.

These workers spend two to six months under the supervision of experienced officers. The federal government and some states have special schools for training corrections officers in programs that last from four to eight weeks.

In many states, applicants have to pass physical fitness, eyesight, and hearing tests. Some states require one or two years of experience in corrections or related police work.

EARNINGS AND OUTLOOK

The average salary for beginning corrections officers is $20,200, although salaries vary widely from state to state and at the different levels of government. Starting salaries for federal corrections officers range from $21,000 to $28,000 per year, depending on location. The average salary for all experienced officers is $33,540 per year, with some officers earning as much as $50,000 per year and more.

Benefits may include health, disability, and life insurance; uniforms or a cash allowance to buy their own uniforms; and sometimes meals and housing.

The employment outlook for corrections officers is good. Crowded prisons have created a need for more officers. New prisons are being built and others are being enlarged.

Most jobs will be found in relatively large institutions located near metropolitan areas, although opportunities for corrections officers exist in jails and other smaller facilities throughout the country. The increasing use of private companies and privately run prisons may limit somewhat the growth of jobs in this field as these companies are more likely to keep a close eye on the bottom line. Use of new technologies, such as surveillance equipment, automatic gates, and other devices, may also allow institutions to employ fewer officers.

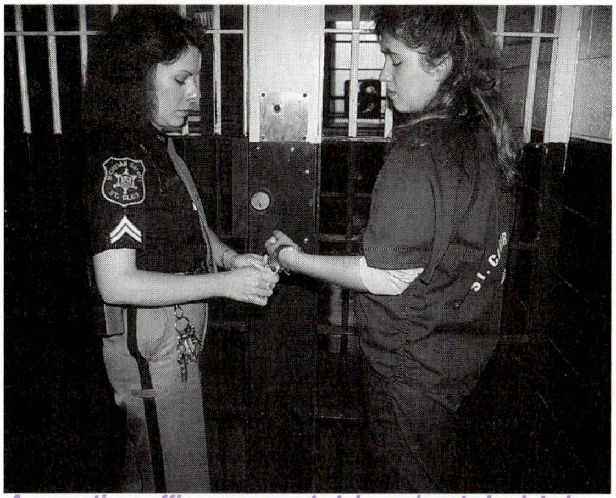

A corrections officer prepares to take an inmate back to her cell.

FOR MORE INFORMATION

Contact the FBP for information on entrance requirements, training, and career opportunities for corrections officers at the federal level.

Federal Bureau of Prisons (FBP)
National Recruitment Office
320 First Street, NW, Room 460
Washington, DC 20534
Email: cmahan@bop.gov
Web: http://www.bop.gov

For more information, contact:

American Correctional Association
4380 Forbes Boulevard
Lanham, MD 20706
Tel: 800-222-5646
Web: http://www.corrections.com/aca

American Probation and Parole Association
c/o Council of State Governments
PO Box 11910
Lexington, KY 40578-1910
Tel: 606-244-8203
Web: http://www.appa-net.org

COSMETOLOGISTS

SCHOOL SUBJECTS:
ART, BUSINESS, HEALTH

PERSONAL SKILLS:
ARTISTIC, HELPING/TEACHING

MINIMUM EDUCATION LEVEL:
SOME POSTSECONDARY TRAINING

OUTLOOK:
ABOUT AS FAST AS THE AVERAGE

OTHER ARTICLES TO LOOK AT:

Barbers
Electrologists
Makeup Artists
Nail Technicians
Pet Groomers

WHAT COSMETOLOGISTS DO

Cosmetologists perform hair-care skills (including washing, cutting, coloring, and perming), esthetics (skin care treatments), and manicures and pedicures. Their services were once considered luxuries and a mark of status, but now a wide variety of people patronize salons on a regular basis. Cosmetology services were also once primarily the domain of women, but today men represent a significant and increasing segment of the market.

Some cosmetologists are experts in makeup and give facials, do makeup analysis, and advise customers on what products to use. Others, called nail technicians, specialize in manicures and pedicures Hairstylists specialize in hair care, and some are even further specialized, such as colorists.

Most cosmetologists work 40 hours a week, although some work more, and their working hours often include Saturdays and evenings, when it is most convenient for customers to come in. With the exception of nail technicians, cosmetologists spend much of their day standing. They are also constantly in the company of others, so it is important that they are friendly, professional, and easily able to carry on light conversation. Since satisfying their clients is paramount to their success, cosmetologists must also be good listeners.

EDUCATION AND TRAINING

Students interested in the cosmetology field should take classes in art, science (especially chemistry), health, business, and communications. Psychology and speech may also be helpful.

Requirements for becoming a licensed cosmetologist vary from state to state. A student must have completed a certain number of classroom credit hours (anywhere from 1,050 to 2,200 hours) at an accredited cosmetology school. This usually takes from 10 to 14 months. To earn a license, the applicant must pass a state-administered examination consisting of a written test and sometimes an oral or practical test as well. Training courses at these schools include classes on hygiene, anatomy, skin and scalp disease, and sanitation. Students often begin practical work on mannequins and on each other. As they become more experienced, they begin styling customers who come into the school shop because of its lower prices.

EARNINGS AND OUTLOOK

You can make an excellent living in the beauty/hair-care industry, but like most careers, it isn't that way when you first start out. While average annual earnings are higher than the national average (approximately $33,000 versus $30,000), you will not begin at that level. Though your raise in salary may start slowly, the curve quickly escalates. Entry-level salaries usually begin around $18,000. On the extreme upward end, some fashion stylists in New York or Hollywood charge $300 per haircut. Their annual salary can go into six figures. Salaries in larger cities are greater than those in smaller towns; but then the cost of living is higher in the big cities, too.

Most shops and salons give a new employee a guaranteed income instead of commission. If you go over the guaranteed amount, then you earn a commission. Usually, this guarantee will extend for the first three months of employment, so that you can focus on building up business before you go on straight commission.

The future looks very good for cosmetology. The demand far exceeds the supply. It has been estimated by a major publisher in the field that each year 29 percent of the jobs available in cosmetology go unfilled. There is an especially high demand for stylists. There is a 2 percent growth in the number of salons each year. The number of salons is increasing each year, and the demand for hair stylists in particular is and will remain high.

FOR MORE INFORMATION

For more information about a career as a cosmetologist, contact the following organizations:

Beauty and Barber Supply Institute/International Salon Association/International Chain Salon Association
11811 North Tatum Boulevard, Suite 1085
Phoenix, AZ 85028-1625
Tel: 602-404-1800 or 800-468-BBSI
Web: http:///www.bbsi.org

A cosmetologist wraps a client's hair between layers of special foil as part of a color treatment.

American Association of Cosmetology Schools
11811 North Tatum Boulevard, Suite 1085
Phoenix, AZ 8528
Tel: 800-831-1086
Email: Jim@Beautyschools.org
Web: http://www.beautyschools.org/

Cosmetology Advancement Foundation
208 East 51st Street, Suite 143
New York NY 10022
Tel: 212-388-2771

Hair International/Associated Master Barbers and Beauticians of America
124-B East Main Street, PO Box 273
Palmyra, PA 17078
Tel: 717-838-0795
Web: http://www.hairinternational.com

National Cosmetology Association
401 North Michigan Avenue
Chicago, IL 60611
Tel: 312-527-6765 or 800-527-1683
Web: http://www.nca-now.com

COST ESTIMATORS

SCHOOL SUBJECTS:
BUSINESS, MATHEMATICS

PERSONAL SKILLS:
TECHNICAL/SCIENTIFIC

MINIMUM EDUCATION LEVEL:
HIGH SCHOOL DIPLOMA

OUTLOOK:
ABOUT AS FAST AS THE AVERAGE

OTHER ARTICLES TO LOOK AT:

Accountants
Assessors and Appraisers
Carpenters
Civil Engineers
Insurance Claims Representatives

WHAT COST ESTIMATORS DO

Cost estimators figure out how much it will cost to build or make something. Builders and manufacturers need cost estimators when they plan a new project or a new product. Cost estimators must have good judgment because their evaluations may involve budgets in the millions of dollars.

Builders first show their plans to a cost estimator who thinks about all the things that go into a large building project. How much will the builder have to pay for labor? What equipment will the builder have to buy or rent? How much will all the materials—stone, wood, plaster, cement—cost? How much will it cost to bring all the materials to the building site?

Cost estimators must gather the necessary information to answer all these questions. Then they put together an estimate. If a project is very complicated, there may be a need for several cost estimators to handle different parts of the project. For example, one estimator may work only on the cost of electrical work, while another covers the cost of transportation. Then the chief estimator puts all these separate reports together in one complete estimate.

Estimators working for manufacturers have to figure out how much it will cost to train workers to produce a new product. They must determine what parts and materials cost and how much labor will be needed to make it. Because a manufacturer will probably be making a product for years, estimators must also predict how much and how fast these costs will rise. They must also consider what equipment is needed and how quickly the equipment will wear out and have to be replaced.

If a builder or manufacturer needs an estimate in a hurry, the cost estimator has to work long hours to get it done on time. Because estimators may have to make decisions very quickly, and because a great deal of money may be involved, cost estimators must work well under pressure.

EDUCATION AND TRAINING

Builders and manufacturers want cost estimators to know all about their particular business. For this reason, on-the-job training is important for any cost estimator. Many cost estimators begin as tradespeople—for example, carpenters or plumbers—who gain experience in figuring out how much a given job will cost.

High school students interested in this profession should take courses in mathematics and English. Many technical schools and community colleges offer two-year programs that specialize in manufacturing and construction processes. Accounting courses are also helpful. The federal government and some other employers require cost estimators to have a college degree in either civil engineering or mathematics.

The American Society of Professional Estimators and the Society of Cost Estimating and Analysis give certification to cost estimators who have three to seven years experience and pass a written and an oral test. This certification is not required; it is a way of proving that estimators know their jobs well.

EARNINGS AND OUTLOOK

Beginning salaries for cost estimators range from $20,000 to $30,000 per year, depending on the candidate's experience, the size of the employer, and the type of work. College graduates with a degree in engineering can earn starting salaries of $30,000 or more. Highly experienced estimators can earn $75,000 or more.

Because the work of cost estimators depends entirely on manufacturing and construction, the employment of cost estimators is sensitive to economic fluctuations. This will continue to be true over the next ten years.

FOR MORE INFORMATION

One way to practice doing what a cost estimator does is to create budgets for various projects, either at home or at school, and then evaluate the accuracy of the budget after the project is completed.

Watching the construction of a building or taking a factory tour will give those interested in a career as a cost estimator an idea of all the different kinds of workers, materials, and equipment involved.

Three cost estimators view a blueprint in an effort to determine the cost of a building.

For more information, contact:

Association for the Advancement of Cost Estimating
209 Prairie Avenue
Morgantown, WV 26505
Tel: 304-296-8444
Web: http://www.cost.org/

American Society of Professional Estimators
11141 Georgia Avenue, Suite 412
Wheaton, MD 20902
Tel: 301-929-8848
Web: http://www.aspenational.com

Society of Cost Estimating and Analysis
101 South Whiting Street, Suite 201
Alexandria, VA 22304
Tel: 703-751-8069
Web: http://www.erols.com/scea

COSTUME DESIGNERS

SCHOOL SUBJECTS:
FAMILY AND CONSUMER SCIENCE, THEATER/DANCE

PERSONAL SKILLS:
ARTISTIC, COMMUNICATION/IDEAS

MINIMUM EDUCATION LEVEL:
HIGH SCHOOL DIPLOMA

OUTLOOK:
ABOUT AS FAST AS THE AVERAGE

OTHER ARTICLES TO LOOK AT:

Actors

Artists

Fashion Designers

Stage Production Workers

Tailors and Dressmakers

WHAT COSTUME DESIGNERS DO

Costume designers create, coordinate, and organize the costumes seen in the theater, on television, and in the movies. They also create costumes for figure skaters, ballroom dancers, circus performers, and others. When a show is to be performed, the costume designer reads the script, then decides what types of costumes are needed for each character. Through the use of a costume's color, style, and texture, the designer can express a character's personality and tell the audience more about a character's lifestyle.

If the story takes place in the past, designers research to make certain that the clothing styles are correct for the time period. For modern settings, a knowledge of styles and trends is necessary. Many costume designers also research previous productions of a play to see the kinds of costumes that were used and how well they worked in the past.

The costume designer consults with the director for design approval, with the stage designer to be certain that the furniture and backdrops do not clash with the costumes, and with the lighting designer to make certain that the lighting will not change the appearance of colors on stage.

The costume designer then makes color sketches, or renderings, of the outfits and accessories needed for each character. The costume designer decides whether to rent, purchase, or sew the costumes, a decision that is often determined by the show's budget. A major part of the costume designer's work consists of shopping for clothing and accessories (often from resale shops), fabrics, and sewing supplies, and in supervising the assistants who do the sewing work.

Typically, the costume shop is a small workroom which is crowded with people working on the various stages of costume creation: sewing, cutting, draping, and fitting. Costume designers need to be able to work in a busy setting, have patience for changes, and get along with people of all dispositions.

Costume designers usually have irregular hours, and when show time approaches, they may work long hours seven days a week to coordinate fittings and last-minute changes. When the show is in production, the work does not end. Costumes need to be cleaned, ironed, and repaired to appear fresh for each camera shoot or stage performance.

EDUCATION AND TRAINING

To become a costume designer, it is necessary to have a high school education and a college degree. If a costume design major is unavailable at a college, working in a strong theater department may provide similar experience.

Such departments usually hire students to help sew and create the costumes.

High school and college students should take as many English and literature courses as possible to learn how to interpret drama. Courses in history are helpful for researching historical costumes and time periods. Courses in sewing, art, designing, and draping are also beneficial.

EARNINGS AND OUTLOOK

Costume designers who work on Broadway or for dance companies in New York City must be members of United Scenic Artists union, which sets minimum fees, protects the designer's rights, establishes rules for billing, and offers group health and life insurance.

A costume designer for a Broadway musical with a minimum of 36 actors earns around $17,500. For opera and dance companies, salary is usually by costume count.

For feature films and television, costume designers earn daily rates for an eight-hour day or a weekly rate for an unlimited number of hours. Designers sometimes earn royalties on their designs.

Regional theaters usually set individual standard fees. Most of them do not require union membership.

Most costume designers work freelance and are paid per costume or show. Costume designers can charge between $90 to $500 per costume, but some costumes, such as those for figure skaters, can cost thousands of dollars. Many costume designers must take part-time or full-time jobs to supplement their income from costume design.

Competition among costume designers is stiff and will remain so throughout the next decade. The number of qualified costume designers far exceeds the number of jobs available.

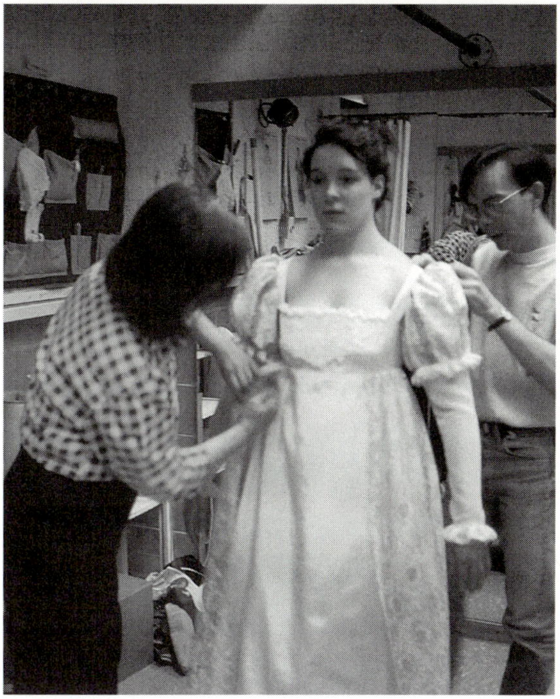

A costume designer works on an elaborate costume that will reflect the personality of the characters wearing it.

FOR MORE INFORMATION

This union represents costume designers in film and television.

Costume Designers Guild
13949 Ventura Boulevard, Suite 309
Sherman Oaks, CA 91423
Tel: 818-905-1557

This organization provides a list of schools and scholarships and a journal. It has a college membership with opportunities to network among other members who are professionals in the costume field.

The Costume Society of America
55 Edgewater Drive
PO Box 73
Earleville, MD 21919-0073
Tel: 410-275-2329
Web: http://www.costumesocietyamerica.com

COUNTER AND RETAIL CLERKS

SCHOOL SUBJECTS:
BUSINESS, MATHEMATICS

PERSONAL SKILLS:
FOLLOWING INSTRUCTIONS
HELPING/TEACHING

MINIMUM EDUCATION LEVEL:
HIGH SCHOOL DIPLOMA

OUTLOOK:
FASTER THAN THE AVERAGE

OTHER ARTICLES TO LOOK AT:

Bank Services Occupations
Cashiers
Clerks
Postal Clerks
Retail Sales Workers
Services Sales Representatives

WHAT COUNTER AND RETAIL CLERKS DO

Counter and retail clerks take orders and receive payments for a wide variety of services. They are the public representatives of businesses that provide goods and services. They work in supermarkets, drugstores, convenience stores, cleaners, computer shops, athletic and footwear boutiques, photo-finishing stores, and many other types of businesses. Many counter and retail clerks work in the rental industry. They may work as clerks at a car rental agency at an airport, in video stores, or at other establishments that rent goods or services to the consumer.

Counter and retail clerks take orders and receive payments from the public. They keep records of receipts and sales using a cash register, computer terminal, or by hand. They are responsible for keeping track of the money in their register throughout the day and balancing their money when their shift ends. Clerks also bag or wrap the customers' purchases, and sometimes arrange for their delivery. Counter and retail clerks are sometimes responsible for the display and presentation of products in their store. They may clean shelves or sweep floors, if necessary. In supermarkets and grocery stores, clerks stock shelves and bag food purchases for customers.

In smaller shops with no sales personnel or in a situation when a salesperson is unavailable, counter and retail clerks assist customers with purchases or rentals by demonstrating the merchandise or answering the customers' questions.

There are many examples of the wide variety of counter and retail clerks. *Video-rental clerks* greet customers, check out tapes, and accept payment. When the customers return their rentals, the clerks check the condition of the tapes and put them back onto the shelves. *Equipment-rental clerks* prepare rental forms and quote rates to customers. They answer customer questions about the operation of the equipment. They often take a deposit to cover any accidents or possible damage. When the customers return the equipment, clerks check it to make certain it is in good working order. *Shoe repair shop clerks* receive shoes that need to be cleaned or repaired. They examine the shoes, quote a price and give the customer a receipt. The clerk marks the shoes with a tag that specifies what work needs to be done and the name of the customer, then sends them to the work department. At the specified date, the clerk returns the repaired or cleaned shoes to the customer and collects payment.

EDUCATION AND TRAINING

There are no formal educational requirements necessary for becoming a counter and retail clerk. Most employers like to hire high school graduates, but there are many jobs available for those who are still in school.

Counter and retail clerks should have a pleasant personality and be able to get along well with people. They should be courteous, responsible, and willing to make the extra effort to satisfy customers. Clerks should be neat and well groomed. They also should have legible handwriting and the ability to perform simple arithmetic quickly.

EARNINGS AND OUTLOOK

Beginning counter and retail workers usually earn minimum wage. Experienced clerks earn between $6 and $9.50 per hour. The most experienced workers with the most responsibility can earn as much as $12.85 an hour. Workers who are members of a union earn considerably more than those are not.

According to the *Occupational Outlook Handbook*, full-time clerks average about $303 a week, or $15,756 annually. Clerks with considerable work experience earn about $631 weekly, or $32,812 a year. Some businesses offer merchandise discounts for their employees.

Approximately 374,000 people were employed as retail and counter clerks in the United States in 1996. About half worked part-time. Because of the proliferation of retail outlets, job opportunities for counter and retail clerks are expected to grow faster than average through the year 2006.

As is currently the case, major employers will be laundry or dry-cleaning establishments, automobile rental firms, and supermarkets and grocery stores. The continued growth in video rental stores and other rental services will also increase the need for skilled clerks. There should also be an increase in

A returns clerk helps a customer exchange a jacket.

the number of opportunities for temporary or part-time work, especially during busy business periods. However, due to the high turnover rate of this field, most job openings will result from the need to replace workers. Employment opportunities for clerks are plentiful in large metropolitan areas, where their services are in great demand.

FOR MORE INFORMATION

For information about educational programs in the retail industry, contact:

National Retail Federation
325 7th Street, NW, Suite 1000
Washington, DC 20004
Tel: 202-783-7971
Web: http://www.nrf.com

COURT REPORTERS

SCHOOL SUBJECTS:
ENGLISH, FOREIGN LANGUAGE, GOVERNMENT

PERSONAL SKILLS:
COMMUNICATION/IDEAS

MINIMUM EDUCATION LEVEL:
SOME POSTSECONDARY TRAINING

OUTLOOK:
FASTER THAN THE AVERAGE

OTHER ARTICLES TO LOOK AT:

Interpreters
Lawyers
Paralegals
Real-time Captioners
Secretaries
Stenographers

WHAT COURT REPORTERS DO

Court reporters record the testimony given at hearings and trials. They use symbols, or shorthand, to rapidly record what is said. In a courtroom, people may speak between 250 and 300 words per minute. Court reporters must record each word that is spoken. They use a stenotype machine to do this. This machine has a keyboard with 24 keys. Each key has a symbol on it and each symbol or combination of symbols stands for a sound, word, or a phrase. As testimony is given, the court reporter records it by striking the proper keys. The symbols are printed on a strip of paper and recorded on a computer disk.

Because court reporters make the official record of trials, they cannot miss a word or phrase. If they do, they must interrupt the trial and ask to have the words repeated. The judge sometimes asks the reporter to read aloud testimony that has already been recorded. Court reporters use computers to help them in their work. Computer programs (called computer aided transcription programs) are used to change the symbols and words of a stenotype machine into standard English. The computer can then print out a record of the trial. That way, the reporter does not have to retype it or read it into a tape recorder.

The court reporter's job doesn't stop in the courtroom, however. The court reporter must edit and proofread the transcript because the computer program only produces a rough draft of the text. After the court reporter cleans it up, the transcript is copied, bound in a durable binder, and sent on to the lawyers and judge.

Most court reporters work in city, county, state, or federal courts. Some work for private companies, recording business meetings and conventions. Others work for freelance reporting companies that provide reporters for trials and business meetings.

Most court reporters work from 40 to 49 hours per week. At times, however, they may have to work much longer hours. They must be on hand before a trial starts, and they have to wait while the jury reaches a verdict.

EDUCATION AND TRAINING

Court reporters must have a high school diploma. High school classes that would be helpful include English, typing, government, and business. Latin classes can also provide instruction on word origins, which may be helpful.

Court reporters also are required to complete a two- to four-year training program in shorthand reporting. Students learn how to type at least 225 words a minute on a stenotype machine. They also study typing, English, law, and medical and legal terms. Programs in shorthand reporting are offered at community colleges, business and vocational schools, and at some universities.

Some states require court reporters to be licensed. Others require them to be certified by the National Shorthand Reporters Association. Court reporters who work for the federal government may have to pass a civil service exam.

EARNINGS AND OUTLOOK

The average salary for a court reporter is about $43,000; a beginning court reporter will earns closer to $30,000. Experienced reporters can earn $55,000 or more depending on skill level. Freelance reporters usually earn between $15 and $35 an hour.

Court reporters who work in small communities or as freelancers may not be able to work full-time. Successful court reporters with jobs in business environments may earn more than those in courtroom settings, but such positions carry less job security.

Those working for the government or full-time for private companies usually receive health insurance and other benefits, such as paid vacations and retirement pensions. Freelancers may or may not receive health insurance or other benefits, depending on the policies of their agencies.

Employment opportunities for skilled court reporters should continue to grow to meet the needs of the rising numbers of both civil and criminal cases. The largest number of openings will probably be found in and around large cities. Those with computer training and the highest level of certification should have the best chance to get high paying jobs.

Court reporters must listen attentively to everything said during a trial and simultaneously record it on a machine.

FOR MORE INFORMATION

To get an idea of what a court reporter does—at least the work they do in public—attend some trials at your local courts. Instead of focusing on the main players—witnesses, lawyers, judges—keep an eye on the court reporter. If you can, watch several reporters in different courtrooms under different judges to get a perspective on what the average court reporter does. Try to arrange a one-on-one meeting with a court reporter so you can ask the questions you really want answers for.

Information on court reporting careers is available from the following associations:

National Court Reporters Association
8224 Old Courthouse Road
Vienna, VA 22182-3808
Email: msic@ncrahq.org
Web: http://www.verbatimreporters.com

National Verbatim Reporters Association
2729 Drake Street, Suite 130
Fayetteville, AR 72703
Email: nvra@aol.com
Web: http://www.nvra.org

CREATIVE ARTS THERAPISTS

SCHOOL SUBJECTS:
ART, MUSIC, PSYCHOLOGY, THEATER/DANCE

PERSONAL SKILLS:
ARTISTIC, HELPING/TEACHING

MINIMUM EDUCATION LEVEL:
MASTER'S DEGREE

OUTLOOK:
FASTER THAN THE AVERAGE

OTHER ARTICLES TO LOOK AT:

Actors and Actresses
Artists
Ceramic Artists
Child Life Specialists
Musicians

WHAT CREATIVE ARTS THERAPISTS DO

Creative arts therapists treat and rehabilitate people with mental, physical, and emotional disabilities. They usually work as part of a health care team with physicians, nurses, psychiatrists, psychologists, and social workers. Therapists often work in hospitals, schools, rehabilitation centers, shelters for battered women, substance abuse programs, hospices, and correctional facilities. Some therapists have their own private practices.

The goal of a creative arts therapist is to improve their patients physically, mentally, and emotionally. Before they begin any treatment, they meet with the team of other health care professionals. After determining the strength, limitations, and interests of their patient, they create a program to promote positive change and growth in the patient. The creative arts therapist continues to confer with the other health care workers as the program progresses, and alters the program according to the patient's progress. How these goals are reached depends on the unique specialty of the therapist in question.

Music therapists use musical lessons and activities to improve a patient's self-confidence, self-awareness, to relieve states of depression, and to improve physical dexterity. *Art therapists* use art in much the same manner. The art therapist may encourage and teach patients to express their thoughts, feelings, and anxieties via sketching, drawing, painting, or sculpting. *Dance/movement therapists* develop and conduct dance/movement sessions to help improve the physical, mental, and emotional health of their patients. Dance and movement therapy is also used as a way to assess a patient's progress toward therapeutic goals.

Drama therapists use role-playing, pantomime (the telling of a story by the use of expressive body or facial movements), puppetry, improvisation, and original scripted dramatization to evaluate and treat patients. *Poetry therapists* and *Bibliotherapists* use the written and spoken word to treat patients.

EDUCATION AND TRAINING

If you plan on becoming a creative arts therapist, you should begin studying the arts as early as possible. Courses such as art, art history, drama, and writing will give you important background skills for whichever arts field interests you. If you are musically inclined, you might consider joining the band or orchestra to learn how to read, write, and play music as a music therapist.

A bachelor's degree is the minimum requirement to become a creative arts therapist. Usually a creative arts therapist will earn an undergraduate degree in a particular field—such as art, music, or drama—and then continue in a master's program. Degree programs in specific creative arts therapy fields are offered at a many colleges and universities. Students who wish to pursue a field that isn't offered at their school often earn a master's degree in education, counseling or a related field. Upon completion of the master's degree, creative arts therapists can apply for certification with the national association that is specific to their specialty. Requirements for certification vary by association. Creative arts therapists who work in public schools must also be licensed by the Department of Education.

EARNINGS AND OUTLOOK

Starting salaries for creative arts therapists generally range between $20,000 and $30,000. Therapists with experience usually earn from $25,000 to $35,000. Those creative arts therapists who have administrative or managerial duties can earn from $35,000 to $50,000 a year. Salaries for therapists who work for the government range from $27,000 to $50,000 per year.

Creative arts therapy programs are growing rapidly. Many new positions are being created each year for trained workers. Job openings in nursing homes will increase as the elderly population continues to grow. Advances in medical technology and the recent practice of early discharge from hospitals should also create new opportunities in managed care facilities, chronic pain clinics, and cancer care facilities. The outlook for creative arts therapists will continue to brighten as more people become aware of the need to help disabled persons in creative ways.

A creative arts therapist leads a group through a movement exercise.

FOR MORE INFORMATION

For more information, contact the following organizations:

American Art Therapy Association
1202 Allanson Road
Mundelein, IL 60060-3808
Tel: 847-949-6064
Web: http://www.arttherapy.org

American Music Therapy Association
8455 Colesville Road, Suite 1000
Silver Spring, MD 20910
Tel: 301-589-3300
Web: http://www.musictherapy.org/

National Association for Drama Therapy
5505 Connecticut Avenue, NW, #280
Washington, DC 20015
Tel: 202-966-7409
Web: http://www.nadt.org

National Coalition of Arts Therapies Associations
2117 L Street, NW, #274
Washington, DC 20037
Tel: 202-678-6787
Web: http://www.ncata.com/

CRIME ANALYSTS

SCHOOL SUBJECTS:
COMPUTER SCIENCE, ENGLISH, PSYCHOLOGY

PERSONAL SKILLS:
HELPING/TEACHING

MINIMUM EDUCATION LEVEL:
BACHELOR'S DEGREE

OUTLOOK:
FASTER THAN THE AVERAGE

OTHER ARTICLES TO LOOK AT:

Deputy U.S. Marshals
Detectives
FBI Agents
Forensic Experts
Police Officers

WHAT CRIME ANALYSTS DO

Crime analysts try to uncover and piece together information about crime patterns, crime trends, and criminal suspects. A crime analyst's work involves collecting crime data from many sources, including police reports, statewide computer databases, and interviews with suspects. Crime analysts also study general factors such as population density, economic conditions (average income and job availability), and crime reporting practices. They then analyze this information. Crime analysts are constantly on the lookout for details that may create patterns. These patterns can help them track and predict criminal activity.

The activities of the crime analyst can change from day to day. One day, for example, an analyst may meet with the police chief to discuss a string of local car thefts. Another day the analyst may work at the computer, gathering statistics. Sometimes the work includes going on "ride-alongs" with street cops, visiting a crime scene, or meeting with analysts from surrounding areas to exchange information. Occasionally, a crime analyst may be pulled off everyday responsibilities to work exclusively on a task force, usually focusing on a rash of violent crimes. Another responsibility of the crime analyst is to monitor activities of "known offenders" such as parolees.

There are three types of analysis: tactical, strategic, and administrative. Tactical crime analysis provides police officers and detectives with prompt, in-the-field information. This is the type of "hot" information that allows police to set up stakeouts and may lead to the arrest of a criminal. Tactical analysis is also used to identify suspects for certain crimes based on their criminal histories.

Strategic analysis deals with finding solutions to long-range problems. For example, an analyst might perform a study to see if the police department is making the best use of its personnel and offer suggestions for improvement.

Administrative analysis provides policy-making information to a police department's administration. This analysis may include a study on the activity levels of police officers that would support a request for hiring more officers. Administrative work could also include creating graphs and charts that are used in management presentations.

EDUCATION AND TRAINING

While you are in high school, you can begin to prepare for a career as a crime analyst by taking English classes that will develop your communications as well as research skills. Both of these skills are necessary for this career since you'll be working with gathering information and communicating with many different people. Math classes, such as algebra, will help you in understanding statistics. Take advantage of your school's computer lab, as basic knowledge of computers, word processing, spreadsheets, and databases is important.

Most agencies require a bachelor's degree for the position of crime analyst, so after high school, plan on going to college. Many crime analysts have degrees in criminal justice, statistics, computer science, and sociology.

Once you have entered the field as a crime analyst professional, you may want to gain certification. Currently, only California offers a formal, state-sponsored certification program for crime analysts. The Society of Certified Criminal Analysts also offers two levels of certification, regular and lifetime.

EARNINGS AND OUTLOOK

The beginning salary for a crime analyst is about $24,000. With several years of experience, crime analysts can expect to earn $34,000 to $42,000, and the most experienced crime analysts earn about $60,000. Salaries tend to be higher in the East and West where crime analysis is more established as a profession and where the cost of living is higher. For instance, in California, a typical starting salary ranges from $27,000 to $40,000.

In the last five years, there has been growing interest in the field of crime analysis. One factor has been the emergence of community-oriented policing in which police officers are sent out to work on the streets of their communities. Crime analysts can help police departments decide where to direct their forces. The field is also growing because better software is becoming available, giving analysts more capabilities. While this growth is expected to continue, it's important to recognize that it is still a competitive job market. Those who want to become crime analysts should be willing to move to find an agency with a job opening.

Crime analysts rely on computers to sort through thousands of pieces of data to help them solve crimes.

FOR MORE INFORMATION

There are plenty of ways that you can begin your own training and education now. First of all, get some exposure to the law enforcement community by volunteering at the local police department.

Contact the ASC for information on careers in criminology.

American Society of Criminology (ASC)
1314 Kinnear Road, Suite 212
Columbus, OH 43212-1156
Tel: 614-292-9207
Email: asc41@compuserve.com
Web: http://www.asc41.com/

For information on certification, contact:

Society of Certified Criminal Analysts
PO Box 631
Cape Neddick, ME 03902
Web: http://www.ialeia.org/scca/

CRUISE SHIP WORKERS

SCHOOL SUBJECTS:
FOREIGN LANGUAGE, GEOGRAPHY

PERSONAL SKILLS:
HELPING/TEACHING
LEADERSHIP/MANAGEMENT

MINIMUM EDUCATION LEVEL:
HIGH SCHOOL DIPLOMA

OUTLOOK:
FASTER THAN THE AVERAGE

OTHER ARTICLES TO LOOK AT:

Cooks, Chefs, and Bakers

Hotel and Motel Management and Workers

Recreation Workers

Resort Workers

Ski Resort Workers

WHAT CRUISE SHIP WORKERS DO

Cruise ship workers provide services to passengers on cruise ships. Besides assisting in the operation of the ship, they serve food and drink, maintain cabins and public areas, lead shipboard activities, and provide entertainment. It takes a staff of hundreds, and sometimes thousands, to ensure the smooth operation of a cruise ship, and the comfort of all passengers. Crew organization is divided into six different departments. The *captain*, or the *master* of the ship, oversees the entire crew.

Deck. This department is responsible for the navigation of the ship, and oversees the maintenance of the hull and deck.

Engine. This staff operates and maintains machinery. Together, deck and engine staffs include officers, carpenters, seamen, maintenance workers, electricians, engineers, repairmen, plumbers, and incinerator operators.

Radio department. *Videographers* are responsible for the maintenance and operation of the ship's broadcast booth, including radio and news telecasts. *Telephonists* help passengers place phone calls shoreside.

Medical department. *Physicians* treat passengers whose illnesses range from seasickness to more serious health problems. *Nurses* assist the doctors, and provide first aid.

Steward. This department, one of the largest on board, is concerned with the comfort of all passengers. The food staff includes specially trained *chefs* that prepare meals, ranging from gourmet dinners to more casual fare poolside. The *wait staff* serves guests in the formal dining room, and provides room service. *Wine stewards* help passengers with wine choices, and are responsible for maintaining proper inventories aboard the ship. *Bartenders* mix and serve drinks at many stations throughout the ship. The *housekeeping staff* is composed of *room stewards and cleaners* who keep cabins and staterooms orderly, supply towels and sheets, and maintain public areas throughout the ship.

Pursers. This large department is responsible for guest relations and services. The *chief purser*, much like a hotel's general manager, is the head of this department and is the main contact for passengers regarding the ship's policies and procedures. *Assistant pursers*, considered junior officers, assist the chief with various duties, such as providing guest services, ship information, monetary exchange, postage, safety deposit boxes, and other duties usually associated with the front desk department of a hotel. The cruise staff, headed by the *cruise director*, plans daily activities and entertainment. The *youth staff* plans activities and games specifically designed for children. Ships with a casino on board employ casino workers, including game dealers, cashiers, keno runners, and slot machine attendants. Many *entertainers* and *musicians* are hired to sing, dance, and perform comedy skits and musical revues. *Dance instructors* teach dance classes ranging from ballroom to country. Also, many employees are hired to work in duty-free shops and souvenir stores, beauty parlors, spas, health clubs, and libraries.

EDUCATION AND TRAINING

Cruise lines require at least a high school education, or the equivalent, for most entry-level jobs. While in high school, you should concentrate on classes such as geography, sociology, and a foreign language. Spanish, French, and Portuguese are some examples of useful languages in this industry. Jobs with more responsibility, say officer level jobs, require college degrees as well as past work experience. Many employees, especially those in the cruise staff, have an entertainment background. Youth staff members usually have a background in education or recreation.

EARNINGS AND OUTLOOK

According to the Cruise Services International, the salary range is about $1,000 to $1,700 per month for cruise ship workers. However, many employees receive tips from passengers that greatly supplements their salaries. For example, restaurant and house staff workers can earn anywhere from $300 to $600 in weekly tips.

Employment for cruise ship workers should grow faster than the average through the year 2006. Today, ships are becoming bigger and offer many different activities onboard such as gambling, dancing, sports

A cruise ship waiter serves drinks on deck.

activities, and spas. With so many mega-ships in operation, the demand for qualified cruise ship workers will increase. Entry-level positions will be fairly easy to obtain with the proper paperwork and credentials. Positions with more responsibility, or officer level jobs will also be plentiful. However, for these positions, a college degree and work experience will be necessary.

FOR MORE INFORMATION

For more information on cruise ship careers, contact:

Cruise Services International
601 Dundas Street West
Box 24070
Whitby, Ontario L1N 8X8 Canada
Web: http://www.intergate.bc.ca/business/jobship

CUSTOMER SERVICE REPRESENTATIVES

SCHOOL SUBJECTS:
BUSINESS, ENGLISH, SPEECH

PERSONAL SKILLS:
COMMUNICATION/IDEAS
HELPING/TEACHING

MINIMUM EDUCATION LEVEL:
HIGH SCHOOL DIPLOMA

OUTLOOK:
ABOUT AS FAST AS THE AVERAGE

OTHER ARTICLES TO LOOK AT:

Business Managers
Labor Union Business Agents
Management Analysts and Consultants
Office Administrators
Secretaries

WHAT CUSTOMER SERVICE REPRESENTATIVES DO

Customer service representatives work with customers to assist with problems or answer questions. Customer service representatives work in many different industries to provide "front-line" customer service. Most customer service representatives work in an office setting, although some may work in the field to better meet customer needs.

Customer service representatives often handle complaints and problems. They should be pleasant and efficient while dealing with customers, no matter how upset those customers might be.

Many customer service representatives answer calls that come in on toll-free telephone lines. While some calls are likely to be focused on complaints or questions, some are simpler. Some people call to order literature or brochures, or to find their nearest dealer location.

Customer service representatives work in a variety of fields and businesses, but one thing is common—the customer. All businesses depend on their customers to keep them in business, so customer service, whether handled internally or by another company, is extremely important.

Some customer service representatives do most of their work on the telephone. Others may represent companies in the field, where the customer actually uses the product or service. Still other customer service representatives may specialize in assisting customers over the Internet.

Some companies have customer service representatives available 24 hours a day, 7 days a week, so a variety of shifts are required. Not all customer service representatives work a varied schedule, though; many work a traditional daytime shift.

EDUCATION AND TRAINING

If you want to become a customer service representative, in high school, you should take classes that focus on communication and business. English and speech classes will help with all forms of communication. Business classes will give an overview of the business world and how customer service fits into that world.

A college degree is not required to become a customer service representative, but any type of postsecondary education through a college or other training programs would help to prepare you for a career as a customer service representative. Communications and business classes are still important, as well as more specific classes in customer relations and leadership.

EARNINGS AND OUTLOOK

Customer service representatives earn an average of $26,000 per year. Entry-level workers may earn as little as $18,000 per year with more experienced representatives earning up to $32,000 per year. Some benefits may be included, depending on the size and type of company. Full-time customer service representatives can expect to receive vacation and sick pay, while part-time workers may not be offered these benefits.

The U.S. Department of Labor predicts that employment for customer service representatives will grow about as fast as the average for all other occupations. While businesses are growing and customers continue to need contact with those businesses, some growth in this field will be offset by growing technological trends. Customer relations handled via the Internet or automated answering machines will eliminate the need for growth in some areas.

For customer service representatives with specific knowledge of a product or business, the outlook is very good, as quick, efficient customer service is valuable in any business. Additional training and education will also make finding a job as a customer service representative an easier task.

A customer service representative assists a customer with an order.

FOR MORE INFORMATION

For information on customer service and other support positions, contact:

The Association of Support Professionals
17 Main Street
Watertown, MA 02472-4491
Tel: 617-924-3944, ext. 14
Email: asp@softletter.com
Web: http://www.asponline.com

For information on jobs, training, workshops, and salaries, contact:

Customer Care Institute
17 Dean Overlook, NW
Atlanta, GA 30318
Tel: 404-352-9291
Email: info@customercare.com
Web: http://www.customercare.com

Help Desk Institute
650 Townsend Street
San Francisco, CA 94103-4908
Tel: 415-551-4600
Email: CSSC@zd.com
Web: http://www.helpdeskinst.com

For more information on international customer service careers, contact:

International Customer Service Association
401 North Michigan Avenue, Suite 2200
Chicago, IL 60611-4267
Tel: 800-360-4272
Web: http://www.icsa.com

CUSTOMS OFFICIALS

SCHOOL SUBJECTS:
ENGLISH, GOVERNMENT

PERSONAL SKILLS:
COMMUNICATION/IDEAS

MINIMUM EDUCATION LEVEL:
HIGH SCHOOL DIPLOMA

OUTLOOK:
FASTER THAN THE AVERAGE

OTHER ARTICLES TO LOOK AT:

Border Patrol Officers
Deputy U.S. Marshals
Detectives
FBI Agents
Forensic Experts
Police Officers

WHAT CUSTOMS OFFICIALS DO

Customs officials work as observant detectives to make sure nothing illegal, such as drugs, is smuggled into the United States. They are employed by the federal government to enforce the laws that regulate goods coming into the country (imports) and goods leaving the country (exports). Customs officials work at airports, seaports, and border crossings of every entry and exit point of the United States. Their main responsibility is to make sure that no illegal merchandise, called contraband, is smuggled into the country. Customs officials need to be observant and crafty to search out all the possible hiding places in luggage or clothes that people might use to conceal contraband. It is possible that they might run into criminals in the course of their work. Federal law prevents other items besides drugs from being transported across borders, including certain plants and foods that could carry insects and disease. The importation of many species of animals, and products made from them, is also prohibited by law. The special customs officials whose job it is to prevent smuggling are called *customs patrol officers.*

Another important part of the job of a customs official is to determine taxes, called duties, on imports and exports. They check the luggage and personal items of airline and shipboard passengers and crew members as well as the ship's or airplane's cargo. They make sure that all merchandise is declared honestly, that duties are paid, and that no contraband is present. Travelers sometimes try to hide expensive imports to avoid paying high duties on them. Customs officials need to be as alert to these tax-evaders as to drug dealers. They also examine packages that are mailed into the country. They check the baggage of travelers who come by car or train across the borders of Canada and Mexico. This allows them to also conduct a first screening of immigrants to the country.

The United States imports many products, which are then sold or used for industry. The merchandise includes bales of cotton from India, rugs from Iran, diamonds from Africa, and wool from Ireland. Customs officials examine, count, weigh, gauge, measure, and sample commercial cargoes in order to check these figures against shipping papers and determine how much import duty (tax) should be paid. Customs warehouse officers guard the goods on the pier or in the warehouse to prevent theft, damage, and fire.

Merchandise for delivery to commercial importers is examined by *customs import specialists*, who consider import quotas and make sure trademark laws are observed.

Customs inspectors check the contents of a traveler's suitcase.

EDUCATION AND TRAINING

If you are interested in working for the U.S. Customs Service, you should take courses in government, geography and social studies, English, and history. If you wish to become a specialist in scientific or investigative aspects of the Customs Service, courses in the sciences, particularly chemistry, will be necessary and courses in computer science will be helpful.

Customs workers must be U.S. citizens, and they must be at least 21 years old. They must have earned at least a high school diploma, but a college degree is preferred. Applicants who do not have a college degree must have at least three years of related work experience. Customs inspectors, like all employees of the federal government, must pass a physical examination and undergo a security check. They must also pass a standardized test administered by the federal government. The test is called the Professional and Administrative Career Examination (PACE).

EARNINGS AND OUTLOOK

Customs workers earn an average annual salary of about $31,200. Beginning customs officials start at either $20,588 or $25,501 per year depending on their level of education or experience.

Employment as a customs official is steady work that is not affected by changes in the economy. With the increased emphasis on law enforcement, including the detection of illegally imported drugs and pornography and the prevention of exports of sensitive high-technology items, the prospects for steady employment are good.

FOR MORE INFORMATION

U.S. Customs Service
Office of Human Resources
1300 Pennsylvania Avenue, NW
Washington, DC 20229
Web: http://www.customs.ustreas.gov

DANCERS

SCHOOL SUBJECTS:
MUSIC, THEATER/DANCE

PERSONAL SKILLS:
ARTISTIC, COMMUNICATION/IDEAS

MINIMUM EDUCATION LEVEL:
HIGH SCHOOL DIPLOMA

OUTLOOK:
FASTER THAN THE AVERAGE

OTHER ARTICLES TO LOOK AT:

Actors
Athletes
Choreographers
Circus Performers
Musicians
Recreation Workers

WHAT DANCERS DO

Dancers perform dances, either as members of a group or as solo performers. Through their body movements they tell a story, express an idea or feeling, or entertain their audience.

There are several types of dancers. *Ballet dancers* require the most rigorous training and perform dances that express a story or theme. Most other types of dancers need some ballet training. *Acrobatic dancers* perform in a difficult gymnastic style. *Interpretive* or *modern dancers* express moods or ideas, often using facial expressions as well as body movements. Jazz dance, for instance, is a form of modern dance. *Tap dancers* keep time with the music by tapping out rhythms with their tap shoes.

Dancers may perform in classical ballets, musical stage shows, folk dance shows, television dance numbers, music videos, or other popular dance productions. Because dancing jobs are not always available, many dancers work as part-time dance instructors. Dancers who create new ballets or dance routines are called *choreographers. Dance directors* are those who train other dancers in performing a new production.

EDUCATION AND TRAINING

Dancers usually begin training around the age of 10, or even as early as age seven or eight. They may study with private teachers or in ballet schools. Dancers who show promise in their early teens may receive professional training in a regional ballet school or a major ballet company. By the age of 17 or 18, dancers begin to audition for positions in professional dance companies.

Many colleges and universities offer degrees in dance. Although a college degree is not required for dancers, it can be very useful. Those who teach dance in a college or university often are required to have a degree. Also, the professional life of a dancer can be rather short. With a college degree, a dancer is better able to move into other career fields.

EARNINGS AND OUTLOOK

The minimum weekly salary for dancers in a ballet and other stage productions is between $610 and $1,275. Dance contracts are rarely done on a yearly basis; most last from 36 to 45 weeks.

Modern dance companies usually pay a base salary of $500 to $1,200 per week for a 42- to 44-week year. In smaller companies, pay is reduced to about $50 per performance and $5 per hour of rehearsal time. The single performance rate for new first-year ballet dancers is $230. Dancers on tour are paid extra to cover their room and board expenses. Minimum performance rates for dancers on television average $569 for a one-hour show, which generally includes an additional 18 hours of rehearsal time.

Pay in other performance areas varies. Dancers on cruise ships can earn between $200 to $500 per week, with free room and board. Opera and stage dancers average about $75 a performance and earn an additional $55 daily while touring. Broadway dancers earn a minimum of $700 per week. Many performing dancers must work other jobs to supplement their income. Union contracts may provide limited benefits.

Job opportunities for dancers through 2006 will be better than average. However, there will still be more dancers seeking jobs than there are openings for them. Local ballet companies are expected to offer the most job opportunities. Because more people have become interested in dance in recent years, there also will be job openings for dance teachers.

FOR MORE INFORMATION

Dancing is a highly competitive profession, and interested students should take advantage of every opportunity to gain experience. It is not too difficult to find places to perform in one's own community, and it is wise to dance publicly early and often. Most dancers continue with classes in dance throughout their professional careers.

For information on all aspects of dance, including job listings, send a self-addressed, stamped envelope to:

American Dance Guild
31 West 21st Street, 3rd Floor
New York, NY 10010
Tel: 212-627-3790

Many hours of practice are devoted to dance routines to achieve the effect of effortless perfection during performance.

A directory of dance companies and related organizations and other information on professional dance is available from:

Dance USA
1156 15th Street, NW, Suite 820
Washington, DC 20005-1704
Tel: 202-833-1717
Web: http://www.danceusa.org

Information on purchasing directories about colleges and universities that teach dance, including details on types of courses offered and scholarships, is available from:

National Dance Association
1900 Association Drive
Reston, VA 22091
Tel: 800-321-0789
Web: http://www.aahperd.org/nda/nda-main.html

A directory of dance, art and design, music, and theater programs may be purchased from:

National Association of Schools of Dance
11250 Roger Beacon Drive, Suite 21
Reston, VA 22090
Tel: 703-437-0700
Web: http://www.arts-accredit.org/nasd/

DATABASE SPECIALISTS

SCHOOL SUBJECTS:
COMPUTER SCIENCE, MATHEMATICS

PERSONAL SKILLS:
MECHANICAL/MANIPULATIVE
TECHNICAL/SCIENTIFIC

MINIMUM EDUCATION LEVEL:
ASSOCIATE'S DEGREE

OUTLOOK:
MUCH FASTER THAN THE AVERAGE

OTHER ARTICLES TO LOOK AT:

Computer Programmers
Computer Trainers
Computer-Aided Design Technicians
Graphic Designers
Software Designers

WHAT DATABASE SPECIALISTS DO

Business, industry, and the government rely on computers to store and organize huge amounts of information. The collection of information stored in a computer is called a database. *Database specialists* work for utilities, stores, investment companies, insurance companies, publishing houses, telecommunications firms, and for all branches of government. They are responsible for setting up and maintaining databases. They purchase computer equipment and create computer programs that will collect, analyze, store, and transmit information.

Some database specialists figure out the type of computer system needed by their company. This means that the database specialist must know all about the latest developments in computer technology. A database manager meets with top-level company officials to discuss the company's needs. Together they decide what type of hardware and software will be required to set up a certain type of database. Then a database design analyst writes a proposal that states the company's needs, the type of equipment that will meet those needs, and how much the equipment will cost.

Another area of responsibility for database specialists is setting up and maintaining the computer system that the company buys. Database managers and administrators must decide how to organize and store the information in the database. This involves creating a computer program or a series of programs and training employees to enter information into those programs. Specialists make decisions on how best to organize data for quick retrieval.

Computer programs sometimes crash, or work improperly. Database specialists must make sure that a copy of the program and the database is available in case of a crash. Specialists also are responsible for protecting the database from people or organizations who are not supposed to see it. A company's database contains important, and sometimes secret, information.

Very large companies may have many databases. Sometimes it is necessary for these databases to share information. Database managers see to it that these different databases can talk, or communicate with each other, even if they are located in different parts of the country.

EDUCATION AND TRAINING

If you are interested in becoming a database specialist, you should take as many computer courses as possible in high school. In addition, you should study mathematics, accounting, science, English, and communications. An associate's degree in a computer-related

Consulting recent publications, a database manager updates a computer file used by clients for information services.

technology is required for entry-level database administrators.

A bachelor's degree in computer science or business administration is necessary for advanced positions. Those with a master's degree will have even greater opportunities.

EARNINGS AND OUTLOOK

Beginning database design analysts with a college education earn about $35,000 per year. Mid-level salaries, offered to professionals with several years of experience, average about $50,000. After even more experience and further training, database design analysts are offered top salaries of over $70,000.

The use of computers and database systems in almost all businesses creates tremendous opportunities for well-qualified database personnel. Database specialists and computer support specialists are predicted by the U.S. Department of Labor to be the two fastest growing occupations through the year 2006. In 1996, there were 212,000 database specialists employed in the United States. By the year 2006, the U.S. Department of Labor expects about 250,000 new jobs in this field—a 115 percent increase. Those with the best education and the most experience in computer systems and personnel management will find the best job prospects.

FOR MORE INFORMATION

Institute for Certification of Computing Professionals
2200 East Devon Avenue, Suite 247
Des Plaines, IL 60018
Web: http://www.iccp.org

Association of Information Technology Professionals
315 South Northwest Highway, Suite 200
Park Ridge, IL 60068-4278
Tel: 800-224-9371
Web: http://www.aitp.org

DEMOGRAPHERS

SCHOOL SUBJECTS:
MATHEMATICS, SOCIOLOGY

PERSONAL SKILLS:
TECHNICAL/SCIENTIFIC

MINIMUM EDUCATION LEVEL:
BACHELOR'S DEGREE

OUTLOOK:
LITTLE CHANGE OR MORE SLOWLY THAN THE AVERAGE

OTHER ARTICLES TO LOOK AT:

Actuaries
Marketing Researchers
Mathematicians
Operations Research Analysts
Sociologists
Statisticians

WHAT DEMOGRAPHERS DO

Demographers collect and study facts about their society's population—births, marriages, deaths, education and income levels, and so on. They use these facts to develop population studies that tell what the society is really like and to forecast economic and social trends. For example, a demographer may discover, through studying birth rates of a particular community, that the population of school-age children is growing faster than expected and that new schools will therefore have to be built. Or the demographer may collect facts about how many of these children have been sick with measles, which in turn could be studied to determine how effective the measles vaccine is.

Demographers work for both government agencies and private companies. Local, state, and federal government agencies use demographers' forecasts to help them provide enough of the right kinds of transportation, education, police, and health services. Private companies (such as retail chains) need demographers' collections of facts, or statistics, for help in making marketing decisions, such as the best location to open a new store. Demographers may also teach in colleges and universities or work as consultants for private companies or communities as a whole.

Whoever they work for, demographers rely on computers to help them gather and analyze the millions of pieces of information they need to make their forecasts. It is up to the individual demographer to know how to interpret the statistics and put them together in a meaningful way.

EDUCATION AND TRAINING

A college degree in sociology or public health with special studies in demography is always required to work as a demographer. Many entry-level jobs require a master's degree. Students interested in this field should be good at solving logical problems and have an aptitude for numbers and mathematics, especially algebra and geometry. Recommended college courses include classes in statistics, public policy, social research methods, and computer applications. High school students interested in this career should take classes in social studies, English, and mathematics. Training in computer science also is advantageous because computers are used extensively for research and statistical analysis.

No licenses or certificates are necessary, but demographers who work for the federal government may need to pass civil service examinations. As the field gets more competitive, many demographers (especially those wishing to work for the federal government) will earn a doctorate in sociology. The most successful demographers keep up with advances in their field by continuing education throughout their careers and by specializing in one area.

After graduation from college, you can apply directly to private research firms or other companies that do population studies. However, because you will most likely need a graduate degree, you should apply to a graduate program. (College placement offices will prove helpful in both cases.) Government jobs are listed with the Civil Service Commission, and if you wish to teach you will find leads through your graduate schools.

EARNINGS AND OUTLOOK

Earnings vary widely according to education, training, and place of employment. Social scientists (including sociologists who specialize in demography) with a bachelor's degree receive starting salaries averaging around $25,000, according to a 1997 survey by the National Association of Colleges and Employers, while those in federal government positions with no experience might start as low as $19,500. A master's degree raises the starting salary to about $29,600, while a Ph.D. degree holder might start at $35,800. Beginning salaries are higher in areas of the country where overall salary levels are higher, such as in large cities. Statisticians in federal government averaged $61,000 in 1997 and $66,000 in mathematical positions.

There is a tremendous amount of fact-gathering and social science research going on in the United States. The need for trained demographers to analyze this research should grow a little more slowly than the average through the year 2006. Job opportunities will be greatest in and around large cities, because that is where many colleges, universities, and other research facilities are located.

A demographer maps population trends on a computer.

FOR MORE INFORMATION

ASA offers many free career publications, lists of accredited schools, and college student membership, as well as job information.

American Sociological Association (ASA)
1307 New York Avenue, NW, Suite 700
Washington, DC 20005
Tel: 202-383-9005
Web: http://www.asanet.org

For information about the U.S. Census Bureau including a list of regional offices, jobs, and a calendar of events, contact:

Census Bureau
Public Information Office
Department of Commerce
Jacob K. Javitz Federal Building
Room 37-130
New York, NY 10278
Tel: 212-264-3860
Web: http://www.census.org

DENTAL ASSISTANTS

SCHOOL SUBJECTS:
BUSINESS, HEALTH

PERSONAL SKILLS:
MECHANICAL/MANIPULATIVE

MINIMUM EDUCATION LEVEL:
HIGH SCHOOL DIPLOMA

OUTLOOK:
MUCH FASTER THAN THE AVERAGE

OTHER ARTICLES TO LOOK AT:

Dental Hygienists
Dental Laboratory Technicians
Dentists
Medical Assistants
Nurse Assistants
Periodontists

WHAT DENTAL ASSISTANTS DO

Dental assistants help dentists examine and treat patients. They also carry out administrative and clerical tasks that make the dentist's office run smoothly.

Dental assistants greet patients, take them to the examining room, and prepare them for examination by covering their clothing with paper or cloth to protect it from water and stains. They also adjust the chair and its headrest to the proper height. Many dental assistants take X rays of patients' teeth and develop the film for the dentist. During examinations and dental procedures, dental assistants hand instruments to the dentist as they are needed and use suction devices to keep the patient's mouth dry. When the examination or procedure is over, assistants give patients instructions for taking care of their teeth and keeping the mouth clean and healthy.

Dental assistants help with a variety of other tasks, such as making plaster casts of a patient's teeth, making dentures, or in some states, applying medications to teeth and gums or removing excess material after cavities have been filled. Dental assistants also may help dentists with any emergencies that arise during dental procedures.

In addition to assisting the dentist with dental procedures, many dental assistants work in the front office on clerical and administrative tasks. They keep patient records, answer telephones, schedule appointments, prepare bills, collect payments, and issue receipts. They may also inventory dental supplies.

Dental assistants are not the same as *dental hygienists*, who are licensed to clean and polish teeth.

EDUCATION AND TRAINING

Many dental assistant positions require little or no experience and no education beyond high school. Assistants in such positions learn their skills on the job. However, some assistants receive training after high school at a technical institute, community or junior college that offers dental assisting programs. Armed forces schools also train some dental assistants. Students who attend two-year college programs receive associate degrees, while those who attend technical schools finish after one year and earn a certificate or diploma. To enter these programs, candidates must have a high school diploma, and some schools require that applicants have received good grades in science, typing, and English.

High school students who wish to work as dental assistants may prepare by taking courses in general science, biology, health, chemistry, and business management. Typing is also important for dental assistants.

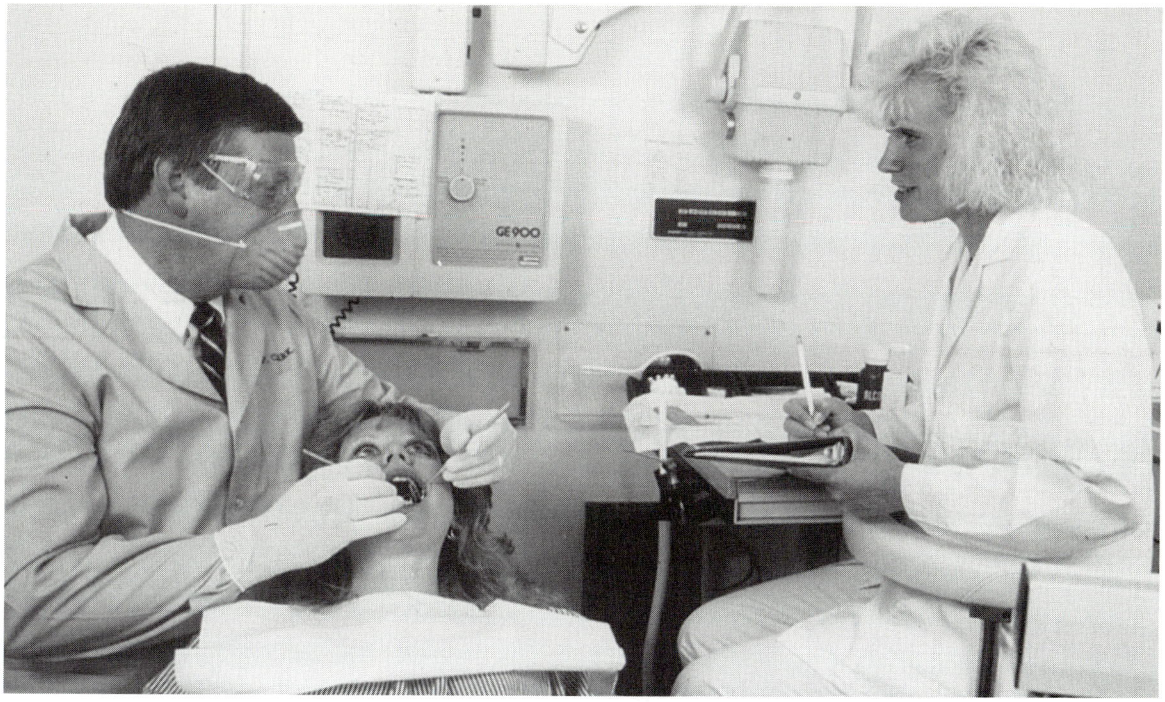

Aiding in a routine procedure, the dental assistant takes notes on the condition of the patient's teeth.

EARNINGS AND OUTLOOK

Salaries of dental assistants vary according to their duties, experience, and geographical location. Full-time dental assistants earn an average annual salary of between $17,000 and $23,000. About 25 percent of dental assistants work part-time. Part-time assistants in entry-level positions earn about $18,000 a year, while those with 15 or more years of experience average about $24,544 a year.

According to the U.S. Department of Labor, employment for dental assistants is expected to grow faster than all occupations through 2006, with about 60,000 more jobs expected to open in the field. As the population grows older and people become more aware that they can keep all of their teeth and be healthy, more people will seek dental services for preventive care and cosmetic improvements. Job openings will also be created through attrition as other assistants leave the field or change jobs.

FOR MORE INFORMATION

For more information on a career as a dental assistant, contact the following organizations:

American Association of Dental Schools
1625 Massachusetts Avenue, NW, Suite 600
Washington, DC 20036
Tel: 202-667-9433
Web: http://www.aads.jhu.edu

American Dental Assistants Association
203 North LaSalle Street, Suite 1320
Chicago, IL 60601
Tel: 312-541-1550
Web: http://members.aol.com/adaa1/

American Dental Association
211 East Chicago Avenue
Chicago, IL 60611
Tel: 312-440-2500
Web: http://www.ada.org/prac/careers/-apl-03.html

DENTAL HYGIENISTS

SCHOOL SUBJECTS:
BIOLOGY, HEALTH

PERSONAL SKILLS:
MECHANICAL/MANIPULATIVE

MINIMUM EDUCATION LEVEL:
ASSOCIATE'S DEGREE

OUTLOOK:
MUCH FASTER THAN THE AVERAGE

OTHER ARTICLES TO LOOK AT:

Dental Assistants
Dental Laboratory Technicians
Dentists
Medical Assistants
Nurse Assistants
Periodontists

WHAT DENTAL HYGIENISTS DO

Dental hygienists are the only assistants working for dentists who are licensed to clean patients' teeth. Their primary job is to remove plaque and other deposits from the teeth, polish teeth, and massage gums. They also promote good oral health by showing patients how to select toothbrushes and use floss, what kinds of foods damage the teeth, and the effects of habits, such as smoking, on teeth. The main goal of a dental hygienist is to help patients prevent tooth and gum decay and maintain a healthy mouth.

Hygienists who work for dentists in private practice may do more than clean teeth. They may take and develop X rays, mix materials to fill cavities, sterilize instruments, assist in surgery, and keep charts of patients' teeth. Some hygienists perform office duties as well, such as answering phone calls and making appointments for patients.

Not all hygienists work for dentists. Some work in schools where they clean and examine students' teeth and show them how to prevent tooth decay. They stress brushing and flossing teeth correctly and eating the right foods. They also keep records of the students' teeth and notify parents of any problems or need for additional treatment.

Some dental hygienists work for local, state, or federal public health agencies. They clean the teeth of adults and children in public health clinics and other public facilities and educate them in the proper care of teeth. A few hygienists work on research projects. Others teach in a dental hygiene school.

EDUCATION AND TRAINING

Dental hygienists must earn a high school diploma, as well as complete two or four years of college at an accredited dental hygiene school, and pass the national board exams or a licensing exam in a particular state.

There are two types of dental hygiene programs: a four-year college program offering a bachelor's degree and a two-year program leading to a dental hygiene certification. More employers now require a four-year degree.

Courses in such programs will include classes in anatomy, physiology, chemistry, pharmacology, nutrition, and other sciences. In addition, students learn to handle delicate instruments, gain experience in the dental laboratory, and practice working with patients in clinics. Before graduation, students are given a test to determine whether or not they are ready to work in the profession.

After graduation from an accredited school, state licensing examinations are required. Upon passing the exam, students are qualified to practice as registered dental hygienists. Dental hygienists must be able to help people relax, because many people are afraid of having work done on their teeth. In addition, hygienists need to be clean, neat, and in good health themselves.

A dental hygienist who wishes to teach, conduct research, or work in a school health program is often required to have a master's degree.

EARNINGS AND OUTLOOK

Dental hygienists' salaries will depend on their education, experience, and employer. Hygienists working in private dentists' offices earn higher incomes than those working in school systems, public health agencies, hospitals, factories, or the armed forces.

According to the U.S. Department of Labor, in 1996, the average earnings of full-time dental hygienists ranged between $24,000 and $39,500 a year. The average hourly wage for full-time hygienists was $20.40; the average for part-time hygienists was $24.50. Beginning hygienists earned an average of $15,200 to $17,500 a year. Salaries in large cities are generally higher than in smaller cities and towns. Additionally, hygienists in research, education, or administration may earn higher salaries.

A salaried dental hygienist in a private office typically receives a paid two- or three-week vacation. Part-time or commissioned dental hygienists in private offices usually have no paid vacation.

Employment opportunities for dental hygienists are very promising through 2006. As the population increases and more employers offer dental insurance, more jobs for dental hygienists will become available.

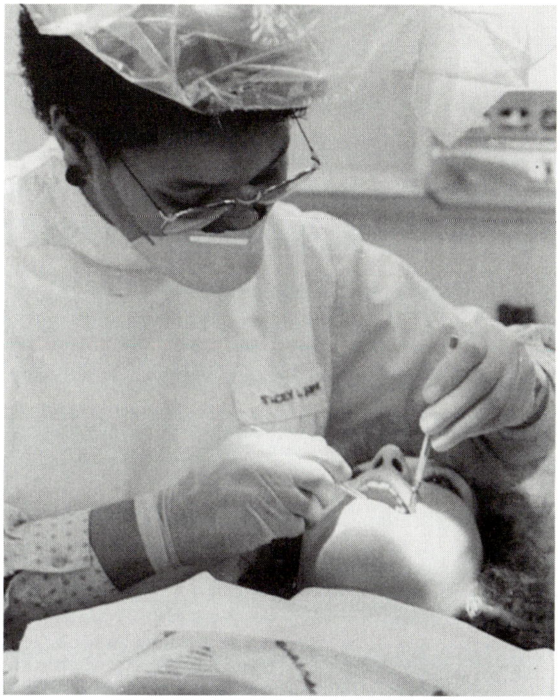

A dental hygienist cleans the teeth of a patient.

FOR MORE INFORMATION

For publications, information on dental schools, and scholarship information, contact:

American Association of Dental Schools
1625 Massachusetts Avenue, NW, Suite 600
Washington, DC 20036
Tel: 202-667-9433
Web: http://www.aads.jhu.edu

American Dental Association
211 East Chicago Avenue
Chicago, IL 60611
Tel: 312-440-2500
Web: http://www.ada.org/prac/careers/apl-03.html

American Dental Hygienists' Association
444 North Michigan Avenue, Suite 3400
Chicago, IL 60611
Tel: 312-440-8900
Web: http://www.adha.org

DENTAL LABORATORY TECHNICIANS

SCHOOL SUBJECTS:
ART, BIOLOGY, CHEMISTRY

PERSONAL SKILLS:
TECHNICAL/SCIENTIFIC

MINIMUM EDUCATION LEVEL:
HIGH SCHOOL DIPLOMA

OUTLOOK:
LITTLE CHANGE OR MORE SLOWLY THAN THE AVERAGE

OTHER ARTICLES TO LOOK AT:

Dental Assistants
Dental Hygienists
Dentists
Endodontists
Orthodontists
Periodontists

WHAT DENTAL LABORATORY TECHNICIANS DO

Even though *dental laboratory technicians* are never seen by the patient, they are very important to the success of many different kinds of dental treatment. When someone loses a tooth, for example, the dentist writes a prescription for a new one and the technician makes it in a laboratory.

There are four main kinds of laboratory work in which a technician can specialize. The first area is orthodontics. *Orthodontic technicians* make braces for straightening teeth by bending wires into complicated shapes that will fit over the crooked teeth. The braces, retainers, or tooth bands that these technicians make are not meant to be permanent, but will stay in a patient's mouth for a long time and so must fit well and feel comfortable.

Dental ceramicists make real-looking porcelain teeth to replace missing ones or to fit over natural teeth that may have been damaged or that are just not attractive. Ceramicists apply porcelain paste over a metal frame to make crowns, bridges, and tooth coverings. Their work involves a great deal of knowledge and creativity, and they are usually the best paid technicians.

Some dental laboratory technicians specialize in making and repairing full and partial dentures. Full dentures are false teeth worn by people who have had all their teeth removed on the upper or lower jaws or on both jaws. Partial dentures are the false teeth that are placed in a jaw between natural teeth to replace a missing tooth or teeth. Dentures are made by putting ceramic teeth in a wax model and then building up wax over it to hold the set in place.

Crown and bridge specialists restore the missing parts of a natural tooth that has broken. They use plastic and metal appliances that are permanently cemented to the natural tooth. Technicians in this area must be skilled at melting and casting metals.

Most technicians work in privately owned labs that employ only about six or seven people. Many large labs specialize in one type of work, while the smaller ones tend to employ technicians who perform a range of jobs.

EDUCATION AND TRAINING

Dental laboratory technicians should have patience and artistic talent, and they must also be able to follow written instructions precisely. High school classes in art (especially ceramics and sculpting) and chemistry are helpful. All technicians must have graduated from high school, but the methods of training following high school vary. Three to four years of on-the-job training is the way some start in the profession. Many others take two-year college courses in applied science. Classwork in such a program includes tooth construction, processing and repairing dentures, and making crowns.

Technicians with at least five years of experience often take a written and practical test that leads to certification by the National Board for Certification in Dental Technology.

EARNINGS AND OUTLOOK

Dental laboratory trainees earn slightly more than minimum wage. As technicians gain experience, however, their salaries increase. The *Occupational Outlook Handbook* reports that the average dental laboratory employee earned close to $24,000 in 1995. According to the National Association of Dental Laboratories, an especially productive or skilled technician may earn as much as $60,000. Self-employed technicians and those who work in smaller laboratories and perform a variety of work exceed the average earnings.

Benefits vary by individual laboratories. Additional benefits available to members of the National Association of Dental Laboratories include major medical and surgical insurance, term life insurance, dental insurance, and disability income coverage.

Although the overall demand for dental laboratory technicians is expected to grow very slowly through the year 2006, some job opportunities will remain favorable. Many trainee jobs may be available, but these positions may pay only a little more than minimum wage. Because fluoridated water has prevented tooth decay and people are keeping their teeth longer, dental laboratories will make fewer complete dentures. This reduced demand may be accompanied by need for more partial dentures, crowns, and tooth-colored fillings.

A dental laboratory technician chips off the plastic impression of a mouth to reveal the positive plaster mold.

FOR MORE INFORMATION

For information on dentistry and dental professions, contact:

American Dental Association
Department of Career Guidance
211 East Chicago Avenue
Chicago, IL 60611
Tel: 312-440-2500
Email: publicinfo@ada.org
Web: http://www.ada.org

For information on certification, contact:

National Association of Dental Laboratories
8201 Greensboro Drive, Suite 300
McLean, VA 22102
Tel: 703-610-9035
Web: http://www.nadl.org/html/certification.html

GLOSSARY

accredited Approved as meeting established standards for providing good training and education. This approval is usually given by an independent organization of professionals to a school or a program in a school. Compare **certified** and **licensed.**

apprentice A person who is learning a trade by working under the supervision of a skilled worker. Apprentices often receive classroom instruction in addition to their supervised practical experience.

apprenticeship 1. A program for training apprentices (see **apprentice**). 2. The period of time when a person is an apprentice. In highly skilled trades, apprenticeships may last three or four years.

associate degree An academic rank or title granted by a community or junior college or similar institution to graduates of a two-year program of education beyond high school.

bachelor's degree An academic rank or title given to a person who has completed a four-year program of study at a college or university. Also called an undergraduate degree or baccalaureate.

certified Approved as meeting established requirements for skill, knowledge, and experience in a particular field. People are certified by the organization of professionals in their field. Compare **accredited** and **licensed.**

commission A percentage of the money taken in by a company in sales that is given to the salesperson as pay, either in addition to or instead of a salary.

community college A public two-year college, attended by students who do not live at the college. Graduates of a community college receive an associate degree and may transfer to a four-year college or university to complete a bachelor's degree. Compare **junior college** and **technical community college.**

curriculum All the courses available in a school or college; or, the courses offered in a particular subject.

degree An academic distinction given by a college or university to a student who has completed a program of study.

diploma A certificate or document given by a school to show that a person has completed a course or has graduated from the school.

doctorate An academic rank or title (the highest) granted by a graduate school to a person who has completed a two- to three-year program after having received a master's degree.

engineering The profession that is concerned with ways of making practical use of scientific knowledge. Typical engineering activities include planning and managing the building of bridges, dams, roads, chemical plants, machinery, and new industrial products.

freelancer A self-employed person who contracts to do specific jobs.

fringe benefit A payment or benefit to an employee in addition to regular wages or salary. Examples of fringe benefits include a pension, a paid vacation, and health or life insurance.

graduate school A school that people may attend after they have received their bachelor's degree. People who complete an educational program at a graduate school earn a master's degree or a doctorate.

humanities The branches of learning that are concerned with language, the arts, literature, philosophy, and history. Compare **social sciences** and **natural sciences.**

intern An advanced student (usually one with at least some college training) in a professional field who is employed in a job that is intended to provide supervised practical experience for the student.

internship 1. The position or job of an intern (see **intern**). 2. The period of time when a person is an intern.

journeyman A person who has completed an apprenticeship or other training period and is qualified to work in a trade.

junior college A two-year college that offers courses like those in the first half of a four-year college program. Graduates of a junior college usually receive an associate degree and may transfer to a four-year college or university to complete a bachelor's degree. Compare **community college.**

liberal arts The subjects covered by college courses that develop broad general knowledge rather than specific occupational skills. The liberal arts are often considered to include philosophy, literature and the arts, history, language, and some courses in the social sciences and natural sciences.

licensed Having formal permission from the proper authority to carry out an activity that would be illegal without that permission. For example, a person may be licensed to practice medicine or to drive a car. Compare **certified.**

life sciences The natural sciences that are concerned with living organisms and the processes that take place within them (see **natural sciences**).

major (in college) The academic field in which a student specializes and receives a degree.

master's degree An academic rank or title granted by a graduate school to a person who has completed a one- or two-year program after having received a bachelor's degree.

natural sciences All the sciences that are concerned with the objects and processes in nature that can be measured. The natural sciences include biology, chemistry, physics, astronomy, and geology. Compare **humanities** and **social sciences.**

pension An amount of money paid regularly by an employer to a former employee after he or she retires from working.

physical sciences The natural sciences that are concerned mainly with nonliving matter, including physics, chemistry, and astronomy.

private 1. Not owned or controlled by the govern ment (such as private industry or a private employment agency). 2. Intended only for a particular person or group; not open to all (such as a private road or a private club).

public 1.Provided or operated by the government (such as a public library). 2. Open and available to everyone (such as public meeting).

regulatory Having to do with the rules and laws for carrying out an activity. A regulatory agency, for example, is a government organization that sets up required procedures for how certain things should be done.

scholarship A gift of money to a student to help the student pay for further education.

social sciences The branches of learning (such as economics and political science) that are concerned with the behavior of groups of human beings. Compare **humanities** and **natural sciences.**

social studies Courses of study (such as civics, geography, and history) that deal with how human societies work.

starting salary Salary paid to a newly hired employee. The starting salary is usually a smaller amount than is paid to a more experienced worker.

technical college A private or public college offering two- or four-year programs in technical subjects. Technical colleges offer courses in both general and technical subjects and award associate degrees and bachelor's degrees. Compare **technical community college.**

technical community college A community college that provides training for technicians (see **community college**). Technical community colleges offer courses in both general and technical subjects and award associate degrees. Compare **technical college.**

technical institute A public or private school that offers training in technical subjects. Technical institutes usually offer only a few courses in general subjects and do not award any kind of degree. Technical institutes that offer a broader range of subjects and award degrees are usually called **technical colleges** or **technical community colleges.**

technical school A general term used to describe technical colleges, technical community colleges, and technical institutes. Compare **trade school** and **vocational school.**

technician A worker with specialized practical training in a mechanical or scientific subject who works under the supervision of scientists, engineers, or other professionals. Technicians typically receive two years of college-level education after high school.

technologist A worker in a mechanical or scientific field with more training than a technician. Technologists typically must have between two and four years of college-level education after high school.

trade An occupation that requires training and skills in working with one's hands.

trade school A public or private school that offers training in one or more of the trades (see **trade**). Compare **technical school** and **vocational school.**

undergraduate A student at a college or university who has not yet received a degree.

undergraduate degree See **bachelor's degree.**

union An organization whose members are workers in a particular industry or company. The union works to gain better wages, benefits, and working conditions for its members. Also called a *labor union* or *trade union*.

vocational school A public or private school that offers training in one or more skills or trades. Compare **technical school** and **trade school.**

wage Money that is paid in return for work done, especially money paid on the basis of the number of hours or days worked.

INDEX

A

account executives, 3:112
accountants, 1:2, 3; 4:147
accounting clerks, 1:150, 151
acoustical experts, 8:2
acquisitions editors, 1:148
active religious sisters and brothers, 7:54
actors, 1:4, 5; 5:48
actuaries, 1:6, 7
acupuncturists, 1:8, 9; 4:70; 6:24, 25
adoption counselors, 1:58
adult and vocational education teachers, 1:10, 11
adult day care coordinators, 1:12, 13
advanced practice nurses, 1:14, 15; 5:148, 150
adventure travel specialists, 1:16, 17
advertising account executives, 1:18, 19
advertising sales workers, 1:20, 21
aerialists, 2:58
aerobics instructors, 1:22, 23
aeronautical and aerospace technicians, 1:24, 25
aerospace engineers, 1:26, 27
agribusiness technicians, 1:28, 29
agricultural consultants, 1:30, 31
agricultural engineers, 1:32, 33
agricultural equipment technicians, 1:34, 35
agricultural inspectors, 4:52
agricultural scientists, 1:36, 37
agronomists, 1:36
air quality engineers, 1:38, 39
air traffic controllers, 1:40, 41
airbrush artists, 6:84
aircraft mechanics, 1:42, 43
airline security representatives, 7:102
airplane pilots, 6:104
alcohol and drug abuse counselors, 1:44, 45
allergists, 1:46, 47
ambassadors, 1:48, 49
amusement park workers, 1:50, 51
analysts, 7:146
anesthesiologists, 1:52, 53
angiographers, 7:142
animal breeders and technicians, 1:54, 55
animal caretakers, 1:56, 57
animal handlers, 1:50
animal shelter employees, 1:58, 59
animal trainers, 1:60, 61; 2:58
animators, 1:62, 63; 4:89
annealers, 4:56
anthropologists, 1:64, 65
antique dealers, 1:66, 67
appliance repairers, 1:68, 69
appliance service technicians, 1:68
application engineers, 5:76
applications programmers, 2:102
appointed and elected officials, 1:70, 71
aquaculturists, 1:72, 73
aquarists, 1:74, 75; , 8:126
aquatic biologists, 1:136
aquatic performers, 2:58
arborists, 8:78, 79
archaeologists, 1:76, 77
architects, 1:78, 79
archivists, 1:80, 81
armored-car guards, 7:102
aromatherapists, 1:82, 83
arson investigators, 3:118
art directors, 1:84, 85
art therapists, 2:134; 5:132
artists, 1:86, 87; 5:110
assemblers, 4:2; 6:38; 7:148
assessors and appraisers, 1:88, 89
assistant equipment mechanics, 4:30
assistant principals, 7:90
astronauts, 1:90, 91; 4:106
astronomers, 1:92, 93

astrophysicists, 1:92
athletes, 1:94, 95; 7:152
athletic coaches, 7:154
athletic directors, 2:78
athletic trainers, 1:96, 97
attendants, 7:63
attorneys, 5:4
auctioneers, 1:98, 99
audio recording engineers, 1:100, 101
audiologists, 1:102, 103
auditors, 1:104, 105
authors, 5:32; 8:118
automatic-equipment technicians, 8:50
automobile collision repairers, 1:106, 107
automobile mechanics, 1:108, 109
automobile sales workers, 1:110, 111
automotive industry workers, 1:112, 113
automotive painters, 1:106
auxiliary equipment operators, 6:134
avionics engineers and technicians, 1:114, 115
ayurvedic doctors and practitioners, 1:116, 117

B

backtenders, 6:44
baggage porters and bellhops, 1:118, 119
baggers, 8:24
bail enforcement agents, 2:6
bailiffs, 1:120, 121
bakers, 2:118, 119
bakery products workers, 3:130
bank clerks, 1:122, 123
bank officers and managers, 1:122
bank services workers, 1:122
bank tellers, 1:122, 123
barbers, 1:124, 125
barker operators, 6:44
barrel platers, 3:60
bartenders, 2:138
beater engineers, 6:44
bed and breakfast owners, 1:126, 127
bell captains, 7:62
bell staff, 7:62
bellhops, 1:118, 119; 4:78
bereavement counselors, 4:40
bibliotherapists, 2:134
bicycle mechanics, 1:128, 129
bilingual consultants, 1:130, 131
billing clerks, 2:68
biochemists, 1:132, 133
biofeedback therapists, 1:134, 135
biological scientists, 1:136; 5:103
biologists, 1:136, 137; 5:103
biomedical engineers, 1:138, 139
biomedical equipment technicians, 1:140, 141
blenders, 6:112
blow-molding machine operators, 6:112
bodyguards, 1:142, 143
boiler operators, 6:134
boilermaker mechanics, 1:144
boilermakers, 1:144, 145
book conservators, 1:146, 147
book editors, 1:148, 149
bookkeepers, 1:150, 151
border patrol officers, 2:2, 3
botanists, 1:136; 2:4, 5
bouncers, 7:102
bounty hunters, 2:6, 7
box-office cashiers, 2:30
bricklayers and stonemasons, 2:8, 9; 4:124
broadcast engineers, 2:10, 11
brokers, 6:152
building custodians, 4:128
building inspectors, 2:114
bus drivers, 7:14
bushelers, 8:38
business managers, 2:12, 13
buspersons, 7:62
bussers, 7:62
butchers, 5:72
butlers, 4:82
buyers, 2:14, 15; 5:78; 7:68

C

cabinetmakers, 4:2
cable splicers, 3:44
cable television technicians, 2:16, 17
CAD technicians, 2:90, 91
calligraphers, 4:88
camera operators, 6:140
camp counselors, 7:44
candy industry workers, 3:130
capsule-filling-machine operators, 6:76
captains, 2:138

car rental agents, 2:68
cardiac monitor technicians, 2:20
cardiologists, 2:18, 19
cardiologists, 6:98; 7:142
cardiology technologists, 2:20
cardiovascular technologists, 2:20, 21
career counselors, 2:22, 23
caretakers, 4:82
carpenters, 2:24, 25; 5:92; 8:12
cartographers, 2:26, 27; 4:14
cartographic technicians, 7:132
cartoonists, 2:28, 29; 4:89
case officers, 7:146
cashiers, 2:30, 31; 4:78; 8:24
caterers, 2:32, 33
celestial mechanics specialists, 1:92
cell site engineers, 8:114
cell site technicians, 8:114
cement masons, 2:34, 35
census takers, 8:16
central office equipment installers, 2:86
central office repairers, 2:86
central office technicians, 8:50
ceramic artists, 2:36, 37
ceramic engineers, 2:38, 39; 6:132
ceramic sculptors, 2:36
certified nurse-midwives, 1:14; 2:40, 41
certified ski instructors, 7:120
chaplains, 4:76
checkers, 2:30; 3:30
check-out clerks, 2:30
chefs, 2:118, 119,138
chemical engineering technicians, 6:70
chemical engineers, 2:42, 43; 6:70
chemical laboratory technicians, 2:44
chemical technicians, 2:44, 45; 4:30
chemists, 2:46, 47; 4:44
chief executive officers, 2:12; 4:54; 8:124
chief financial officers, 2:12
chief information officers, 2:12
chief operating officers, 2:12
child care workers, 2:48, 49
child life specialists, 2:50, 51
chippers, 6:44
chiropractors, 2:52, 53; 4:70; 5:83, 132
choreographers, 2:54, 55, 144
cinematographers, 2:56, 57
circulators, 8:28
circus performers, 2:58, 59
city managers, 2:60, 61
city planners, 2:62, 63
civil engineering technicians, 2:64, 65
civil engineers, 2:66, 67; 4:44
claims adjusters, 4:110
cleaners, 4:128, 129; 7:62
clerks, 2:68, 69; 3:34; 5:104; 8:24
clinical chemists, 2:70, 71
clinical geneticists, 4:12
clinical nurse specialists, 1:14
clinical psychologists, 7:8
clowns, 2:72, 73
coaches, 7:152
coal mining technicians, 2:74, 75
coaters, 6:76
collection workers, 2:76, 77
college administrators, 2:78, 79
college professors, 2:80, 81; 6:43, 122, 123
color mixers, 6:112
columnists, 2:82, 83; 8:118
comedians, 2:84, 85
commercial decorators, 5:92
commercial or graphic artists, 1:86
communications equipment mechanics, 2:86, 87
composers, 2:88, 89
compositors, 6:140
computer aided design technicians, 2:90, 91
computer and electronics sales representatives, 2:92, 93
computer and office machine technicians, 2:94, 95
computer and video game designers, 2:96, 97
computer animation specialists, 7:140
computer network administrators, 2:98
computer network specialists, 2:98, 99
computer numerical control (CNC) programmers, 5:144
computer operators, 2:100, 101
computer programmers, 2:100, 102, 103; 7:128
computer security specialists, 2:104, 105
computer specialists, 5:104
computer systems analysts, 2:106, 107
computer trainers, 2:108, 109
concierges, 4:78, 80, 81; 7:62

conference coordinators, 3:78
congressional aides, 2:110, 111
conservators and conservation technicians, 2:112, 113; 5:116
construction boilermakers, 1:144
construction inspectors, 2:114, 115
construction laborers, 2:116, 117
contemplative religious sisters and brothers, 7:54
convention planners, 3:78
cooks, 2:118, 119; 4:82; 5:104
cooks, chefs, and bakers, 2:118, 119
copy editors, 1:148; 5:134
copywriters, 8:118
coremakers, 2:120, 121
corrections officers, 2:122, 123
correspondents, 7:56, 57
cosmetologists, 2:124, 125; 5:48
cosmologists, 1:92
cost estimators, 2:126, 127
costume designers, 2:128, 129; 8:12
counselors, 4:66, 67; 7:90
counter and retail clerks, 2:68, 130, 131
court reporters, 2:132, 133; 7:40
creative arts therapists, 2:134, 135
crime analysts, 2:136, 137
crime lab technologists, 3:142
criminologists, 7:126
critics, 8:118
crown and bridge specialists, 2:154
cruise directors, 2:138
cruise ship workers, 2:138, 139
cryptographic technicians, 7:146
cultural anthropologists, 1:64
custom shoemakers, 7:112
customer service representatives, 2:140, 141
customs brokers, 3:84, 85
customs inspectors, 4:52
customs officials, 2:142, 143
customs patrol officers, 2:142
cutters, 1:112; 7:110

D

dairy products workers, 3:130
dance directors, 2:144
dance/movement therapists, 2:134; 5:132
dancers, 2:144, 145
darkroom technicians, 6:84
data entry clerks, 2:68
data entry keyers, 8:82
data recovery operators, 2:98
database specialists, 2:146, 147
dealers, 3:28
deans, 2:78; 7:90
decorators, 4:26
demographers, 2:148, 149
dental assistants, 2:150, 151
dental ceramicists, 2:154
dental hygienists, 2:152, 153
dental laboratory technicians, 2:154, 155
dental practitioners, 6:29
dental specialists, 6:29
dentists, 3:2, 3; 6:58
departure controllers, 1:40
deputy U.S. marshals, 3:4, 5
dermatoimmunologists, 3:6
dermatologists, 3:6, 7; 6:98
design engineers, 5:76
designers, 8:58, 60
desk clerks, 7:62
desk top analysts/specialists, 8:36
desktop publishers, 6:140
desktop publishing specialists, 3:8, 9
detailers, 3:30
detectives, 3:10, 11
development directors, 3:12, 13
developmental psychologists, 7:8
diagnostic medical sonographers, 3:14, 15
dialysis technicians, 3:16, 17
die makers, 6:138
diesel mechanics, 3:18, 19
dietetic technicians, 3:20, 21
dietitians, 5:152, 153
digester operator, 6:44
diocesan priests, 7:80, 81
direct company representatives, 3:28
directors of housing, 2:78
directors of religious activities, 2:78
directors of student activities, 2:78
directors, 7:28
directory assistance operators, 8:56
disc jockeys, 3:22, 23; 7:24, 30
dishwashers, 7:62
dispensing opticians, 3:24, 25
display workers, 5:92
divers and diving technicians, 3:26, 27
DJs, 3:22

dockworkers, 8:20
doctors, 6:98, 99
dog walkers, 6:66
doorkeepers, 4:78
doormen, 7:62
door-to-door sales workers, 3:28, 29
drafters, 3:30, 31
drama therapists, 2:134
drawing-kiln workers, 4:26
dressers, 8:12
drier operators, 6:76
drivers, 8:20
drug developers, 3:32, 33
druggists, 6:78
dry cleaning and laundry workers, 3:34, 35
drywall installers and finishers, 3:36, 37

E

echocardiographers, 2:20
ecologists, 2:4; 3:38, 39
economists, 3:40, 41
edgers, 7:88
editorial assistants, 5:135
editors, 5:32, 42, 43, 80, 134, 135
education directors, 3:42, 43
education secretaries, 7:98
educational directors, 5:114
EEG technologists, 3:54, 55
electric power workers, 3:44, 45
electrical and electronics engineers, 3:46, 47
electrical engineers, 4:104
electrical inspectors, 2:114
electricians, 3:48, 49; 7:88; 8:12
electrocardiograph technicians, 2:20
electroformers, 3:60
electrologists, 3:50, 51
electromechanical technicians, 3:52, 53
electroneurodiagnostic technologists, 3:54, 55
electronics engineering technicians, 3:56, 57
electronics experts, 5:104
electronics service technicians, 3:58, 59
electronics technicians, 3:56, 57
electroplaters, 3:61; 7:116
electroplating workers, 3:60, 61
elementary school teachers, 3:62, 63; 5:121
elevator constructors, 3:64
elevator inspectors, 2:114
elevator installers and repairers, 3:64, 65
embalmers, 3:154, 155
emergency medical technicians, 3:66, 67
employment agency managers, 6:60
employment consultants, 6:60
employment counselors, 2:22
EMTs, 3:66, 67
END technologists, 3:54
endodontists, 3:2, 68, 69
energy conservation and use technicians, 3:70, 71
energy specialists, 5:76
engineering assistants, 8:104
engineers, 5:138
entertainers, 1:50; 2:139; 7:63
entomologists, 8:128
environmental engineers, 3:72, 73
environmental health inspectors, 4:52
environmental technicians, 4:51; 6:124
equipment maintenance and sales technicians, 8:104
equipment managers, 3:74, 75; 4:30
equipment manufacturing technicians, 1:34
equipment operators, 4:30
equipment sales technicians, 1:34
ergonomists, 3:76, 77
estheticians, 7:122
estimators, 8:104
etymologists, 5:30
event planners, 3:78, 79
executive chefs, 7:62
executive recruiters, 3:80, 81
exhibit designers, 3:82, 83
export managers, 3:84, 85
export-import specialists, 3:84, 85
exterminators, 6:62, 63
extractor operators, 6:76
extruder operators, 6:112

F

fabricators, 6:114
fact checkers, 1:148; 7:58
family and consumer scientists, 3:86, 87
family practice physicians, 4:10

farm crop production technicians, 3:88, 89
farm equipment mechanics, 3:90, 91
farm operators and managers, 3:92
farmers, 3:92, 93; 4:32
farriers, 4:72
fashion designers, 3:94, 95
fashion illustrators and photographers, 3:96, 97
fashion models, 5:110, 111
fast food workers, 3:98, 99
FBI agents, 3:100, 101
fiber optics engineers, 6:16
fiber optics technicians, 3:102, 103
field contractors, 7:16
field service representatives, 6:38
field service technicians, 6:38
field technicians, 2:10
file clerks, 2:68
filers, 7:88
film and television directors, 3:104, 105
film and television producers, 3:106, 107
film editors, 3:108, 109
film strippers, 6:140
financial planners, 3:110, 111
financial services brokers, 3:112, 113
fine artists, 1:86
fingerprint classifiers, 3:142
finish carpenters, 2:24
finishing workers, 7:110
fire captains, 3:118
fire chiefs, 3:118
fire control and safety technicians, 3:114, 115
fire inspectors and investigators, 3: 116, 117
fire marshals, 3:116, 118
firefighters, 3:118, 119
firers, 6:134
fish farmers, 1:72
fish scientists, 1:72
fishers, 3:120, 121
fitting room workers, 7:110
flame-hardening-machine setters, 4:56
flight attendants, 3:122, 123
floor covering installers, 3:124, 125
floral designers, 3:126, 127
florists, 3:126, 127
fluid power technicians, 3:128, 129
flying instructors, 6:104
foam-machine operators, 6:112
food and beverage managers, 7:66
food and drug inspectors, 4:52
food concession attendants, 1:50
food production workers, 3:130, 131
food service workers, 3:132, 133
food technologists, 3:134, 135
foreign correspondents, 3:136, 137
foreign service officers, 3:138, 139
foreign-student advisors, 2:78
foremen, 4:30
forensic accountants and auditors, 3:140, 141
forensic experts, 3:142, 143
forest ecologists, 3:144
forest engineers, 3:144
foresters, 3:144, 145; 5:40
forestry technicians, 3:146, 147
forge shop workers, 3:148, 149
forklift drivers, 7:88
forming-machine workers, 4:26
franchise owners, 3:150, 151
freight forwarders, 3:84
fumigators, 6:62
fund-raisers, 3:152, 153
funeral directors, 3:154, 155
furniture finishers, 4:2
furniture manufacturing workers, 4:2, 3
furniture movers, 4:4, 5

G

game attendants, 1:50
gang bosses, 8:20
gasfitters, 6:106
gate tenders, 7:102
gear workers, 8:20
gene therapists, 4:12
genealogists, 4:6, 7
general maintenance mechanics, 4:8, 9
general office clerks, 2:68
general practitioners, 4:10, 11
genetic counselors, 4:12
genetic engineers, 4:12
genetic scientists, 4:12, 13
geneticists, 4:12; 5:103
geochemists, 3:38
geodetic surveying technicians, 8:30
geodetic technicians, 7:132
geographers, 4:14, 15

geographic information systems specialists, 4:16, 17
geologists, 4:18, 19, 44; 6:68, 72, 74
geophysicists, 4:20, 21
geriatric social workers, 4:22, 23
geriatricians, 4:24, 25
gift shop attendants, 1:50
glass grinders, 4:26
glass manufacturing workers, 4:26, 27
glaziers, 4:28, 29
golf course superintendents, 4:30, 31, 153
graders, 7:88
grain buyers, 7:16
grain merchants, 4:32, 33
grant coordinators, 4:34, 35
grant writers, 4:34, 35
granulator machinery operators, 6:76
graphic designers, 4:36, 37, 88
graphics programmers, 4:38, 39
grief therapists, 4:40, 41, 76
grinders, 3:148
grinding machine operators, 6:112
grocery clerks, 2:30
ground helpers, 3:44
groundskeepers, 4:30, 42, 43
groundsmanagers, 4:42, 43, 152
groundwater professionals, 4:44, 45
guards, 7:62
guidance counselors, 2:22; 4:46, 47
gynecologists, 5:154, 155

H

hairstylists, 8:12
hammersmiths, 3:148; 7:116
hand carvers, 4:2
hand dry cleaners, 3:34
hand finishers, 8:72
hand packers, 6:77
hardware engineers, 4:48, 49
hazardous waste management technicians, 4:50, 51
head coaches, 7:154
head sawyers, 7:88
headers, 8:20
headmasters, 7:90
headmistresses, 7:90
health and regulatory inspectors, 4:52, 53
health care administrators, 4:55
health care managers, 4:54, 55
health services administrators, 4:55
heat treaters, 4:56, 57
heating and cooling technicians, 4:58, 59
heat-treatment technicians, 5:96
helicopter pilots, 6:104
herbalists, 4:60, 61
herpetologists, 8:128
highwire or wire walkers, 2:58
histologic technicians, 4:62, 63
historians, 4:64, 65
HIV/AIDS counselors, 4:66, 67
hold workers, 8:20
holter monitor technologists, 2:20
home health care aides, 4:68, 69, 76
home inspectors, 2:114
homeopaths, 4:70, 71
horse grooms, 4:72, 73; 7:63
horticultural technicians, 4:74, 75
horticulturists, 4:30
hospice workers, 4:76, 77
hospital attendants, 5:146
hostesses, 7:62
hosts, 7:62
hotel and motel managers, 4:78, 79
hotel clerks, 2:68
hotel concierges, 4:80, 81
household workers, 4:82, 83
housekeepers, 4:82; 7:62
housekeeping staff, 2:138
human resource workers, 8:25
human resources managers, 6:60
human services workers, 4:84, 85
humane educators, 1:58
humane investigators, 1:58
hydrogeologists, 3:38; 4:44
hydrologists, 4:20; 6:74
hypnotherapists, 4:86, 87

I

ichthyologists, 8:128
identification technicians, 3:142
illustrators, 4:88, 89
immigration inspectors, 4:52
import-export agents, 3:84
independent auditors, 1:104
indexers, 4:90, 91
industrial chemicals workers, 4:92, 93
industrial designers, 4:94, 95
industrial engineering technicians, 4:96, 97

industrial engineers, 4:96, 97
industrial machinery mechanics, 4:98, 99
industrial safety and health technicians, 4:100, 101
industrial traffic managers, 4:102, 103
information clerks, 7:42
information operators, 8:56
information security technicians, 2:104
injection molders, 6:112
inside salespersons, 8:112
inspectors, 1:112; 8:60
instrument makers, 4:104, 105
instrument repairers, 4:104, 105
instrumentation technicians, 4:106, 107
insulation workers, 4:108, 109
insurance claims representatives, 4:110, 111
insurance policy processors, 4:112, 113
insurance underwriters, 4:114, 115
integrated circuit technicians, 4:116, 117
intelligence officers, 7:146, 147
interior designers and decorators, 4:118, 119
internal auditors, 1:104
Internet content developers, 4:120, 121
Internet security administrators, 2:104
Internet security engineers, 2:104
Internet security specialists, 2:104
interpreters, 4:122, 123; 5:30
investigative accountants, 3:140
investigators, 3:100
iron and steel industry workers, 4:124, 125
ironers, 3:34
ironworkers, 4:126, 127
irrigation specialists, 4:30

J

janitors, 4:128, 129
jewelers, 4:130, 131
job and die setters, 4:132, 133
job development specialists, 4:134, 135
job superintendents, 8:2
jockeys, 4:136, 137
journalists, 5:80
judges, 4:138, 139
jugglers, 2:58
justices, 4:138
juvenile court workers, 6:50

K

kennel attendants, 1:58
kindergarten teachers, 6:142, 143
kinesiologists, 4:140, 141
kinesiotherapists, 4:140, 141
knit goods industry workers, 4:142, 143
knitters, 4:142

L

labor relations specialists, 6:60
labor union business agents, 4:144, 145
laboratory testing technicians, 2:44
land acquisition professionals, 4:146, 147
land trust or preserve managers, 4:148, 149
landscape architects, 4:42, 150, 151
landscapers, 4:152, 153
laser and fiber optics engineers, 6:16
laser technicians, 4:154, 155
last assemblers, 7:110
lathers, 5:2, 3
laundry spotters, 3:34
lawyers, 4:138, 139; 5:4, 5, 10, 118
layout artists, 4:36
layout workers, 5:6, 7
leather tanning and finishing workers, 5:8, 9
legal assistants, 6:46
legal secretaries, 5:10, 11; 7:98
legislative advocates, 5:34
lens technicians, 5:12, 13
librarians, 5:14, 15, 18
library media specialists, 5:16, 17
library technicians, 5:18, 19
licensed practical nurses, 5:20, 21, 150
life insurance agents, 5:22, 23
life insurance brokers, 5:22, 23
life scientists, 1:136
lifeguards, 5:24, 25; 7:63
lighting designers, 8:12
lighting technicians, 5:26, 27
lighting-equipment operators, 8:12
line installers and cable splicers, 5:28, 29
line installers, 3:44
linesmen, 8:84
linguists, 5:30, 31

literary agents, 5:32, 33
lithographers, 6:140
load dispatchers, 3:44
lobbyists, 5:34, 35; 7:12
local controllers, 1:40
locksmiths, 5:36, 37
locomotive engineers, 5:38, 39; 7:32
logging industry workers, 5:40, 41
longshore workers, 8:20
lyricists, 7:136

M

machine molders, 6:76
machine operators, 7:148
machine repair personnel, 8:60
machinery builders, 6:38
machinists, 1:112
magazine editors, 5:42, 43
magicians, 5:44, 45
mail carriers, 5:46, 47
maintenance administrators, 2:86
maintenance and operations engineers, 5:76
maintenance staff, 7:88
maintenance workers, 1:112; 6:70; 7:62
makeup artists, 5:48, 49; 8:12
make-up effects specialists, 7:140
mammalogists, 8:128
management analysts and consultants, 5:50, 51
managing editors, 5:134
manufacturers' sales representatives, 5:52, 53
manufacturing engineers, 5:76
manufacturing supervisors, 5:54, 55
marble setters, tile setters, and terrazzo workers, 5:56, 57
marine biologists, 5:58, 59
marine biologists, 6:4
marine engineers, 5:60, 61
marine services technicians, 5:62, 63
markers, 3:34; 7:88
marketing researchers, 5:64, 65
marshals, 3:4, 5
massage therapists, 5:66, 67, 132
mathematicians, 5:68, 69
meat packing workers, 5:70, 71
meatcutters, 5:72, 73
mechanical effects specialists, 7:140
mechanical engineering technicians, 5:74, 75
mechanical engineers, 4:104; 5:76, 77
mechanical inspectors, 2:114
mechanics, 5:104
media planners and buyers, 5:78, 79
media relations professionals, 6:144
media relations specialists, 5:80, 81
medical assistants, 4:70; 5:82, 83
medical examiners, 3:142
medical illustrators, 5:84, 85
medical record technicians, 5:86, 87
medical secretaries, 5:88, 89; 7:98
medical technologists, 5:90, 91
meeting planners, 3:78
membership secretaries, 7:98
merchandise displayers, 5:92, 93
merchant mariners, 5:94, 95
metallographers, 5:96
metallurgical engineers and technicians, 5:96, 97
meteorological technicians, 7:132
meteorologists, 4:20; 5:98, 99
meter readers, 5:100, 101
microbiologists, 5:102, 103
microcomputer support specialists, 8:46
microwave technicians, 8:50
military careers, 5:104, 105
millwrights, 5:106, 107; 7:88
mineralogists, 6:74
mining engineers, 5:108, 109
model dressers, 5:92
model makers, 7:116; 8:72
models, 5:110, 111
mold and tool makers, 6:114
mold makers, 6:138
molders, 5:112, 113
morticians, 3:154, 155
museum attendants, 5:114, 115
museum curators, 5:114, 116, 117
museum directors, 5:116, 117
museum guards, 5:114
museum teachers, 5:114, 115, 116
music producers, 5:118, 119
music teachers, 5:120, 121
music therapists, 2:134; 4:76
musical instrument repairers, 5:122, 123
musicians, 5:120, 121, 124, 125; 6:22

mycologists, 2:4

N

nail technicians, 5:126, 127
nannies, 5:128, 129
narcotic squad detectives, 3:10
naturalists, 5:130, 131
naturopathic physicians, 4:60; 5:132, 133
naturopaths, 4:60, 61, 70; 5:132, 133
nephrology technicians, 3:16
network control technicians, 8:50
network security consultants, 2:104
network security specialists, 2:98
news reporters, 7:26
newscasters, 7:26
newspaper editors, 5:134, 135
newswriters, 8:118
nuclear engineers, 5:136, 137
nuclear instrumentation technicians, 5:138, 139
nuclear medicine technologists, 5:140, 141
nuclear reactor operators, 5:142, 143
numerical control tool programmers, 5:144, 145
nurse aides, 5:146
nurse anesthetists, 1:14
nurse assistants, 4:76; 5:20, 146, 147
nurse practitioners, 1:14; 5:148, 149
nurse-midwives, 2:40, 41
nurses, 4:70; 5:150, 151
nursing home administrators, 4:55
nutritionists, 4:70; 5:152, 153

O

obstetricians/ gynecologists, 5:154, 155
occupational dermatologists, 3:6
occupational safety and health inspectors, 4:52
occupational therapists, 4:76; 6:2, 3, 94
occupational therapy assistants, 4:141
oceanographers, 4:14; 6:4, 5
office administrators, 6:6, 7
office assistants, 4:30
office managers, 6:6
official scorers/statisticians, 8:6
oncologists, 6:8, 9
on-farm equipment managers, 1:34
operating engineers, 6:10, 11
operations research analysts, 6:12, 13
operations workers, 6:70
operators, 7:146
ophthalmologists, 6:14, 15, 20
optical engineers, 6:16, 17
opticians, 6:20
optometric technicians, 6:18, 19
optometrists, 5:83; 6:14, 18, 20, 21
oral pathologists, 3:2
oral surgeons, 3:2
orchestra conductors, 6:22, 23
orderlies, 5:146
organ technicians, 6:102, 103
Oriental bodywork therapists, 6:24, 25
Oriental medicine practitioners, 4:60, 61; 6:24, 25
orientation and mobility specialists, 6:26, 27
ornithologists, 8:128
orthodontic technicians, 2:154
orthodontists, 3:2; 6:28, 29
orthotic and prosthetic technicians, 6:30, 31
orthotists, 6:32, 33
osteopathic physicians, 6:34, 35
osteopaths, 6:34, 35
overhaul mechanics, 1:42

P

packaging engineers, 6:36, 37
packaging machinery technicians, 6:38, 39
packaging technicians, 6:36
packers, 7:110
pad cutters, 6:112
painters, 5:92; 6:40, 41
paleontologists, 4:18; 6:42, 43
paperhangers, 6:40, 41
paper-machine operators, 6:44
papermaking workers, 6:44, 45
paralegals, 6:46, 47
park rangers, 6:48, 49
parking attendants, 1:50
parole officers, 6:50, 51
party planners, 3:78; 8:100, 101
paste-up workers, 6:140
pathologists, 5:90; 6:52, 53
patrollers, 7:102
PBX installers, 8:54
PBX operators, 7:62; 8:56
PBX repairers, 8:54
PBX systems technicians, 2:86; 8:50

PC set up specialists, 8:36
pediatric dermatologists, 3:6
pediatricians, 6:54, 55, 98
pedodontists, 3:2
perfusionists, 6:56, 57
periodontists, 3:2; 6:58, 59
personnel recruiters, 6:60
personnel specialists, 6:60, 61
pest control workers, 6:62, 63
pet groomers, 6:64, 65
pet sitters, 6:66, 67
petroleum engineers, 6:68, 69
petroleum refining workers, 6:70, 71
petroleum technicians, 6:72, 73
petrologists, 6:74, 75
pharmaceutical industry workers, 6:76, 77
pharmacist assistants, 6:83
pharmacists, 6:78, 79, 82, 83; 8:24
pharmacologists, 6:80, 81
pharmacy assistants, 6:82
pharmacy technicians, 6:82, 83; 8:24
pharmacy technologists, 6:82
philologists, 5:30
photo lab workers, 6:84, 85
photo stylists, 6:86, 87
photo technicians, 6:146
photographers, 4:88
photographers, 5:110; 6:88, 89; 8:108, 109
photographic equipment technicians, 6:90, 91
photographic retouchers, 6:84
photojournalists, 6:92, 93
physical anthropologists, 1:64
physical science technicians, 7:132
physical therapists, 4:76, 141; 6:94, 95
physician assistants, 6:96, 97
physicians, 2:138; 6: 98, 99
physicists, 6:100, 101
piano technicians, 6:102, 103
pier superintendents, 8:20
pilling-machine operators, 6:112
pilots, 6:104, 105
pipefitters, 6:106, 107
planers, 7:88
planetary astronomers, 1:92
plant cytologists, 2:5
plasterers, 6:108, 109
plastic products manufacturing workers, 6:113
plastics engineers, 6:110, 111
plastics form makers, 6:112
plastics pattern makers, 6:112
plastics products manufacturing workers, 6:112, 113
plastics technicians, 6:114, 115
platemakers, 6:140
playwrights, 8:118
plumbers, 6:116, 117
plumbing inspectors, 2:114
podiatrists, 6:118, 119
police officers, 6:120, 121
policy analysts, 6:122
political consultants, 6:144
political scientists, 6:122, 123
pollution control technicians, 6:124, 125
polygraph examiners, 6:126, 127
pop/rock musicians, 6:128, 129
postal clerks, 6:130, 131
pottery and porcelainware industry workers, 6:132, 133
power plant workers, 6:134, 135
precision machinists, 6:136, 137
precision metalworkers, 6:138, 139
pre-flight technicians, 6:140
prep cooks, 7:62
preparators, 6:42
prepress workers, 6:140, 141
preschool teachers, 6:142, 143
presidents, 2:12
press operators, 3:148
press secretaries, 6:144, 145
pressers, 3:34
principals, 7:90
printed-circuit-board technicians, 6:146, 147
printed-circuit-board x-ray technicians, 6:146
printing press operators, 6:148, 149
private detectives, 6:150, 151
private investigators, 6:150, 151
probation officers, 6:50
process engineers, 5:76; 6:44
procurement engineers, 7:16
producers, 3:104, 106, 107; 5:32; 7:28
production editors, 1:148
production managers, 8:60
production potters, 2:36
professional athlete coaches, 7:154
project managers, 8:2

proofreaders, 1:148
prop makers, 8:12
property and casualty insurance agents and brokers, 6:152, 153
property and real estate managers, 6:154, 155
prosthetists, 6:32, 33
prosthodontists, 3:2
protestant ministers, 7:2, 3
psychiatric technicians, 7:4, 5
psychiatrists, 7:6, 7
psychologists, 6:94; 7:8, 9
public opinion researchers, 7:10, 11
public relations specialists, 7:12, 13
public transportation operators, 7:14, 15
public works inspectors, 2:114
pulp-and-paper lab testers, 6:44
purchasers, 3:84, 85
purchasing agents, 7:16, 17
pursers, 2:138
pyrotechnics effects specialists, 7:140

Q

quality assurance testers, 7:18, 19
quality control engineers, 7:20, 21
quality control technicians, 7:20, 21; 8:58, 62
quality-control inspectors, 7:148

R

rabbis, 7:22, 23
radiation therapists, 8:120
radio and television announcers and newscasters, 7:27
radio and television announcers, 7:24, 25
radio and television newscasters, 7:26, 27
radio and television program directors, 7:28, 29
radio astronomers, 1:92
radio producers, 7:30, 31
radiologic technologists, 7:142
radiologists, 8:120
railroad clerks, 2:68
railroad conductors, 7:32, 33
railway system drivers, 7:14
range conservationists, 7:34, 132
range ecologists, 7:34
range managers, 7:34, 35
range scientists, 7:34
real estate agents and brokers, 7:36, 37
real estate developers, 7:38, 39
real-time captioners, 7:40, 41
real-time reporters, 7:40
receptionists, 7:42, 43
recreation center directors, 7:44
recreation leaders, 7:44
recreation workers, 7:44, 45
recruiters, 3:80, 81
recycling coordinators, 7:46, 47
referees, 8:84, 85
reflexologists, 7:48, 49
refuse collectors, 7:50, 51
registered nurses, 4:76; 5:20, 146, 150, 151
registered representatives, 3:112
registrars, 2:78
rehabilitation counselors, 6:2; 7:52, 53
religious priests, 7:80
religious sisters and brothers, 7:54, 55
renal dialysis technicians, 3:16
reporters and correspondents, 5:80, 134; 7:56, 57
research assistants, 7:58, 59
research engineering technicians, 2:64
reservation and ticket agents, 7:60, 61
reservation clerks, 7:62
residence counselors, 2:78
resort workers, 7:62, 63
respiratory therapists, 7:64, 65
restaurant managers, 7:66, 67
retail clerks, 7:62, 68
retail managers, 7:62
retail sales workers, 7:68, 69
retail store managers, 7:70, 71
retirement planners, 7:72, 73
ride attendants, 1:50
ride operators, 1:50
riggers, 4:126; 8:12
ringmasters, 2:58
risk managers, 7:74, 75
road conductors, 7:32
road crew workers, 7:76, 77
robotics engineers, 7:78, 79
robotics technicians, 7:78, 79
roman catholic priests, 7:80, 81

roofers, 7:82, 83
roustabouts, 7:84, 85
rubber goods production workers, 7:86, 87

S

sales and service workers, 6:114
sales clerks, 7:68
sales engineering technicians, 2:64
sales representatives, 6:76
sales route drivers, 3:34
salespeople, 5:52; 7:68
sand molders, 5:112
sanitary engineers, 4:128
sawmill workers, 7:88, 89
scanner operators, 6:140
school administrators, 7:90, 91
school directors, 7:90
school psychologists, 7:8
screenwriters, 7:92, 93; 8:118
scriptwriters, 8:118
seamstresses, 7:148
secondary school teachers, 5:121; 7:94, 95
secret service special agents, 7:96, 97
secretaries, 7:98, 99
secular priests, 7:80
securities sales representatives, 3:112
security consultants, 7:100, 101
security guards, 7:102, 103
security workers, 1:50
seismologists, 4:20
semiconductor technicians, 7:104, 105
senior salesperson, 7:68
service and sales representatives, 6:77
services sales representatives, 7:106, 107
sewage plant operators, 8:94
shaping-machine operators, 6:112
sheet metal workers, 7:82, 108, 109
shelter administrators, 1:58
shelter managers, 1:58
shipping and receiving clerks, 2:68
shoe industry workers, 7:110, 111
shoe repairers, 7:112, 113
shop tailors, 8:38
shorthand reporters, 8:18
showcase trimmers, 5:92
sign language interpreters, 7:114, 115
silversmiths, 7:116
silverware assemblers, 7:116
silverware designers, 7:116
silverware industry workers, 7:116, 117
silviculturists, 3:144
singers, 7:118, 119
ski instructors, 7:63
ski lift operators, 7:120
ski patrol, 7:120
ski resort workers, 7:120, 121
ski technicians, 7:120
skin care specialists, 7:122, 123
social directors, 7:44
social psychologists, 7:8
social secretaries, 7:98
social workers, 4:67, 76; 7:124, 125
sociologists, 7:126, 127
soft-tool technicians, 6:146
software designers, 7:128, 129
software engineers, 7:130, 131
soil conservation technicians, 7:132, 133
soil scientists, 6:68; 7:134, 135
solar astronomers, 1:92
songwriters, 7:136, 137
sonographers, 3:14
sound mixers, 1:100
sound technicians, 8:12
sous chefs, 7:62
special agents, 3:100
special education teachers, 7:138, 139
special effects technicians, 7:140, 141
special procedures technologists, 7:142, 143
specification writers and estimators, 8:2
spectrographic technicians, 5:96
speech therapists, 4:76; 7:144
speech-language pathologists, 7:144, 145
spies, 7:146, 147
spin doctors, 6:144
sporting goods production workers, 7:148, 149
sports agents, 7:150, 151
sports broadcasters, 7:152, 153
sports coaches, 7:154, 155
sports facility designers, 8:2, 3
sports physicians, 8:4, 5
sports statisticians, 8:6, 7
sportscasters, 7:152
sportswriters, 8:8, 9
sprinkle fitters, 6:106

stadium ushers, 8:10, 11
stadium vendors, 8:10, 11
stage production workers and technicians, 8:12, 13
stage technicians, 8:12, 13
stand-up comedians, 2:84
stationary engineers, 8:14, 15
statistical clerks, 2:68
statisticians, 8:6, 7, 16, 17
stellar astronomers, 1:92
stenographers, 8:18, 19
stevedores, 8:20, 21
stevedoring superintendents, 8:20
stock clerks, 2:68
stock handlers, 7:110
stock personnel, 8:24
stockbrokers, 3:112
stonemasons, 2:8
store detectives, 8:24
store managers, 8:24
stove tenders, 4:124
streetcar drivers, 7:14
stress test technologists, 2:20
structural designers, 8:2
stucco masons, 6:108
studio technicians, 1:100
stunt coordinators, 8:22
stunt performers, 8:22, 23
submarine cable equipment technicians, 8:50
substation operators, 3:44
subway drivers, 7:14
superintendents, 7:90
supermarket managers, 8:24, 25
supermarket workers, 8:24, 25
surgeons, 5:84, 150; 8:26, 27
surgical technicians, 8:28
surgical technologists, 8:28, 29
surveying and mapping technicians, 8:30, 31
surveying technicians, 7:132
surveyors, 8:32, 33
swimming pool servicers, 8:34, 35
switchboard operators, 6:134
switching equipment technicians, 8:50
systems programmers, 2:102
systems set up specialists, 8:36, 37

T

tailors and dressmakers, 8:38, 39
tapers, 3:36
tax auditors, 1:104
tax interviewers, 8:40
tax preparers, 8:40, 41
taxidermists, 8:42, 43
teacher aides, 8:44, 45
teachers, 3:62, 63; 6:142, 143; 7:94, 95; 8:44
team physicians, 8:4
technical analysts, 7:146
technical editors, 8:48, 49
technical secretaries, 7:98
technical support specialists, 8:46, 47
technical support technicians, 8:36
technical writers and editors, 8:48, 49
technical writers, 8:48, 49
telecommunications technicians, 8:50, 51
telemarketers, 8:52, 53
telephone installers and repairers, 8:54, 55
telephone operators, 8:56, 57
telephonists, 2:138
television program directors, 8:90
textile manufacturing technicians, 8:58
textile technicians, 8:58, 59
textile workers, 8:60, 61
ticket agents, 2:30
ticket attendants, 1:50
ticket sellers, 2:30
tire technicians, 8:62, 63
title examiners, 8:64, 65
title searchers, 8:64, 65
toll collectors, 8:66, 67
tool and die makers, 1:112; 7:116
tool makers, 6:138
tour guides, 8:68, 69
toxicologists, 8:70, 71
toy designers, 8:72
toy industry workers, 8:72, 73
tracers, 3:30
traffic agents, 2:68
traffic engineers, 8:74, 75
trail guides, 7:63
translators, 4:122, 123; 5:30
trapeze artists, 2:58
travel agents, 8:68, 76, 77
tree department workers, 7:110
tree experts, 8:78, 79
trimmer sawyers, 7:88
trouble shooters, 3:44
truck drivers, 8:80, 81

typesetters, 6:140
typists, 8:82, 83

U

umpires, 8:84, 85
undertakers, 3:154
urban anthropologists, 1:64
user support specialists, 8:46

V

vascular technologists, 2:20
veterinarians, 8:86, 87, 88
veterinary assistants, 1:56
veterinary technicians, 8:88, 89
video technicians, 8:90, 91
videographers, 2:138
visual artists, 4:88

W

wait staff, 2:138
waiters, 7:62; 8:92, 93
wardrobe supervisors, 8:12
washing machine operators, 3:34
wastewater treatment plant operators, 8:94, 95
wastewater treatment plant technicians, 8:94, 95
watch and clock repairers, 8:96, 97
weather forecasters, 5:98
Web designers, 4:120
Web developers, 4:120
webmasters, 8:98, 99
wedding planners, 8:100, 101
welders, 1:112; 7:88; 8:102, 103
welding analysts, 8:104
welding equipment salespeople, 8:104
welding operators, 8:104
welding process-control technicians, 8:104
welding qualification technicians, 8:104
welding technicians, 8:104, 105
wholesale sales workers, 8:106, 107
wholesalers, 3:84
wildlife photographers, 8:108, 109
wildlife shelter workers, 1:56
winch operators, 8:20
window dressers, 5:92
wine stewards, 8:92
winemakers, 8:110, 111
wireless sales workers, 8:112, 113
wireless service technicians, 8:114, 115
wood products engineers, 8:116
wood products technicians, 8:116
wood science and technology workers, 8:116, 117
wood scientists, 8:116
wood technologists, 8:116
woodworkers, 4:2
word processors, 8:82, 83
wranglers, 7:63
writers, 5:32, 135; 8:118, 119

X

X-ray technologists, 8:120, 121

Y

yard conductors, 7:32

Z

zoo and aquarium curators, 8:122, 123
zoo and aquarium directors, 8:124, 125
zookeepers, 8:126, 127
zoologists, 1:136; 8:128, 129